"A model of what a book on sex written for adolescents should be."
—*New York Times*

"An excellent book . . . comfortable reading for either the young or their parents. . . . Reading [it] made me want to know the authors personally for their warmth and respect for individuals (and differences among individuals)."
—ROBERT A. HATCHER, M.D., *The Nation's Health*

"Intelligent, responsible high school and college students can gain much understanding . . . by studying this needed book."
—*Library Journal*

"Concepts of sex and birth control are fully explored in lucid prose especially for young people in this frank book."
—*Los Angeles Times*

"[The authors] marshal arguments to persuade their readers that irresponsibilty in sexual matters can lead to emotional harm but that in America today, the dangers can be avoided with some reasonable effort and regard for one's partner, oneself, and society."
—VICTOR GOLDIN, M.D.,
International Journal of Mental Health

"Splendid . . . I would have no hesitation in putting this book into the hands of young people."
—DR. LOUISE BATES AMES

Sex & Birth Control

A Guide for the Young

Sex
&
Birth
Control

A Guide for the Young

Revised Edition

E. James Lieberman, M.D., & Ellen Peck

Introduction by Mary S. Calderone, M.D., M.P.H.

SCHOCKEN BOOKS • NEW YORK

First published by Schocken Books 1982
10 9 8 7 6 5 4 3 2 1   82 83 84 85
Sex & Birth Control (Revised Edition) Copyright
© 1981 by E. James Lieberman, M.D. & Ellen Peck

Published by arrangement with Harper & Row, Publishers

Library of Congress Cataloging in Publication Data
Lieberman, E. James, 1934–
Sex & birth control.
Includes index.
1. Sex instruction for youth.   2. Birth control—
United States.   I. Peck, Ellen, 1942–
II. Title.   III. Title: Sex and birth control.
[HQ35.L544   1982]   613.9′5   81–16674
AACR2

Manufactured in the United States of America
ISBN 0–8052–0701–5

To our families:

Susan and Bill
Karen, Daniel
and
our parents

Contents

Acknowledgments

We wish to express thanks to the following persons for their kind help in preparing this book. Bruce Abel; Thelma Baker; Doris Bernhein, Planned Parenthood, New York; Audrey Bertolet; Cindy Blakeslee; Dr. George Brock Chisholm, *in memoriam;* Nancy Cox; Dr. Hugh J. Davis, Johns Hopkins Hospital, Baltimore; Dr. James Henderson Dorsey; Judy Falk; Terry Fleishman; Norman Fleishman, Center for Population Options; Dr. Sadja Goldsmith; Margery Greenfeld; Mark Horlings, attorney at law, San Francisco; Jimmye Kimmey, Association for Study of Abortion, New York; Nan Tucker McEvoy and the Preterm staff, Washington, D.C.; Margaret Miner; Sally Minshew; Dr. Lonny Myers, Midwest Population Center, Chicago; the staff of Planned Parenthood Teen Clinic, Chicago; Lorena Ragland, Birth Control Institute, Los Angeles; John Rague; Jan Shaw; James Shriver, III, Director, The Gallup Youth Survey; Dr. Jerome J. Siegel, Emko Company, St. Louis; Dr. Bruce Sklarew; Myra Sklarew; Libby Smith, Abortion Information Data Bank, San Francisco; Doug Stewart, Planned Parenthood, New York; Harriet Surovell; Lydia Vuynovich; Elizabeth D. Ward; Wendy J. Wertheimer and the American Social Health Association. Particular appreciation is expressed to Carol Cassell and Timothy P. Lannan, Education Department, Planned Parenthood World Population, New York City.

Preface

... we can never learn to reverence life until we know how to
understand sex.

Havelock Ellis, 1897

This is not a biology book or a marriage manual. There are plenty of
those already. We took care to be scientifically accurate, and we hope
and believe the book will help young—maybe even older—marriages.
But we did not wish to repeat what has been done well enough, even
overdone, elsewhere.

What has been missing and much needed, in our view, is a practical
presentation on sexual freedom and responsibility. Many young people, married or not, are making decisions to have sex without benefit
of sound birth control information. While such information is becoming more readily available, there is a long way to go—witness the large
number of young people obtaining abortions under recently liberalized laws.

Teachers in high schools and colleges have told us repeatedly that
there are enough materials on anatomy and physiology. What they
need for their students, and themselves, is a straightforward discussion dealing with both practical questions and social and psychological issues—values and emotions. We have attempted to do this.

Of course, any discussion of values is subjective; science cannot
decide certain vital issues, and several points of view will be helpful
to young people in making up their own minds. That's one of our basic
assumptions. On many issues, therefore, we do offer several points of
view, leaving the reader to decide what is best for him or her. Indeed,
we two authors do not always agree. No one can make universal
judgments in an area as diverse, changing, and private as sexual

behavior. We speak out strongly on some matters and leave others alone, recognizing the variety of behavior around us without approving or disapproving of everything we see.

Perhaps this can best be regarded as a self-help book on health—not just physical health, but mental health as well! As far as anybody's total, overall well-being is concerned, sexual attitudes and understanding of sexuality is vitally important!

Planning a first pregnancy is a good indicator of success in this regard, and failures are still legion, mainly among the young. We oppose the idea that if people want to have sex, they have to have babies too. For almost everyone in society except the young, sex and reproduction are separated now by ready access to good contraception. Young people are last to have this benefit of modern science, having been denied it by the prejudice, ignorance, or timidity of their elders. This book is an expression of faith in the readiness of young people to learn and do what will help them cope better with vital relationships, and to govern their own futures wisely.

We are gratified by the favorable response to this book, which justifies a new revision; even more, we are pleased at the progress made since the first edition toward a better informed, better protected young adult population.

The changes for this edition were made by Dr. Lieberman with the approval of Ms. Peck. Every reader's comments and suggestions will be helpful in preparing future editions.

E. James Lieberman, M.D.
Ellen Peck

Introduction

Over the centuries, most older people have found talking about sex and sex-related behavior to be uncomfortable or impossible. Some try to cover up their discomfort by telling sex jokes, usually dirty; others, by trying to appear learned or super-solemn; still others, by being as dully matter-of-fact as if they were discussing taking a suit to the dry cleaners. Furthermore, when they talk about sex with younger people (up to age twenty), most adults tend to emphasize what they themselves consider to be important about sex–an aura of romance, of mystery, of sacrament, of repressive moralism, or sometimes of *laissez faire* total freedom. Still others refuse to talk about sex at all with the young, convinced that this will simply "put ideas into their heads."

James Lieberman and Ellen Peck do none of these things, and, as to putting ideas into any heads, they know very well that no one has to do this, for the ideas are already there–as they should be. Instead of falling into any of the above traps, they come to young people via these pages with good clear prose, lucid understanding, a wealth of solid facts of the kinds most relevant for those just entering the fullness of sexuality–and above all, a feeling of warmth, comradeship and sharing about the whole thing.

Dr. Lieberman and Ms. Peck talk as people talking with other people, about things that are important for all people to learn to talk about with each other. In fact, although they have subtitled their book "A Guide for the Young," it's a book for all ages, and they have obviously learned as much *from* the young as they expect to convey *to* the young. Therefore, they create an atmosphere of candor, veracity, and composure that fits well into the mood and life-styles of today's young people: sex *is* a big thing, but not all *that* big.

So parents who also read these pages will be doing themselves a great favor, because the book grants them an opportunity to begin to perceive their children's generation for what it is. The authors, in trying to meet the needs of children whose parents have not met these needs, have succeeded in illuminating the young for the parents themselves to see more clearly. Here are the young, then, reaching out for identity, for a sense of belonging, of intimacy, in a crowded, feverish, hostile world; reaching out for self-respect in a world that accords respect to very few, but especially not to the young or the old; asking for information that is denied them, in a world that exploits commercially the very life force they want to learn about; asking for the privacy and confidentiality of medical and guidance counseling services geared to their special needs, in a world that fails to supply these adequately to anyone, but especially not to the young and the old.

We all share a world that grows more different every day from any world ever lived in before—a world that asks more of people while giving less to them, a world getting very short indeed of the basic commodities for human and humane living. One of these essential commodities is closeness—real closeness—of human beings to one another. Young children deprived of this closeness can die—or stay alive and still feel dead inside. Sex is one way to closeness, and young people are using it for this, often prematurely, but in a sometimes despairing effort to stay alive inside. So are adults, for that matter, only they are afraid or ashamed to admit it. Talking about sex with other people in the way that this book does has been found to lead to more closeness between people, of the same age, of different ages—and even sometimes between husbands and wives and between young people and their own parents!

Reading this book about sex will help people to learn how to talk about it with each other–and that's the first big step.

Mary S. Calderone, M.D., M.P.H.
Executive Director of SIECUS
(Sex Information and Education
Council of the U.S.)

Sex & Birth Control

A Guide for the Young

1
Sex and the Teen-ager: Living in Limbo

Since children are able to have babies at thirteen and fourteen years of age, do you believe in sex at that age? If not, why did nature make it possible?

An eighth-grader

We believe that youngsters are not ready for sex at the beginning of puberty. Yet some do start, ready or not, and the result is some 30,000 pregnancies annually to girls under fifteen. That seems like a large number, but there are about 5 million girls in the age group from twelve to fourteen in our country. Divide 30,000 by 5,000,000 and you find that less than 1 percent are getting pregnant, 99.4 percent are not. About 13,000—less than half this very young group—actually have babies: The abortion rate is very high. Early teen-age pregnancy is a tragedy for most families; fortunately, it is a relatively rare occurrence.

The real cause for concern is an older group, from fifteen up to twenty. About 10 percent of the women in this age group get pregnant each year: 1 million pregnancies—600,000 births, about 300,000 abortions induced, another 100,000 miscarriages. The vast majority of these pregnancies are unplanned and unwanted at the time they occur. Saying "no" to sex is one way, perhaps the best way, to prevent such accidents. If you say "yes," at least do so with confidence that pregnancy won't result. For those who choose to have sex, the knowledge and means to protect against unwanted pregnancy should be made available much more widely than at present. Even older, married women still have many accidental pregnancies.

Young people are sexually adult sooner than they used to be, and socially adult later. There is a "sex gap" of about ten years between the time of puberty—about twelve—and the time when mature couples are ready for parenthood. While quite a fuss is made about teen-agers and sex, little has been done to help them cope successfully with a decade of living in limbo.

Experts believe that the average age of puberty has fallen in the last century. The change is probably due to better health and nutrition, which also account for the greater average height, and better athletic and possibly better learning abilities, of today's young people. The average girl nowadays begins her physical development and menstrual periods earlier than her mother and grandmother. Boys reach physical manhood sooner than their fathers and grandfathers.

But social readiness for parenthood takes longer. Young adults need an increasing amount of education and job experience in order to cope with the complex society of today and tomorrow. While parenthood can be one of life's great joys, it can also be a serious setback, depending on when the first baby comes. Parenthood by accident has always been common, has always created problems, but the consequences to teen-agers are particularly serious now, and teen-agers know it. Yet most first pregnancies are still unplanned. Although some young people do remarkably well as parents under trying circumstances, and love their children, many would rather have waited a while longer for marriage, parenthood, or both. They feel, and experts agree, that a few years' delay is a big advantage in starting a family.

The older generation is well aware that the most serious consequence of sexual intercourse is pregnancy; from time immemorial youngsters—especially girls—have been warned away from premarital sex because of the risk of pregnancy. The warnings stopped many, but millions of others had their sex and had their babies. Everyone knows these facts. But parents, teachers, doctors, and clergymen have not found a way to deal with them so that more teen-agers can find a sensible pathway through the dilemma of sex.

Now, with modern contraception, it is quite possible to have sex without babies. Indeed, most married and older couples in the United States currently practice contraception. And even more of these couples have a choice in the matter: If they do not use contraceptives it is usually because they have decided not to. With younger people, however, the situation is different. If they do have sex and do not use contraception, it is most often because they have not been taught how contraception works, they are not sure how to obtain or use contraceptives, or they feel too guilty about sexual activity to think ahead and take precautions. As a matter of fact, most teen-agers have not had sexual intercourse, and those who are experienced have sex quite infrequently—but they have a high risk of pregnancy because they are not protected by effective contraception. For many teenagers the "sex gap" leads straight into the baby trap.

Another danger that has traditionally been used to discourage premarital sex is the possibility of getting venereal disease. This is a real danger, for VD has presently reached epidemic proportions. There is wide agreement, however, that people, whether old or young, are not going to give up sex in order to avoid VD. The "answer" involves providing better education for both doctors and the general public and making good health care available to all.

Young people are physically ready for sex before they are emotionally ready for intimate relationships—and *long* before they are ready for marriage or parenthood. When it comes to sex before marriage, the usual teaching of the older generation has been "don't." That message is well-intentioned, since it is supposed to preserve the moral values of society, protect young people from emotional harm, and strengthen American family life. Good intentions, however, are not enough. Widespread ignorance about sex and contraception has caused innumerable human tragedies.

Many young people have observed strict chastity but have married too soon under pressure of normal, strong sexual urges; young marriages have notoriously high divorce rates, and it is clear that the vow "till death do us part" has little meaning in the face of the difficulties young couples experience.

It is time to change from "don't" to "it depends" when talking about premarital sex. The goals of a sane and moral society can be met with greater trust given to developing young adults, if all relevant knowledge is made available. It is time for society to wake up to the facts of teen-age life. "Respectable" adults seem to have both eyes closed to premarital sex, even while deploring hundreds of thousands of premarital pregnancies and babies. Now let's admit that the stork didn't bring them.

The risk of pregnancy can, with a little knowledge and planning, be reduced almost to zero. If young people are not ready to obtain the knowledge and do the planning, they ought not to be having sexual intercourse. Even if they don't care about themselves, an innocent third party must be considered.

If pregnancy and VD can be avoided, are there other cautions about teen-age sex? Definitely, yes. The most convincing cautions come from teen-agers themselves, from whom we will hear more later.

When there is no risk of pregnancy, questions about premarital sex move to a different level—moral and psychological, rather than biological and social. Many individuals have suffered as a result of early sexual experiences even when no pregnancy or venereal disease occurred. Many others have found premarital sex to be a positive experience. No one can resolve the complex question of premarital sex for any other individual, but it is a good beginning to admit that there is no longer any easy answer. The eminent scientist and philosopher René Dubos has stated that "For the first time in the history of mankind, the biological and social experience of the father is almost useless to his son." By understanding the biological and social changes in the area of sex, we can make use of the psychological and moral insights which come from the past, a lasting heritage of value and wisdom.

When people argue about morals and sex, a key issue is what they think is the purpose of sex. Not many people believe any more that the *only* function of sex is making babies. (Those who do are entitled to, but they should not make rules for the rest of us, any more than we should impose ours on them.) Some people still believe that the most important function of sex is reproduction, but even that is open to question. Certainly most couples are not usually hoping to have a child when they have sex—and this has long been true, even before the days of modern birth control. It is also true that the survival of the race depends on some degree of procreation, and therefore on sexual intercourse. But this does not mean that for human beings reproduction is the most important aspect of sex, or even that it is always biologically helpful. In animals as well as human beings sexual activity is not always connected with reproduction. There is also evidence that among social animals mating behavior may serve a variety of social purposes other than producing offspring. And certainly, among human beings, there is no longer need for a high level of reproduction matching the level of our sexual drives. Advances in public health have brought the world to the point where human reproduction is hurting rather than helping the survival of the race because births far outnumber deaths and the population is growing everywhere with no place to go. Unlike other animals, human beings are committed to keeping their offspring alive, their death rates down, even when there is overpopulation. The only acceptable way to do this is to keep birth rates down.

The nonreproductive side of sex—its physical and emotional satisfaction—is no less natural than the procreative function, and has always been the usual reason for people to engage in sexual relations. Much as a couple may wish to make a baby, the prospect hardly can account for the passionate arousal that makes sex possible. There has always been a great deal of discussion of the morality of nonreproductive sexual activity, but most people agree that sex contributes uniquely to the most valuable human experiences—love, loyalty, intimacy, sharing.

Unfortunately, people have been taught off and on throughout history that sex is bad, pleasure is wicked, and intercourse is excusable only for making babies, i.e., to preserve the race. As a result many people feel guilty about enjoying sexual feelings, even in married love, when having a baby is not their intent. This is one reason some people "forget" to use birth control: They feel guilty about sex unless it can lead to pregnancy. In those cases pregnancy becomes the price or penalty that people pay for having pleasure, when they feel the pleasure is not deserved, or in some way sinful.

Of course, we, the authors, don't accept the idea that sexual love is sinful or that pleasure is wicked. If the pleasure is at someone else's expense, or it involves lying or deception, then it should be criticized, but not because it is enjoyable. Sexual ignorance and guilt have taken a massive toll of human life and happiness throughout history. Today more people, and especially young people, hope for and expect full understanding and enjoyment of sex; and they are concerned with how to combine this with responsible moral standards.

Bridging the Sex Gap

One way to cope with that long period between puberty and marriage is to compromise between total sexual avoidance and intercourse: The obviously sensible thing to do, most teenagers realize, is to "start" having some sexual experiences—but stop short of "going all the way." This is still the most common solution, at least in the teen-age years. Sexual excitement and release (orgasm), can take a number of different pathways. We will have more to say about this in a later chapter, but a few comments are in order now.

Among young people masturbation is the most usual form of sexual pleasure. Today experts agree that masturbation is normal for both sexes, the only harm being caused by ignorance and guilt. In fact, it is believed that masturbation (or what might better be called solitary sex) is not only a normal and natural phase of sexual development but a very important one, helping young people to deal with sexual experiences in fantasy without involving another person. It's only half of sex but it fulfills a practice function—it's a part of normal development which can contribute to better sex later on without risking personal hurt in the present.

Another channel of sexual release is involuntary: the wet dream, or nocturnal emission, which occurs among males. During sleep sexual arousal occurs which may lead to orgasm; in the male this is accompanied by ejaculation of seminal fluid. (A girl may also have an erotic dream with or without orgasm.) Wet dreams occur with varying frequency, more commonly when other sexual outlets are not available, but sometimes a wet dream may occur after a prior orgasm the same night. The dream may or may not be remembered; sometimes the sleeper wakes, sometimes not. The subject of the dream may be surprising or even disturbing, e.g., if it involves a sister, brother, parent, or friend of the same sex. Such dreams are not cause for alarm (although daytime preoccupations with such disturbing subjects might well be discussed with a professional counselor).

Petting is another normal sexual activity which can lead to orgasm without intercourse. This solution is practically an American tradition, and widely accepted. Some other cultures find this odd. For example, Danes and Swedes tend to believe that going all the way with one partner is respectable but find American petting patterns shockingly promiscuous because many American virgins have had so many petting partners. The idea that not having intercourse is somehow morally superior is something they can't understand. They consider our much-petted women to be only technical virgins! It seems that an increased number of young Americans today agrees with this point of view.

Prostitution is another outlet. Consider the boy who wants to "protect" his girl, and protect himself from deeper emotional involvement with her based on sex. He'll visit prostitutes or go out with someone who is free with her body, but he wouldn't think of doing it with "his" girl, whom he hopes to marry (and who he wants to be a virgin when he does). This is an aspect of the absurd but still common "double standard" which is supported by many men and women. Some of the many rules of the double standard are that sex is alright for *all* men but not for (good) women; therefore only bad girls are fun in bed and good ones are to be wives and mothers; there is a time for men to sow wild oats and then a time for them to settle down to the serious business of marriage. Such attitudes are not consistent with good sex or happy marriage in a time when human beings, male and female, are regarded as equals.

Young people are moving away from the double standard. They are trying to be more natural and honest with sex. Sometimes they reduce this to a different kind of absurdity—an attempt to be casual about passion. They want to get away at all costs from the commercialism, the sexism, the gross "adult" distortions of intimate and compassionate human relationships. They may make many mistakes but they're not likely to go back to the old double standard, which made sex the husband's right and the wife's duty. The wholesomeness of today's young lovers shows up in their declining use of prostitutes, as couples decide that premarital sex—with birth control, of course—is a legitimate expression of love.

The double standard is breaking down, but it will take time to reach real equality between the sexes. Meanwhile, the effort to reach this goal is leading to changes in sexual attitudes, and it is young people who have to make many of the most difficult decisions. For example, a girl may be aware that many men prefer their wife to be a virgin. She may also be aware of what is equally true: Many of these men are insecure, afraid that a sexually experienced woman will criticize their performance, and in general more apt to believe that the status of women should stay below that of men. Under these circumstances giving up one's virginity involves some long-range considerations, and it is not surprising that so many girls want to take their time about the decision.

On the other hand, young men are often equally doubtful about what is expected of them and what they want for themselves. They are the first generation to cope with a meaningful women's liberation movement, with widespread criticism of the double standard, with girl friends who accuse them of being sexists, and with fiancées who don't want to be housewives and may not even want to be married. Equality between the sexes is an important human goal, but it is also true that with standards changing so rapidly, it's difficult for anyone to know what's right. On balance, though, thinking through one's personal decisions is morally and psychologically preferable to following rules blindly—even though it's harder.

Mental health means an ability to cope with life, to adapt to circumstances, and to better one's circumstances when possible. Today there is more freedom, and with it, more uncertainty. Coping with uncertainty requires a balance of emotional security and intelligence: Your head and your heart have to be "in tune."

A young girl and a young boy is a tormented tangle, a seething confusion of sexual feelings and sexual thoughts which only the years will disentangle. Years of honest thoughts of sex, and years of struggling action in sex will bring us at last where we want to get, to our real and accomplished chastity, our completeness, when our sexual act and our sexual thought are in harmony, and the one does not interfere with the other.*

Using Your Head Before Bed

Sex takes intelligence—brains as well as body feelings. Learning and thinking about sex is the responsibility that goes with the freedom, and the healthy way to cope with the exciting and hazardous unknown. Getting married young, and having babies in the teen-age years, is simply not the way to cope with the realities of today and tomorrow.

In making sensible decisions about your personal lives, it is essential to understand what choices are open to you. In the years between coming of age sexually and being ready to think about parenthood, young people theoretically have the choice of having sexual intercourse without pregnancy resulting. But in practice, it often doesn't work out this way. This isn't because it couldn't: If you know how your body works and how birth control works, you need not become a parent before you want to. Most of you do not have this basic information, however. Others understand some of the facts but do not know the details of how to buy and use contraceptives. Our generation is largely to blame for this. What adults decide to explain in the way of sex education most often leaves out the facts of life that matter most. In this book we try to answer the practical questions about birth control that most books and courses don't cover. But to some extent young people themselves are to blame. There is no getting around the fact that some mental and emotional effort is needed if you are going to control your sex life.

One of the most popular methods of contraception among young

*D. H. Lawrence, "Apropos Lady Chatterley's Lover" from *Sex, Literature, and Censorship* (New York: Viking Press paperback, 1959).

people is hope, or crossed fingers. This is no better than the "It can't happen to me" approach. But simple mathematics gives a very different and more reliable answer.

What percentage of couples mating on a random day of the month will achieve pregnancy with a single act of intercourse? Based on the length of time an ovum is ready to be fertilized—about twenty-four hours—and the survival time of sperm deposited in the vagina—about forty-eight hours—the chances of becoming pregnant with a single sex act are about one in 25. So about 4 in 100, or 4 percent of careless couples, will get caught the first time they have intercourse. If no contraception is used by couples who have intercourse a dozen times, half will be pregnant; the chances for any one couple will be 50 percent.

In discussing the effectiveness of contraceptives, we use the measure "woman-year." One woman exposed to unprotected normal marital relations—intercourse 2 or 3 times a week—for a year counts as one woman-year. If 4 percent get pregnant with each exposure, practically all women will be pregnant after 25 exposures (4 percent × 25 = 100 percent). At the end of a year—about 120 exposures to intercourse—you'd expect all women to be pregnant. And you'd be almost right—studies have shown that about 80 pregnancies will result from 100 woman-years of risktaking; in the second year of exposure, another 10 women will become pregnant, making 90 percent; and of the last 10 percent, some will have babies later on, and some never will. Another way of putting all this is: If you want to get pregnant, it takes an average of three to five months of trying; if you don't want to, it may take only once! To understand this, you need to know some biology and some mathematics. Whether you understand it or not, don't take chances where lives are involved.

In rating contraceptive methods, you need to know how many sexually active women will get pregnant if a particular method is used faithfully. With the pill, the answer is almost zero—officially 0.5 percent, or one woman in 200: That means 99.5 percent protection. Compare that with relying on the so-called safe period just before, during, and after normal menstruation; this is called the rhythm for Catholics). Of 100 women, 30 to 40 will have babies after a year on the rhythm method, depending on how carefully it's used. That's a lot—but still 50 percent less than using no method at all (80 women pregnant out of 100). So you ought not to rely on rhythm unless you have to, but everyone should know about it anyway. If you are stuck sometime without a contraceptive or want to use combinations, you can estimate the risk of pregnancy better if you understand the monthly cycle. More on that later.

In this brief introduction to a large subject, we must leave a great deal unsaid. It is difficult to put sex in perspective, without distortion or prejudice. We do not want to take sex out of its context of human relationships, but cannot do justice to communication, commitment, intimacy, ethics, optimism, harmony, conflict, maturation, equality, fidelity, idealism, failure, frustration, patience, empathy, love and joy —to mention some important themes.

With sexual inhibitions diminishing, people with scruples about chastity and fidelity feel defensive, in need of some (reasonable) support, as did sexual nonconformists of generations past. There are good reasons for premarital chastity, as there are for other choices (more on this in the chapter on abstinence).

Literature, the arts, and science can all help in understanding the role of sex in people's lives. Talking discreetly with individuals and couples who are more experienced is a good way of learning more about successful and unsuccessful approaches to sexuality.

The moral principles that apply in other aspects of life also apply in sexual relations. Among the most important, we feel, are: to do no harm, to be truthful with tact, to regard people as individually unique, to value them as equals, to help when you can. Knowledge, understanding, freedom of inquiry and expression, justice, and sensitive respect for the rights and feelings of others are necessary to the good life, including the good sex life.

The most private and personal element in our lives, sex, has the most public and planetary consequences. No one has seen this and said it more clearly than Walt Whitman:

Sex contains all, bodies, souls,
Meanings, proofs, purities, delicacies, results, promulgations,
Songs, commands, health, pride, the maternal mystery, the seminal milk,
All hopes, benefactions, bestowals, all the passions, loves, beauties,
    delights of the earth,
All the governments, judges, gods, follow'd persons of the earth,
These are contain'd in sex as parts of itself and justifications of itself.

Without shame the man I like knows and avows the deliciousness of his
    sex,
Without shame the woman I like knows and avows hers.

from *A Woman Waits for Me*

2

Research on
Teen Sexuality

In 1971 and again five years later, in 1976, national surveys of teen-age women (fifteen to nineteen years old) were conducted by researchers at Johns Hopkins University. Professors John Kantner and Melvin Zelnik are widely known and respected for their studies of sexual knowledge, experience, birth control, and pregnancy among young unmarried American women. We will tell you about a few of their findings, and offer some interpretations of our own.

1) In 1971 27 percent of these single young women reported having sexual intercourse at least once. In 1976 the experienced, or non-virgin, group increased to 35 percent. That is a substantial change in five years. If the trend were to keep up, virgins would soon be in the minority. However, this is unlikely to happen.

Considering the loosening of strictures on sexual discussion and behavior in recent years, teen-agers have remained relatively conservative. Overall, 65 percent of these women are still virgins; at age fifteen, 82 percent are virgins. Among the eighteen- and nineteen-year-olds about half are sexually experienced. But remember: A few years ago, many more women of that age would have been married already. Nowadays women (and men) are waiting longer before making that long-term commitment. Some of them are having sex while single. Instead of viewing this as moral breakdown, we can interpret it as a result of delayed marriage, with the total *level* of sexual activity not increasing very much at all. Indeed, except for couples living together, premarital sex is rather infrequent compared with marital sex. Those who feel that premarital sex is better than premature marriage—which it seems to have replaced—have grounds for optimism in this trend. Protection against accidental pregnancy remains a problem, as we shall see. But would you say we are a sexually revolutionary society when, in 1976, almost half of single women were still virgins at their twentieth birthday?

2) In 1971 less than half the women said they used contraception the last time they had intercourse; in 1976 two-thirds used some protection. The older the woman, the more likely she was to have used birth control. The change over five years was dramatic: Younger teen-agers were as well protected in 1976 as the older ones were in 1971. Still, only 30 percent *always* used contraception in 1976 (compared with 18 percent in 1971). We see improvement, but much remains to be done.

3) Half of the non-virgins have had only one sex partner; another one-third report two or three partners. Premarital sex seems to be guided by rules of monogamy and fidelity, as is marital sex. More than one partner does not mean promiscuity: It usually means one relationship ended and another began. A small group of women—under 10 percent—report having had six or more partners. This small group is not typical, and we might not dwell on them at all except that they are at much higher risk for venereal disease (see Ch. 13). Obviously, this group provides sexual experience to a relatively large number of males, and this helps explain why young men generally have more sex experience than most women of comparable age.

4) Not only are so-called sexually active women in this study relatively monogamous, they are also rather inactive sexually. About half the non-virgins reported no intercourse in the previous month, and only one-fourth had sex three or more times in that period. Although there were fewer virgins in 1976, the non-virgins abstained more than in 1971. Our explanation: More teen-age women in the later study had tried sex, but many of them didn't like it, or decided they didn't need or want it at this time in their lives. Apparently, quite a few have sex once or twice and then give it up until much later. Certainly, for the vast majority, premarital sex does not lead to the lewd and lascivious

life traditionally pictured as the fate of the "fallen" woman.

In 1979, Drs. Zelnik and Kantner found that 50 percent of urban area women fifteen to nineteen had had premarital sex. More of these teen-agers used contraception than in the past, but there was a shift toward less effective methods—withdrawal and rhythm—from the pill and IUD, so the pregnancy rate was high: 32 percent of the sexually active group.

Why Teens Take Chances

Very few young women want to become pregnant, yet less than one-third always use contraception. Zelnik and Kantner included questions about birth control in their study (*Family Planning Perspectives,* September 1979). It seems that most of those surveyed thought they couldn't get pregnant, either because of the time of month, because they were too young, or because they had intercourse too infrequently. While the first two reasons might have some validity, the research also showed that most of the young women did not understand the "safe" period well enough to rely on it at all. As for those who knew they might get pregnant, about half said they simply hadn't expected to have intercourse when it happened. A few said their boyfriends objected to contraception, and some gave other reasons: They "didn't know about contraception or where to get it"; it was "difficult to use" or "interfered with pleasure"; or they "believed it was wrong or dangerous."

To sum up, the main reasons (75 percent) for nonuse of birth control were these: 1) thinking you cannot get pregnant, or 2) thinking you won't have intercourse. Teen-agers are wrong on one or both of these points so often that they have been experiencing about 1 million pregnancies each year, most of them unwanted. Those are costly misconceptions. Think about it and act accordingly: Unless you have a rare medical condition, you *can* get pregnant as a young couple. Therefore, if you plan to have sex, be prepared; if you're not prepared, wait; if you can't wait, at least don't be caught off guard a second time.

Teens Want Information and Services

The Gallup Youth Survey interviewed 1,174 young people by telephone in 1978 on sexual attitudes. The respondents, thirteen to eighteen years old, were mostly tolerant of premarital sex, and favored sex education in schools and making birth control devices available to teen-agers. This survey is intended to be representative of American young people across the country.

By a majority of two to one, the respondents felt that premarital sex was not wrong. More boys (66 to 22 percent) than girls (52 to 38 percent) believed premarital sex to be acceptable. Older teen-agers were more accepting than younger ones. Those who live in more conservative areas—the Midwest and South—disapproved more than those living in the East or Far West. As you would expect, those approving sex before marriage placed less importance on whether they later married a virgin. But from other research there are still signs of a double standard: Both sexes tend to accept premarital intercourse for males more readily than for females.

Should contraceptives be made available to teen-agers? Those polled by Gallup answered "yes" 59 percent and "no" 27 percent, while 14 percent were undecided. Attitudes differed depending upon age and region of the country: Older teen-agers, and those in the East and Far West, were more affirmative. *Similarities* in responses were more remarkable than differences. Girls were only slightly more interested than boys in having contraception made available: 61 and 56 percent favored it, respectively. Between Protestants and Catholics there was essentially no difference, with 58 and 57 percent approval, respectively. This occurred in spite of strong opposition by the Catholic Church to contraception. Finally, a comparison of teen with adult attitudes on this question is possible. The Gallup Poll asked adults the same question in 1977 and found 56 percent in favor of providing birth control to unmarried teen-agers and 35 percent against—not very different from the opinions (59 percent for and 27 percent against) of the younger generation.

Fewer than half the teen-agers in the poll had taken a classroom course in sex education. Of those who had, one-fourth said nothing was included about contraception. When contraception was included, it made a big difference in the value of the course: 88 percent in those classes found them to be "very" or "fairly" helpful, compared with 67 percent who did not learn about birth control. Conversely—and more dramatically—33 percent of the latter group found the course "not very helpful," compared with only 12 percent of the former. Teen-agers want sex education, and they like it better when it is complete with contraceptive information. That seems perfectly reasonable to us.

Consider the implications of ignorance and misinformation: In the first of the studies by Zelnik and Kantner, all the girls were asked if they knew when a woman can first become pregnant. The answers were divided between "when periods begin" and "sometime later." (It is true that the periods begin about a year before most girls ovulate and can get pregnant; however, one cannot be sure of the timing, and girls who are menstruating and have intercourse ought to take precautions against unwanted pregnancy.)

"During what part of the monthly cycle is a girl most likely to get pregnant?" Only half of the girls knew the correct answer: about two weeks after a menstrual period (or, more correctly, about fourteen days before the next one). The rest of the girls thought either "any time" or "right before, during, or after a period" was the fertile point —wrong! (but the "any time" respondents are less likely to be careless). The older girls knew more about it than the younger ones, but even among the sexually experienced eighteen- and nineteen-year-olds, 40 percent did not understand at what time during their cycle they ran the greatest risk of pregnancy. Very few of the girls admitted that they didn't know; most of those who are mistaken are blissfully unaware of the ignorance which can ruin their lives. It is bad enough not to know, much worse to have the facts backward: Some of these girls will avoid intercourse when it would be safer and arrange to have it in mid-cycle—when it is least safe!

Where did these girls get their sex information? We are not even talking about contraception now, but simply about the facts of the menstrual cycle. Evidently their mothers, teachers, sisters, and friends —male and female—failed to transmit accurate information.

Knowledge of contraception among girls tends to be greater as they become older, and if they have had intercourse. Birth control pills are known to practically everyone. Eighty percent of the sexually experienced girls in the first Johns Hopkins survey had heard about most of the other methods (including douching, which is *not* a useful birth control method at all); seventy percent of them had at least heard of the safe period—that portion of the monthly cycle during which pregnancy is unlikely to occur. However, half the girls would not have been able to follow the rhythm method properly because they didn't know *when* the safe period comes (and in any case, the safe period is only *relatively* safe). The overwhelming majority of all the girls interviewed—over 80 percent—thought responsibility for contraception should be shared by male and female partners.

What About Males?

A recent study of teen-age boys from a well-to-do Illinois community may surprise some readers who believe that boys are way ahead of girls in sexual experience. Dr. Daniel Offer reported in 1971 that about 50 percent of the high school boys he studied did not even date until their sophomore year. By the junior year about 30 percent dated regularly, and about half of these boys had experienced heavy petting. By the end of high school about 10 percent of the boys had experienced sexual intercourse; this rose to about 30 percent after the freshman year of college and to about 50 percent by the end of the junior year in college.

A more significant—and also surprising—study in terms of numbers and representativeness appeared in the November 1972 issue of *Journal of Marriage and the Family.* A Michigan research team reported on answers to a questionnaire by 4,220 students in grades eight through twelve. The survey took place in 1969 in three west-shore Michigan communities where there were more blue-collar than white-collar families. Students indicated their personal experience by level of heterosexual behavior.

Table I*
The Progress of Sexual Experience

		BOYS			GIRLS		
	Up to age:	13	15	17+	13	15	17+
I	Held hands (%)	79	91	94	78	90	96
II	Held arm around (%)	64	83	92	68	88	93
III	Kissed (%)	64	78	89	65	83	93
IV	Necked (%)	46	63	81	44	68	84
V	Light petting, above waist (%)	36	54	74	22	45	70
VI	Heavy petting, below waist (%)	28	40	65	16	27	54
VII	"Gone all the way"—coitus (%)	19	21	33	7	12	26
VIII	Coitus with two or more partners (%)	12	11	16	4	4	7

*Adapted from "The Sexual Behavior of Adolescents in Middle America: Generational and American-British Comparisons" by Arthur M. Vener, Cyrus S. Stewart, and David L. Hager. *Journal of Marriage and the Family* 34:696–705 (November) 1972.

The experience for both sexes was found to be about the same through level IV (necking): Two-thirds of the boys and girls had done some necking by age fifteen. Experience with sexual intercourse was higher among boys than girls, but at age seventeen and older, the difference was only about 7 percent. The rate reported by girls at seventeen—26 percent—matches that found in the Johns Hopkins interview survey—27 percent—which tends to support the validity of both studies. The findings for boys aged seventeen (33 percent had intercourse) are *identical* with those in a study done almost thirty years ago with a similar social group by Glenn V. Ramsey (*American Journal of Psychology,* 1943). The authors of the present study conclude: "Apparently for boys in middle America, the alleged revolution in sexual behavior has not yet come to pass." A follow-up study done in 1973 showed slight but significant increases in sexual experience among Michigan—and possibly all—teens.

The Teen Scene in Britain

Males as well as females were interviewed a few years ago in a survey of unmarried English teen-agers. This study, *The Sexual Behavior of Young People* (1966), by Michael Schofield, reports findings from 1,873 young people fifteen to nineteen years old. One-third of the boys and one-fourth of the girls were sexually experienced. Over 80 percent of the boys and girls, experienced or not, claimed to know something about birth control. But, as in the American group, there was considerable misinformation. Only 20 percent of the experienced girls always used birth control; over half the girls said they never took precautions; and many used contraception (including male methods) only occasionally. Among the boys, 43 percent said they always used some form of birth control—including withdrawal. Girls were asked if they insisted that their partners use something; only one-third said they insisted. One nineteen-year-old girl said, "Well, I suppose I am too shy to bring the subject up." A seventeen-year-old girl said her partner claimed that "if it were natural to use them we'd have been born with them on us."

These young people were also asked whether they considered the possibility of pregnancy, since it is often assumed that the fear of pregnancy is a serious barrier to premarital sex. About half of the experienced boys and 70 percent of the experienced girls had worried about pregnancy, but the rest said they had not. Apparently up to 80 percent of the non-virgins were taking chances with pregnancy. This did not seem to be due to lack of available contraceptives, but because "social disapproval means that many of their sexual adventures are unpremeditated." Except in the case of engaged couples who regularly slept together, many of the teen-agers had sexual relations on impulse, and not very regularly.

Here we face a situation which is not really new but is being talked about more: Many teen-agers have premarital intercourse, most of these wish to avoid pregnancy, but only a few take adequate precautions. One reason most don't take precautions is because they feel they are not supposed to be having sex in the first place; another reason is that they feel it is unromantic to be prepared for it. Many young people enter a sexual relationship on impulse. It's as though planning for it is somehow wrong, while being swept away in the heat of passion is somehow more acceptable—at least for girls—in the hush-hush climate of proper manners.

Young people who really think *planned* sex is wrong but will allow *unplanned* sex to occur will not be affected by having birth control available. They might become more careful if their basic attitudes would change so that they could think about this aspect of their lives without feeling guilty. In a follow-up study, *The Sexual Behavior of Young Adults* (1973), Schofield found a pregnancy-filled gap of about five years between the first experience of sexual intercourse and the regular use of contraceptives. This gap "is the cause of many personal tragedies, some of them irreparable."

Attitudes Toward Love and Sex

Dr. Winston Ehrmann, in his book *Premarital Dating Behavior* (1959), pinpointed some trends among college students that are still of interest today. On the basis of interviews with 1,000 students, he found that among girls there was a closer association between feelings of love and sexual activity than among boys. The sexually experienced girls *all* were or had been involved with someone they loved; some had also had affairs with people they did not love. Only *some* of the sexually experienced boys had been involved with someone they loved. About one-third of the boys held to the double standard: They would not have sex with the girls they cared for seriously but did or would have sex with others. Interestingly, differences between the sexual experience and behavior of the males and females tended to disappear when both were in love. Dr. Ehrmann wrote that ". . . love tends to equate the sexual behavior of males and females."

Today males and females are more equal in sexual experience than in the past. Some of this is probably because of the strong feeling among women that they have the right to the same sexual freedom as men, including the freedom to have sex without love or commitment. But our own interviews with young people indicate that the increasing equality between young men and women goes along with a greater stress on friendship and a complete relationship, and the end of the double standard. There is less seeking out of prostitutes and more interest in combining sex with feelings of respect, affection, and love.

3

Abstinence?

He that is chaste and continent not to impair his strength, or honest
for fear of contagion, will hardly be heroically virtuous.
                                Sir Thomas Browne, *Christian Morals*

It's okay to say NO WAY.
Teensex, Planned Parenthood Federation of America pamphlet

This chapter is for those who have had sexual intercourse as well as
those who have not. Abstinence or virginity is where everyone starts
in sex, and long after they have exchanged innocence for experience,
people still feel strongly about how they began, and how it is best to
begin.

You cannot go back to virginity, but you can and sometimes must
return to abstinence. There are times in life when it becomes necessary
or desirable to leave off sex—sometimes for the sake of having or
saving a good sexual relationship.

Abstinence is the backdrop for sex, like the silence around music.
The reasons for abstinence are complex, as complex as the reasons for
having sex. You can say No to sex for better reasons or worse, just
as you can say Yes to it—because you are strong or because you are
weak, because you are loving or because you are spiteful, because you
know yourself or because you don't.

Abstinence need not be a requirement for all teen-agers; the old
insistence on it was rigid, repressive, sometimes useless, sometimes
destructive. But abstinence can be a healthy and respectable *option,*
particularly for limited periods of time. If abstinence was once the
only "correct" behavior before marriage, it now seems opinion may

have swung too far in the opposite direction. The New Sexual Liberationists ("What? You've never done it? Ha!") can be just as rigid as the Old Sexual Moralists ("What? You did it? Shame!").

Many American college athletes used to sign pledges not to engage in sexual relations during the season of their sport. Some artists and writers have said that abstinence is necessary for their creativity. Many people believe that abstinence is good because it proves and strengthens self-discipline. And others are afraid that each person has a quota of orgasms, which should be rationed carefully (it was once believed that seminal fluid, not blood, was the source of a man's stamina). Now we know better. Dr. Craig Sharp, adviser to a British Olympic team, wrote recently that sex before competition may very well help to relax an athlete and improve his rest and later performance. Many creative individuals can have good sex without sacrificing artistic achievement. Seminal fluid is not limited in quantity, but is produced in response to hormone levels and sexual activity, and the frequency of orgasm varies tremendously from one man or woman to another, with no known relationship to length of life or physical strength.

If abstinence is not a requirement for health and strength, creativity and longevity, neither is it a mark of sickness or abnormality. Although sexual intercourse is natural and healthy, it is not necessary to a sane and healthy life. Bearing children is natural but not necessary, and is even undesirable for some people. One does not need sex any more than a vegetarian needs meat to be healthy. Nonvegetarians may think it odd to forego meat, but they cannot say that such restraint is harmful or unhealthy. The same goes for sexual abstinence. People who claim that abstinence is "bad for you" usually are just as uninformed as the people who claim that sex is harmful. It depends on the individual and the circumstances.

Reasons for Waiting

To many, total abstinence is easier than perfect moderation.
St. Augustine, *On the Good of Marriage*

Why do so many teens decide to remain virgins? (That word, by the way, applies to males as well as females.) The reasons vary from "It is my personal decision to remain chaste for Jesus" to "I couldn't find anybody to do it with me if I tried."

Perhaps a few personal stories will seem familiar:

Stephanie's reason for "no sex now" is a result of some fairly sophisticated thinking on her part. At seventeen she is sure that having sex with any of the boys she now dates would mean hard-to-handle dependency problems for her. "When a boy I like so much as touches me, I practically fall in love with him," she explains, "and then I become too involved and too possessive. So what would happen if I went all the way instead of just part way? I might easily make a fool of myself by getting too emotional about him, causing embarrassment for myself—and him. I will consider having sex with a boy before marriage. I don't have any moral hangups, just emotional ones; but for that reason it's best for me to wait until I can be more independent emotionally. When I can say to myself, 'I dig him, I want him, but if the relationship ends in six weeks, I'll survive'—well, when I can say that and truly mean it, I may consider that I'm ready for sex."

Eileen, almost eighteen, practices abstinence but is not a virgin. Two years ago she had a sexual experience which turned out badly. Describing her former lover as "a real MCP" (male chauvinist pig), she explains that "I was simply used, not cared for."

"I'm not turned off to guys or anything like that," Eileen emphasizes, "but at this point I'm almost virgin again. Really, I do think of myself as a virgin—and I'll go into any other sex experience feeling like one. I do not count my first 'episode' at all. I do not think it was what sex is supposed to be. I regret it, but I won't let it ruin my love life: I'll remember it just enough to be sure I'm ready—and that, next time, the guy will be the right one."

"A bad experience" or the risk of it is also cited as a reason for abstinence by males. Paul, seventeen, tells this story: "When I was sixteen I had relations with a girl, also sixteen. Neither of us knew just what we were doing. It happened awkwardly, in a car. It was far from pleasurable. I kept wishing I could think of something to say. But neither of us said anything; we were not 'in love' enough to be very romantic. I was scared she'd be pregnant. In trying to find out whether I was going to be a father or not, I obtained most of my sex information that I have today." Paul, like Eileen, feels that he will not have sex again until a relationship offers "what sex is supposed to be."

Laurie, who is sixteen, comes from a conservative background. Her parents have never censored the movies she attends or prevented her exposure to the sexuality of the modern media, but they have counteracted its effects with their own strong beliefs and with the example of their own life-style. Laurie's parents feel that waiting until marriage for sex is best. Her mother did not sleep with Laurie's father prior to marriage—and says she feels very good about this choice. Laurie believes this; her parents seem very happy, and she has never known them to lie to her. Since she has always been treated with respect and love by her parents, she is impressed by the straightforward and sincere moral ideas they have to offer—ideas that, in some other family situations, might be or seem to be hypocritical. Laurie is not positive that she will always hold to her "no sex before marriage" idea, but at this point she thinks she will. And she thinks so enough to wait.

Jeanne, also sixteen, is a class leader. She was recently voted into the National Honor Society by a panel of classmates and teachers. She feels deeply in love with her boyfriend, Carl, and they have been dating nearly a year. Their sex activities have reached the petting stage, and she knows that Carl would go all the way if she let him—and Jeanne finds that thought somewhat tempting. Jeanne's expressed reason for holding back is simple: "If it didn't work out, I can't be sure Carl would keep quiet about it." Shortly after meeting Carl, Jeanne overheard a discussion in which he was involved. A certain girl was mentioned. Carl laughed meaningfully and said, "Oh, yes—I knew her for a while—*very well.*" Jeanne is not sure how much the other girl may have meant to Carl . . . whether she might once have meant as much to him as Jeanne herself now seems to . . . and Jeanne does not want to risk being reduced to the level of "a casual remark." This would jeopardize the high standing in which she is held by her school, which she describes as "fairly conservative." There is, for Jeanne, a lack of complete trust or confidence, even though she is in love. That kind of trust takes time, and she is wise to wait rather than risk spoiling her first sexual experience and even her basic attitude toward men.

Boys report reasons for waiting similar to those of Laurie, Jeanne, and Stephanie. Not all the moral and emotional concerns or all the fears of reputation or pregnancy fall to the girls. Just as Jeanne was worried that her boyfriend might talk of their relationship, some boys express concern that their girls will "tell it to the whole school so they'll 'have' you for the rest of the year." Some boys echo Laurie's moral convictions; others feel, like Stephanie, that they might become too involved. And thoughtful boys are also concerned about their responsibility for a pregnancy. Take the case of George, now nineteen:

"I had gone steady with my girl for over two years. Twice during our relationship we became emotionally involved and were very close to going all the way. . . . We were very much in love with each other and were planning marriage in the future, but for some reason we stopped before we did go all the way—it was she who put the brakes on both times. Now I find I don't love her any more and I want to break up with her. Had we gone all the way last year, we may have had to get married, because we felt emotionally obligated, maybe unfit to marry another person, or she might have gotten pregnant. If we had gotten married we'd probably be getting a divorce now."

There are still boys who will sleep with an "easy mark" for fun but want to marry a virgin; other boys realize this will lead to an emotional split between sex-for-fun and loving sex. So they wait. Finally, there are boys who decide to save sex for a special girl, boys who prefer to wait until they're engaged or married.

Which of the above reasons for abstinence are valid? *All of them.* Laurie's conservative position certainly deserves respect. While it might seem regrettable that Jeanne must worry about a ruined reputation if she sleeps with a boy she cares for, she probably is right about the situation, and she made a responsible decision. Stephanie's desire to maintain a measure of emotional independence is also responsible and mature. And although Eileen was hurt by one bad experience, she shows only a healthy reluctance to repeat that experience—not a neurotic fear of sex or men in general.

Next question: Which of the above teen-agers should, at this point, be concerned about contraception? *All of them.* Even if moral principles do not change, Laurie should be aware that moral perspectives do change with experience; and Laurie's emotions, thus far, have not been seriously tested. Contraception should be on Jeanne's mind, too: What if Carl shows he has grown beyond the kind of behavior that worried her and *would* keep a sex experience a private and personal matter—just between them? What if Stephanie, sometime this year, in the process of overall maturing, finds the emotional independence she wants as a prerequisite to sex? What if Eileen's next boyfriend wants sex with her for reasons of affection, not exploitation? And certainly Paul, who would not want to ruin "what sex is supposed to be about" with another pregnancy scare, should be thinking about contraception.

Any or all of these young people may soon find themselves seriously involved. And unfortunately the excitement of love or passion all too frequently interferes with taking the time to get one's facts straight about pregnancy and contraception. Moreover, all of these people have friends. And one favor that young people can do for each other is to stop relying on rumors, and start learning and communicating sound information.

Readiness for Sex: Responsible Seduction

If there is a common feeling underlying what was said by all these teen-agers, it might be summed up in these three words: "I'm not ready." For them—and for you, if you have similar feelings—sexual abstinence makes sense. "No sex" has a value; and that value is much more than biological safety or protection against criticism. It has to do with this sense of readiness, a wish to make sex (when it does eventually occur) a special experience both physically and emotionally.

"Readiness" in human development is a concept useful in considering many types of learning experiences. In education "reading readiness" is a common term: Your vision, your concentration, your brain functions must be adequately developed. Readiness means development of potential to a certain stage. The nerves and muscles must be formed and teachable, the mind must be ready to acquire and digest new information, the emotions must be in harmony with the task ahead. In sex, emotional readiness includes the confidence to be intimate (which means being vulnerable) and the confidence to trust the other person to give and receive honestly, lovingly. *Not everyone reaches this ideal of readiness and many who do not are disappointed by sex.* Those who reach it do so in different ways, at different times, and all go through anxiety and doubt in the process.

Are there any ways to tell whether you are ready for a sexual experience? We think there are.

If a ten-year-old were physically eligible for sex—and a few are—most people would say "too young." Doctors, clergymen, parents, and teen-agers would perhaps give different explanations for their positions, but they would all add up to pretty much the same thing: too young. Age is something of an indicator, and until we find something better, we should pay attention to it, which is not to say worship it.

Let's take a tougher example. Age fourteen. Most young people have at least the awakenings of adult sexual urges by then. But most people in our society, including fourteen-year-olds, would say that fourteen-year-olds are not ready for intercourse. Nevertheless, a small but significant number are having sex relations at that age or younger: In 1968, over 9,000 babies were born to girls under fifteen in the United States. Even those few people who might argue that sex is fine at fourteen would undoubtedly say that pregnancy is not desirable at that age. And the fact that these girls became pregnant is an indicator that they were not ready to deal realistically with a sexual relationship.

In our judgment, most fourteen-year-olds having sex are not coping very well whether or not they become pregnant. That is still a rather tender age, as readers over sixteen will probably attest. There are studies which indicate that the very young sexually active girls and boys are frequently also emotionally, educationally, or economically deprived. Life hasn't given them the support they need and—unfortunately at this age and stage—aren't likely to get from sex. On the contrary, at this age sexual experiments (for this is what they are) usually make one's problems worse. It tends to be the less popular kids who get caught up in premature sex. They feel more desperate, less confident of friendships than the popular kids, who know enough not to risk a relationship on impulse and don't have to worry if they back off from a sexual opportunity that doesn't seem right.

There were *28,863* babies born to fifteen-year-olds in 1978, and *64,923* to sixteen-year-olds. What about sixteen, then? As we have seen, sexual experience increases with age. And the older the group, the larger the percentage who have the maturity to decide Yes and not be sorry later. At sixteen, doubtless some are mature enough, but no one can say what the proportion is at any particular age. There were 25,000 babies born to fifteen-year-olds in 1968, and 60,000 to sixteen-year-olds. That's a tragic outcome of sex for most at that age. Having a baby doesn't bring a young girl the love and support she seeks, although many unhappy girls think it can. Some people may be mature enough at sixteen, but again, becoming a parent at that age is pretty good evidence of *not* being ready.

The road to maturity is long. Everything seems to have been speeded up in the jet age, but some things cannot be rushed. Sixteen-year-olds still think of fourteen as pretty young, and eighteen-year-olds look back at sixteen as rather immature. In fact, looking back on how one has changed can be a humbling thing.

The rate of change slows down, though. The difference between eighteen and twenty is not so great, and the older you get, the less difference a couple of years makes in maturity—and the easier it is to feel sure about what you want to be and do. If good and responsible sex is your goal, you will choose with care and love. When desperation, impulse, arrogance, or competition lead to sex, it's likely to be an unhappy experience for one or both of the people involved.

Young women are propositioned by men all the time; the reverse is less common, but far from rare. Many girls are told, "If you can't do it with me now, it means you may be frigid later. I'll help you avoid that terrible fate." And, "Until you try it, you don't know if you can do it." Such comments play upon the inexperience and normal concern of a virgin who looks forward to a good sex life later but isn't sure she wants to start yet. The boy who offers to introduce her to the joys of sex may not be as altruistic as he sounds, as is obvious when he uses pressure tactics, exaggerations, or falsehoods.

One boy told his girl that premarital sex was associated with better marital sex adjustment. She believed him but couldn't bring herself to take the plunge, and worried a great deal. Then she learned from an objective authority that no one knows whether this is true, and even if it were statistically so, it might not apply to her in particular. If a boy—or girl—makes general arguments of this type, and you aren't sure, ask for the reference source!

Good sex is not a con job. Partnership and trust and informed consent are needed for the adventure of responsible seduction. In this era love has a single standard, not a separate one for male and female; love is joined by equals. Each is seducing and being seduced, although one may be more active, and each remains responsible in the midst of pleasure, play, and romance.

Where a single mutual standard cannot exist, seduction is irresponsible, or just plain wrong. To take the extremes: Seduction of children or the mentally handicapped, or the use of force or threat, are all incompatible with love and fairness. Lying and deception also violate the standard of mutual decision and consent. If, for example, a boy says he will use a rubber and doesn't, then sex is reduced to a selfish gamble at the girl's expense. If a girl sleeps with a boy because she wants to keep going out with him in order to meet more of his attractive friends, then she's using the boy as a stepping stone, not a partner.

You might ask, "Well, it may not be right or nice but does it really interfere with enjoying sex?" To some extent, you'll have to take our word for it, but the answer is Yes. People who exploit other people in bed generally do not have good sex lives. The relationship between a prostitute and client is usually an extreme of exploitation and famous for being unsatisfactory. If you want to study the subject further, there are thousands of novels, plays, books on psychology, biographies, and autobiographies that cast light on the problem.

Couples thinking of marriage sometimes ask, "How do we know

we're compatible unless we try it?" Very often the question isn't sincere. It's an argument, not a question. The couple is looking for an excuse, but consenting mature people do not need to look for this kind of excuse. However, if the question is sincere, the answer is that going to bed together doesn't prove anything. If it does not work out well, the reason may be that one or both of the people feel pressured, tense, or guilty in a situation of trying to prove sexual adequacy. This is very common and no proof of lack of sexual potential. If it does work out well, this still isn't proof that the couple will be compatible in a married relationship. What's more important is really knowing, liking, admiring, and being attracted to each other. If a couple has experienced and enjoyed sexual arousal together (necking and petting), then they can be reasonably well assured that they will have a good sexual relationship. There are a few cases where special counseling may be needed before marriage. And there are some cases of couples who felt sexy together before going to the altar but not after. But going to bed together before the wedding day doesn't solve those problems anyway. Sometimes girls worry if their boyfriend is a virgin —they don't want the wedding night bungled by a novice. Love should overcome such fears: If he and she don't trust enough to teach and learn their sex together, there may be something deeper missing in their love.

Asking the Right Questions

Here are some ideas and cases which can help you form guidelines for yourself if you are trying to decide between abstinence and sex.

Can the two of you discuss birth control? Working out the details of contraception should be shared by a couple; it reflects your maturity and shows you care enough about each other to act in a way that will protect both of you.

Estelle is one of many teen-agers we know who does not know how to bring up the subject with her boyfriend. "I'd be too embarrassed —what could I say?" What you can say is very simple: "If we have sex, what will we use for protection?" If you don't have enough respect for yourself to say that, you should not be sleeping with anybody. If two people can't talk about birth control without embarrassment, they are not ready for sex. In fact, those like Estelle who feel they can't ask for, or discuss, birth control may inwardly fear that their partner does not care for them enough to bother with protection.

Of course, the fact that you *would* use contraception is not in itself a reason for having sex. It only works the other way; if you *wouldn't* have the protection you want, that's a good reason (a *very* good reason) for not having sex.

Are you hoping that sex will significantly improve your relationship? Are you hoping that sex will make him (or her) call more, care more? Don't count on it. Nor should you count on sex to rekindle an interest that is beginning to fade away. It may not. It may, in fact, be the end of a relationship.

Leonard, an eighteen-year-old boy, tells this story: "I think Mary was using sex to try and keep me dating her. For all our early dates, she would barely let me touch her, and then I started getting interested in another girl. Suddenly Mary's *no* turned to *go.* We were watching TV in her basement and I was pulling her bra strap, and she whispered to me to undo it. On our next date, we were lying on a sofa at somebody's house and she undid my pants. On our final date, she tried again. We were at a party about an hour from her house. She drank a little, and on the long drive home, she lay her head on my lap. I thought she was going to sleep, but she started kissing and stroking me. That got to me. I pulled the car off the road at the first opportunity and let her have what she wanted—just hoping all the while that I'd pull myself out in time. I kept thinking what a mess it would be if she got pregnant, with me not even liking her any more. I stopped seeing her after that night."

Many teen-agers learn this lesson the hard way. That's what we call desperate sex. If the relationship between two people is not good, then consummating that relationship with sex will simply reduce sex to the level of the poor relationship.

You should also ask yourself honestly, "Do I have any guilt feelings about the amount of physical involvement I have had so far?" Guilt can take many forms; it's not always as simple and clear as knowing within yourself "I think we went too far." Sheila, who enjoys petting to climax with her boyfriend, is inwardly unable to think that what they are doing is "moral" or right. Her guilt shows itself in a number of ways: She is irritable at home (particularly on mornings following her dates) because she is unhappy with herself. She tries to push back her guilt by being scrupulously "good" in her high school studies. Following a date, she will sometimes "punish" herself by staying home and studying all evening, until after midnight. Her inner, unconscious reasoning seems to make this bargain: "If I get good grades, that will pay for my bad morals." Eventually Sheila will probably resolve her problem and accept petting as a normal part of maturing. But it goes without saying that if you feel any guilt, doubt, or conflict about going as far as you already *have* gone—then you are not ready to go farther.

Do you feel that you're thinking about sex all the time, and that having sex will get it out of your system? Many teen-agers, especially boys, have strong sexual urges and frequent sexual daydreams. Having sex just to get it out of your system doesn't work, and acting only out of desperation usually leads to disappointment or failure.

If you're obsessed with sexual thoughts before you have intercourse, you're apt to be just as obsessed with those thoughts—and the consequences of your actions—*after* the experience. If masturbation does not reduce sexual urges to a tolerable level, intercourse probably won't either. If masturbation causes guilt, or a persistent need for intercourse interferes with normal friendships and social activities, then professional counseling is indicated.

As sex becomes a more regular part of your life, the feeling of being obsessed with it will be diminished. In the meantime, having sex just to get it done, so to speak, won't solve your problem and may cause some new problems.

Are you very jealous of the person you're dating, or vice versa? A certain amount of jealousy is probably inevitable, and not always bad, but extreme jealousy destroys freedom, growth, and the very love it guards so fiercely.

Lisa, sixteen, provides a typical example. When her boyfriend talks to other girls at parties, she seethes inside. She feels hurt and angry. Conversations such as this follow:

LISA: Well, you certainly seemed to be having a good time.
BEN: Yeah, weren't you?
LISA: Well, I might have had a good time if you hadn't neglected me most of the evening.
BEN: For heaven's sake, I was just talking to Pat and Linda for a few minutes.
LISA: Oh, they're more interesting to talk to than I am, I suppose . . .

That last remark gets at the heart of Lisa's problem. She feels insecure when compared to other girls. She is truly afraid that she is, indeed, less interesting than they. Lacking self-confidence, she is quick to see other girls only as competitors.

Would the situation be different if Lisa were having sex with Ben as part of their relationship? Yes, the situation would indeed be different—and much worse for Lisa. She, at this point, would feel doubly "damaged," hurt, and angry. If she is bothered that a boy she *dates* talks to other girls, she would feel outrage that a boy she *slept with* would talk to other girls. Lisa needs to gain confidence in herself before she is ready for sex. She needs to stop seeing other girls as competitors, and boyfriends as exclusive possessions. Being or having a "one and only" should leave room for friends of the opposite sex. This is true for couples who are intimate sexually as well as for those who abstain. Though our example here is Lisa, *boys are equally prone to jealousy.* (Try switching boys' and girls' names in the dialogue above.)

What do you imagine as a possible result of a sexual involvement? Random thoughts, fantasies, or daydreams can provide clues to your underlying motives for wanting sex; they can help tell you whether your motives are healthy or not. Do you envision sudden, dramatic gossip among your friends? ("Guess who's sleeping together . . . ?") If so, you may only want sex as an attention-getting technique, and you'd be wise to explore other ways to get the recognition you are seeking.

Do you have fleeting thoughts of parental outrage or handwring-

ing? ("Where did we go wrong . . . ?") If so, then you are regarding
sex partly as a means of rebellion—not just as an expression of affection. And, in fact, you are exploiting your partner in order to gamble
with your parents' outrage.

Are you trying to prove something by having sex? Do you imagine
ways in which sex will do away with doubts about your attractiveness,
your sexiness, your worth as a person? If so, you may be bringing to
sex a load of worries that it cannot solve and that will interfere with
a good sexual relationship. Few of us, of course, are completely secure, but if you are feeling emotionally shaky already, a poor sexual
relationship can seem like, and sometimes be, a disaster. If you're
thinking about your own problems and worries and not truly concerned with your partner's feelings, you may not be ready for sex at
this time.

These questions are particularly important if you are thinking not
only about sex but about becoming a parent. If you have serious
fantasies about pregnancy or would be likely to "gamble" with pregnancy, you are not ready for sex. This gamble involves serious consequences not only for you and your partner, but possibly for a child
as well.

Girls who entertain thoughts of having babies young may be
searching for affection they are not finding elsewhere ("A baby will
love me") or attention they are not getting elsewhere ("Everybody
will notice me"). Girls who are not mature may see this as a way to
announce to the world that they are "grown up." Or, if they feel
unpopular or unsure of their femininity, they may view pregnancy as
a dramatic way to prove that *somebody* slept with them, *somebody*
wanted them. A degree of failure and fantasy is often woven into a
teen-age girl's desire for pregnancy. Some examples may show what
we mean:

Gina was the second oldest of seven children. She had never been
given much parental guidance or attention. Her father did not live
with the family, and, as she was growing up, she saw her mother's
attention directed away from her and toward each new baby brother

or sister who entered the household. At age thirteen she deliberately led a neighborhood boy to the point where intercourse was inevitable. Immediately after the experience she told her mother, "I did it, and I'm going to have a baby." When her startled mother took her to a clinic, Gina told the counselor, "I know how babies are made and I'm making one, that's all." Gina, following her mother's repeated example, did indeed produce a baby and thus gained, at least for a while, her mother's attention. Gina *herself* wanted—directly or through the new infant—the "babying" she felt cheated of. The sex act held no meaning for her. Her resultant pregnancy and premature motherhood brought attention, but mostly hostile, and sidetracked her social development, reducing her chances to establish a loving, more responsible relationship later on.

Linda, age sixteen, was an eighth-grade student at a Baltimore public school. Because of a reading handicap, she had been held back from promotion two years in a row. Though she was older than her classmates, she had difficulty keeping up and understanding assignments, and she had few friends among the younger students. She hated school and was often absent. In the fall semester of 1971 she wrote a short essay for English class entitled "I Wish I Could Disappear from Here." But not very many avenues of escape were open. And no one was watching Linda closely enough to see that she was *trying* to escape; no one was able to help draw her back into a productive school life. The teachers who always had time to report her absences to the school's home visitor did not have the time to help her overcome the reading problem that was indirectly causing her such humiliation. Linda thought a lot about becoming pregnant, because it was easy to observe that girls who were pregnant could leave school—with few questions asked. Linda's pregnancy was her way of "disappearing," of "dropping out."

There are many "Lindas." Counselors in virtually any school system will report that girls who are lower achievers and have fewer friends than their peers have higher pregnancy rates. And often the reasons are similar to Linda's.

Linda's problems in adjusting to school were partly due, of course, to a school system that did not have time for her individual needs. But her problems were only made worse by her pregnancy.

Paula, just barely seventeen, often daydreams about motherhood. She is still a virgin and is not dating anyone steadily. Right now, she has no strong desire for sex. Still she feels that "if I did sleep with a guy, I'd like to get a baby from it." Asked why, she explains, "School is a hassle, my mom and dad don't get along with me. What I'd really like to do is shove it all and just live alone, with a baby to take care of. Taking care of a baby would be easy—it would be fun."

At the very least, Paula's attitude is unrealistic. Babies deserve parents who have at least some idea of the complexities of child raising. (If taking care of babies were "easy," we might not need the hundreds of books now available on the subject of how to do it!)

Mary Ann, sixteen and a half, who lives in Silver Spring, Maryland, had similar ideas about what fun it would be to have a baby. But she wanted marriage, too. She and her boyfriend knew little about birth control, but they were strongly attracted to each other and discussed having sex. Mary Ann says, "I asked Bill what if I got pregnant, and he said we'd get married—and I figured that wouldn't be so bad. I loved him and thought I'd really like to have his baby." However, when Mary Ann did become pregnant about three months later, the two were in no position to start out married life on their own; instead, they lived with Bill's parents. Mary Ann's father and mother were furious about the forced marriage, and relationships were somewhat strained with Bill's parents as well. Mary Ann had only Bill to lean on, but his enthusiasm for the arrangement seemed to wear off as her pregnancy progressed.

One evening late in her pregnancy, Bill told her that he was going out to meet some friends and that she should not accompany him, since these particular friends "wouldn't approve" of her being pregnant. Bill's evening absences began to occur more often—leaving

Mary Ann in the uncomfortable position of spending a lot of time alone with her non-too-friendly in-laws.

Whether or not Bill has another girl friend is something Mary Ann is not sure of, but it is certain that marriage and parenthood, thus far, are not working out the way she had anticipated. (The week we spoke with Mary Ann, she had seen Bill only at school.) Bill's parents are making no effort to help their son live up to his new responsibilities; Mary Ann even thinks they are glad to see her face emotional humiliation as "punishment" for a situation they regard as totally "her fault."

Girls who feel that "it wouldn't be so bad if I got pregnant" or "I'd like to have a baby" should realize that such attitudes carry a great deal of risk. Pregnancy cannot be counted on to solve problems, improve one's status or self-image, or provide one with a superior "new" life.

Teen-age boys can fantasize about pregnancy as well—it is not exclusively a female trait. Dr. Ner Littner of the Chicago Institute for Psychoanalysis has studied hundreds of young unmarried fathers. He feels that there are several significant reasons which may cause a boy (though he may not realize it is deliberate) to set out to make a girl pregnant.

Such a boy may have a desire for revenge against all women. A boy may be hostile, for example, to women in his household: a restrictive mother, sisters who he feels are favored over him. He may resent female teachers or other female authority figures. His determination to impregnate a girl doesn't result from the fact that he dislikes her personally or wants to hurt her—but from a generalized inner feeling that he would like to "get even" with someone of the female sex.

A boy may need to "prove himself" in the masculinity race. Traditionally, men "compete" where issues of masculinity are concerned. The boy who secretly fears he is not as "manly" as others may impregnate a girl in order to boost his ego.

Lester David, who has done a sensitive job of analyzing the teen-age father in an article for *Seventeen* magazine (October 1970), tells of one such boy, Jon.

Jon was haunted by the thought that he might have homosexual tendencies. "As boys mature sexually, they pass through various stages of physical and emotional development," Lester David points out, "one of which involves a strong interest in other males. Most can accept these feelings. Jon, however, could not; to him [such feelings] were terrifying. In his case, the triggering incident occurred one afternoon when he was wrestling playfully with his best friend. . . ."

Jon felt, or imagined he felt, stirrings of a sexual nature. His reaction was panic and confusion. "It was," concludes the author, "no coincidence that Jon's girl friend Ellie, whom he had known for almost a year, became pregnant after their next date—for Jon had deliberately set out to father a child to prove his manhood to himself."

Dr. Littner feels that about *half* the instances of unwed fatherhood are due to negative psychological motives: insecurity, identity crisis, destructive impulse.

Often, a natural partner for a boy who has doubts about his masculinity is a girl who fears she may not be feminine enough; both may seek refuge for troubled egos in reproduction. When pregnancy occurs, both feel an unhealthy sense of gratification: *She* is pleased with whisperings of "Joanne's pregnant, and Ted's the father," and *he* is sure his doubts about his sexual identity have been hidden from public view when he can tell friends, "Yeh, I got Joanne knocked up."

If you are mature enough for sex, you will care enough about yourself and your partner to use a contraceptive—every time. Sexual intimacy requires this mutual consideration.

The last question to ask yourself before deciding to begin a sexual relationship might be: How much deception will be likely to result? Consideration not only for yourself but for your parents, the community in general, and even for your good friends will require that you not broadcast the facts of your affair. On the contrary, discretion or even secrecy may be required.

Discretion about a sexual affair, however, is different from deceit. If a girl tells her parents "We'll be at Karen's house" when she and her boyfriend are actually going to a friend's apartment, there is always a risk that parents may call Karen's house to "check up." The beauty of sexual intimacy can easily be spoiled by the tension that results from false stories and alibis. You may be ready for a sexual affair—but circumstances won't permit it without deception or outright lies. In that case, patience is in order.

There is a very delicate balance here. Your sex life is a private matter, and you don't have to discuss it with anyone, and usually probably shouldn't unless you are talking to your lover, a doctor, or a counselor. This means that there may be times when you do not tell your parents or others the "whole truth and nothing but the truth." But most people find that if they get involved in a web of deceptions and outright lies, the price is high—in terms of guilt that interferes with sexual pleasure, and in the loss of trust from friends and family if the truth comes out (it often does).

We have not asked the question "Are you in love?" It's too difficult to arrive at a meaningful answer. If sex is OK when you're in love, then it's all too easy to say and even believe, "Well, we're in love, so sex is OK."

The spoken words "I love you" do not prove that the underlying *feeling* of love really exists. Real love involves feelings of esteem for yourself and your partner; and to discover if you really hold those feelings of esteem, it's necessary to ask deeper questions than just "Am I in love?"

But this does not mean that love is not relevant to sex. If you consider the *quality* of a sexual experience, or affair—Was it all you hoped it would be? Did it bring happiness?—then love becomes extremely important. Each person defines love differently, but however it's defined, most people feel that sex without love is a compromise. The ideal—and for many people the only situation they really want —is sex *with* love.

In conclusion, if a person is totally inhibited sexually or governed by a rigid moral philosophy which brooks no questioning whatsoever, then his or her chastity doesn't mean very much. No chastity medals for impotence.

There is more to it when abstinence results from restraint when you know very well that you could proceed with sexual relations but for good reasons decide not to. These reasons may be religious. There is nothing psychologically wrong with religious reasons. But they should be reasons which you can uphold thoughtfully. Obeying the law—including religious law—should be based on principles of reasonableness and rightness rather than "Somebody told me to do it that way" or "I'm scared to think about it." *How* one decides is as important as what one decides.

If sex is regarded as evil, abstinence automatically becomes good. And when the pendulum swings and "everyone" says sex is good, the same simple-minded logic makes abstinence seem bad, or odd at least. When the pendulum is somewhere in the middle, sex and abstinence both can be seen as normal and healthy aspects of human relations, not ends in themselves, but capable of being used well or badly.

As with every important choice in life, saying Yes to sex responsibly is only possible if you are capable of saying No. If you cannot abstain, you cannot choose—you merely react. Animals don't abstain or choose; people can. Choosing sex means your mind is in it as well as your body. Many young people find abstinence easier than "perfect moderation"—even necessary, as a platform on which to be secure, to observe, to better prepare.

Questions Often Asked About Abstinence

Q. Isn't it unhealthy to refrain from sex? After all, you're repressing a natural drive, aren't you?

A. Sex is not necessary to life in the same way as are eating, sleeping, or breathing. Sex is "natural" but not biologically essential. Sexual drives vary from person to person, and from time to time. Furthermore, most teen-agers with strong sexual urges find masturbation or petting an outlet that helps them abstain from premature intercourse.

Q. If you don't have sex when you're in your teens, are you apt to be frigid or impotent when you're an adult?

A. There is no evidence to suggest this. It all depends on why you do or don't have sex. Teens who abstain from sex do so for a variety of reasons: These reasons include morality, anxiety, or just plain choosiness.

Q. Can you have oral sex and still call it abstinence?

A. It is not actual intercourse, and pregnancy cannot result. But that's only technical abstinence. In practice, oral sex is just as intimate and involving as intercourse—or more so.

Some teenagers find oral sex fully satisfying, and a few, in fact, consider it their means of birth control. Most, however, do not engage in oral sex until after they have had intercourse for some time; culturally, it seems to be considered a more sophisticated sexual practice.

Q. Do adults ever practice abstinence?

A. Of course. Single men and women abstain from sex often, when a satisfactory partner is not available. Married couples may abstain when they are in the midst of an argument, when one partner is ill, when the usual method of contraception is not available, when husband or wife is out of town—or for other reasons. And for married couples who attempt to use the rhythm method of birth control, periods of abstinence are a *must!*

4

Rhythm and
the Reproductive Cycle

If, then, there are serious motives to space out births, which derive
from the physical or psychological conditions of husband and wife,
or from external conditions, the Church teaches that it is then licit
to take into account the natural rhythms immanent in the generative
functions . . . and in this way to regulate birth without offending the
moral principles. . . .

Pope Paul VI, Encyclical Letter

"I like the rhythm method," one girl told us, "because it's organic
birth control—no chemicals!"

Unfortunately, science and the experience of many ordinary women
prove that rhythm also results in a large number of organic unplanned
babies. Still, rhythm, which is based on an understanding of human
reproduction, is essential to intelligent use of other forms of birth
control, and to the process of having a baby when you want to.
Rhythm is the only method of birth control approved by the Catholic
Church; while not an effective method compared to others, it is much
better than nothing (about 35 percent of the women using rhythm will
be pregnant at the end of a year, as against 80 percent who use no
method). And you can use rhythm along with other methods to
improve the reliability of contraception.

A college freshman said, "It's an unlikely method for somebody at
this school, and most of my friends think it's pretty square. But you
don't need prescriptions. All you need is a knowledge of how your
body works, and regular periods! I would not use rhythm, however,
if my periods weren't very regular."

You will recall from Ch. 2 that most American girls have heard of rhythm, and many think they are using it—but they are often mixed up about what time of the month is safe and what time is fertile. *The usual fertile time is midway between periods. The safest time is just around or during the menstrual period itself.* Do you know what a couple is called when they get mixed up about rhythm? Parents. (It's embarrassing and costly—like heading for the wrong goal in a football game.)

Why isn't rhythm good enough birth control by itself? Because there is no way known as yet to tell *exactly* when ovulation—release of an egg from the ovary—will occur during the woman's monthly cycle. Women whose cycles are not regular are walking in the dark, so to speak, and almost bound to stumble. With regular cycles, a calendar, and a special thermometer you can map your way better and reduce, at least by half, the chances of getting pregnant.

Pregnancy results from the union of sperm and egg, one of each. Rhythm, like other birth control methods, helps prevent this union of two cells while permitting sexual relations. Fertilization of the egg is only possible for twelve to twenty-four hours during the month; the egg decays quite rapidly after release. But sperm survive for up to forty-eight hours—and sometimes longer—after deposit in the female reproductive tract. Theoretically, if sex were avoided for about two days before ovulation and one day after, pregnancy would be prevented. Three days' abstinence would not be very difficult—but the problem is knowing which three days are fertile, or "unsafe."

The unsafe days are sometime in the middle of the cycle; ovulation typically precedes menstruation by fourteen days. In these fourteen days the egg, if not fertilized, dies; the built-up lining of the uterus withers and disintegrates, and is expelled from the womb with some blood—this is the menstrual flow. But it is almost impossible to figure out exactly when you are going to ovulate. You must keep a careful record of many monthly cycles in order to figure out an average or *most probable day for ovulation,* starting from the most recent menstrual period. All the counting begins with the first day of the most recent menstrual flow.

The lucky girl with very regular twenty-eight-day cycles can expect to ovulate about day 14. But in order to use rhythm successfully, even she will have to abstain more than three days: at the very least, experts advise *no sex for eight days* around the time of ovulation. Their formula, from which Table II is derived, indicates that the fertile or unsafe period for this girl would be days 10 to 17. For women with irregular periods the unsafe time is longer, as you will see, but calendar and thermometer will help to locate them.

For those who are using a chemical or mechanical contraceptive but wish to supplement protection during the fertile time, there is one main idea to remember: The fertile days are in mid-cycle. The days immediately before and after, as well as during, menstrual flow are relatively safe from the risk of pregnancy.

Precision Rhythm

Eight days is the minimum time to abstain if rhythm is to work at all well. The longer you abstain around the middle of the month, and the more precisely you can pinpoint ovulation, the better rhythm works. Some women have their strongest sexual feelings just before or after their menstrual period (which is safe—almost no pregnancy risk). Other women have stronger sexual feelings near mid-cycle, the time of ovulation—and rhythm is not designed for them!

This is an uncertain method. You never know until your next period comes whether it is working, and anxiety itself can alter the time of ovulation. An egg may be released sooner or later than expected, due to fatigue, travel, illness, nervousness. It is even possible that intercourse itself sometimes plays a role in the timing of ovulation, as it does normally in some other mammals (cat, rabbit, and ferret).

There is also the problem of scheduling sex. Pat, who is seventeen, complains that she has had to avoid intercourse with her boyfriend after a particularly loving evening "because it's the wrong day." At other times Pat and her boyfriend feel that they are having "programmed sex" because they don't want to miss a "safe" day. Another problem for teen-agers is the change in menstrual periods as they mature. Suppose a girl's monthly cycle has never been longer than thirty days, but suddenly she goes thirty-three or thirty-four days before her period comes. Is her cycle changing, is it a fluke, or is she pregnant? She waits several anxious days. At worst, she finds she has something more to worry about: pregnancy. Used very carefully, rhythm is said to have a failure rate of 30 to 35 pregnancies per 100 woman-years. Without charts and thermometer, there are more failures. With those rates, it is hard to avoid anxiety even if you manage to avoid pregnancy.

The first thing you do if you use the rhythm method is to keep a written record of every menstrual cycle. Eight to twelve cycles are needed for reliable calculations. Count from the first day of one period until the first day of the *next* period; then start a new count.

For example, here is a typical record after six months:

1st month: 29 days from first day of period until first day of next period	*3rd month:* 30 days
	4th month: 28 days
	5th month: 26 days
2nd month: 26 days	*6th month:* 32 days

After a record has been kept for eight to twelve months (preferably the full year), you can then consult the standard chart on page 48, which has been used by doctors as a guide to rhythm birth control for many years.

Note: To keep current, you must continue to record the length of your cycles, calculating again each month by dropping the oldest recorded cycle (now a year old) and adding the latest one to keep the total list at twelve.

The way to figure the unsafe time is first to subtract 18 from the length of the shortest monthly cycle of the twelve cycles you have recorded. This gives you the first unsafe day. Then subtract 11 from the longest cycle; this gives you the last unsafe day. For example, if the shortest cycle is twenty-six days, and the longest has been thirty-two days, then the first unsafe day will be the eighth day of the cycle and the last unsafe day will be the twenty-first day of the cycle. So, to be fairly sure of avoiding pregnancy, intercourse must be avoided between the eighth and the twenty-first days counting from the first day of each period. In other words, you must abstain for at least fourteen days—or about half the days in each month. This is not

Table II
The Rhythm Method
HOW TO FIGURE "UNSAFE" DAYS FOR INTERCOURSE

Length of shortest cycle	First unsafe day after start of any period	Length of longest cycle	Last unsafe day after start of any period
21 days	3rd day	21 days	10th day
22 days	4th day	22 days	11th day
23 days	5th day	23 days	12th day
24 days	6th day	24 days	13th day
25 days	7th day	25 days	14th day
26 days	8th day	26 days	15th day
27 days	9th day	27 days	16th day
28 days	10th day	28 days	17th day
29 days	11th day	29 days	18th day
30 days	12th day	30 days	19th day
31 days	13th day	31 days	20th day
32 days	14th day	32 days	21st day
33 days	15th day	33 days	22nd day
34 days	16th day	34 days	23rd day
35 days	17th day	35 days	24th day
36 days	18th day	36 days	25th day
37 days	19th day	37 days	26th day
38 days	20th day	38 days	27th day

unusual among teen-age girls, who often have extremely irregular periods. Some may even have to abstain *more than 50 percent* of the days each month.

A calendar can be made up to show the safe and unsafe days. The following would be the calendar for the example just given, with three days added for extra safety.

Table III
Menstrual Calendar—One Cycle

(1) Menstru- ation begins	(2)	(3)	(4)	(5)	6	7
					Intercourse on these days may leave live sperm to fertilize egg	
8	9	10	11	12	13	14
	Unsafe: Ripe egg may be released on any of these days					
15	16	17	18	19	20	21
	Unsafe: Ripe egg may be released on any of these days					
22 Egg may still be present	(23)	(24)	(25)	(26)	(27)	(28)
(29)	(30)	(31)	(32)			

Numbers in parentheses: Safe days—conception is unlikely
Other numbers: Unsafe (fertile) days—pregnancy may occur

Note that in Table III, some of those "safe" days at the end of each month may be lost. If menstruation begins again on day 26, then day 26 becomes, in effect, day 1. And counting begins again from that point.

That, essentially, is the calendar method of using "rhythm" for birth control.

For those girls and women who are willing to go to the trouble, the calendar method can be refined by using a special thermometer to help make sure that ovulation does not occur at a surprising time.

As a result of hormonal activity at the time of ovulation, the release of the egg coincides with *slight* changes in a woman's temperature. The temperature change is noticeable *only* with a *basal thermometer* on which you can accurately read *tenths* of a degree. To learn what slight signal your own body sends out when ovulation occurs, you must use this thermometer to take your temperature *every morning at the same time, before getting out of bed.* The thermometer may be used orally or rectally: Oral is easier, rectal more accurate. Whichever you decide on, you must stick with. Any kind of activity can throw off the reading by a crucial tenth of a degree, so you cannot go to the bathroom, eat something, or even raise your voice before taking your temperature.

Suppose you find that your resting morning (basal) temperature is usually 97.7 degrees (typically this morning temperature is lower than normal daytime temperature). Just before ovulation your temperature should drop about three-tenths (0.3) of a degree—to about 97.4. When you do ovulate, your temperature will suddenly start to rise about five or six tenths (0.5 or 0.6) of a degree *higher than usual*—to about 98.3.

If the egg is not fertilized, it will disintegrate within three days, during which the temperature remains at least 0.5 degrees above the basal level. The average temperature in the second half of the cycle is usually slightly higher than in the first, but your temperature should drop toward basal level after a few days if you are not pregnant. (Of course, if you are sick and running a temperature, this will throw off your calculations.)

Using a temperature chart like the example shown on page 51, you will see that your unsafe days begin from the fifth day following the start of your period and continue until your temperature has peaked for three days and dropped back to normal range.

To have the best chance of working, the rhythm method should employ both calendar and thermometer. The thermometer helps provide a check on your calendar calculation of unsafe days and saves you from surprises (such as an unusually early ovulation). And the calendar helps in those months when you have a cold or sore throat which brings fever along with it.

A basal thermometer costs $3 to $4 and should come with instructions and temperature chart—from your local drugstore or Planned Parenthood clinic.

Many devices are available as supposed aids to better use of the rhythm method. These include slide rules, special calendars, and even a clock whose face turns red on unsafe days. Most of these items are fairly expensive, and they are not necessary. The standard chart

Chart That Might Be Kept by a Girl Using a Basal Thermometer

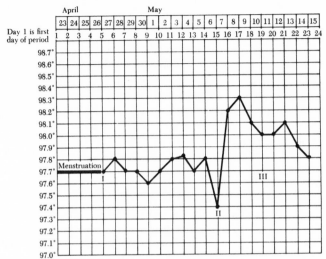

I   Temperature readings begin when period ends
II Lowered temperature followed by rise signals ovulation
III Safe period begins here, after rise of at least 0.5° has continued for three days

shown in this book, which has been used for years by doctors and Catholic family planning clinics, is just as accurate as any special devices or gadgets.

There is also a new Fertility Testor available in drugstores. To use the Testor, you insert a thin tape into your vagina. If the tape turns blue, you may be in your fertile period. (The test is based on the fact that glucose appears in the vagina at the time of ovulation.) Dr. Frank Ewers, inventor of the Fertility Testor, stresses, however, that this is only a supplemental safeguard to the standard rhythm method, and you should use it *only with* the basal body temperature method.

Another recent suggestion has to do with changes in the mucus secretions from the cervix (the neck of the uterus, which projects into the upper part of the vagina). With instructions, women can detect changes in the mucus that occur at the time of ovulation: It becomes clear, slippery, and stretchy (less dry and flaky) at the fertile time. This observation has been used by doctors to help infertile couples who are trying to get pregnant. Now couples can use the method for either purpose—to get pregnant or avoid it.

Not surprisingly, very few teen-age girls use such a complicated procedure as rhythm. Many cannot, for while other methods of birth control require you to anticipate first intercourse by only a matter of days or weeks, using rhythm effectively requires that you anticipate first intercourse by one full year while you keep an accurate record of your menstrual periods. (Occasionally, for various reasons, girls record their periods on a calendar anyway—making rhythm somewhat simpler, perhaps, for them.) And sooner or later, this method will probably fail. Even strictly followed, it has a high failure rate.

Some girls do use the rhythm method, however, and you might be interested in their reasons:

A seventeen-year-old Los Angeles girl explained, "When my older sister was engaged to be married, she got the chart and some other things, too—even a slide rule of some sort. I think she got them from a Pre-Cana conference, or maybe from her doctor. Anyway, I asked her what all that stuff was, and she explained the rhythm method. Since I already knew about it, I figured I'd just start keeping my own chart."

A nineteen-year-old Winnetka girl feels, "Using rhythm means that my boyfriend and I have only about ten safe days a month. That keeps sex a special occasion—it keeps us from taking sex for granted in our relationship, or from treating sex too casually."

One reason for using rhythm seems to be *shyness:*

"I could never bring myself to discuss birth control with a guy."

"When you use rhythm, nobody else is involved. You don't have to have any embarrassing conversations."

"I went to a gynecologist a friend has recommended. After the pelvic exam, I wanted to ask him about the pill. But when he said, 'Do you have any questions?' I didn't know how to ask. So I just use rhythm."

"I'd be glad to use some other kind of birth control, but I don't even have the nerve to phone a doctor or a clinic to get an appointment.

I wrote a question about the IUD and turned it in during Health and Hygiene class, but it wasn't answered. So just watching the calendar is the only thing I can do."

For these girls, rhythm is not really the method of first choice, but a last resort better than nothing. Embarrassment about sex keeps them from a surer method of birth control. If you're too shy to talk about birth control, you're risking a lot by having intercourse.

Some girls simply operate on the principle that the middle of the month is "unsafe" and have sex at times close to their period. Luck and the law of averages will keep some of them from becoming pregnant—but not all.

Which would ultimately prove *more* embarrassing: to say to a boy, "I think you should use a condom" or to say to him a few weeks later, "I think you've gotten me pregnant"? Which is easier to say in a gynecologist's office: "I want birth control information" or "I had sex without birth control and . . . now I've missed a period . . . and . . ."? This is worth considering—since with *only* the rhythm method for protection, pregnancy is a very real risk.

Using rhythm *in combination with* another birth control method is another matter. Many teen-age girls do this.

If you use the pill properly, there is no need to use rhythm, since there is no ovulation. But since the diaphragm, condom, and especially foam can sometimes fail, *knowledge of your unsafe days is a good supplement* to these methods—and one we recommend. If you are using either foam or the condom, you can improve protection by calculating the *fertile* days and using both together at that time. There are no statistics on the effectiveness of this combination of three methods, but it is probably very close to 100 percent—and is perfectly safe from the standpoint of side effects.

Though the rhythm method is endorsed by the Catholic Church as the only "natural" method of birth control, it requires a great deal of dedication plus a collection of pencils, charts, calendars, graphs, thermometers, and the scientific research which backs them up. If it is all you can do, do it right.

Successful lifelong family planning is an arduous but worthwhile journey. Like every journey, it begins with a single step. You need to learn to walk, even though you may be riding most of the way. Like walking, the rhythm method is natural—nothing but the body's own machinery—inexpensive, and requires practice and stamina.

Women who have to rely on rhythm *only* are likely to have some missteps in their reproductive years. Though it's good to understand rhythm, and how your body works, this method is best regarded as a supplement to other contraceptive practices.

Questions Often Asked About Rhythm

Q. Are there some women who shouldn't try to use rhythm?

A. About 15 percent of women have such irregular cycles that they cannot rely on the rhythm method. It would not suit a girl whose cycles vary by more than 10 days—for example, longest cycle 32, shortest 21; her unsafe days go from the third to the twenty-first. That's 19 days, and sometimes it will be essentially the whole cycle. Women with very long cycles—over 33 days—are advised to visit a doctor or nurse who is experienced in rhythm counseling if they are limited to this method.

Q. Do Catholics use rhythm only?

A. Many Catholics do use other methods of contraception and even abortion; more than half the Catholics interviewed in recent surveys, including Catholic obstetricians' wives, reported using methods of contraception other than rhythm. In areas where safe, legal abortion was available before the Supreme Court legalized it throughout the country (e.g., Rochester, New York), the proportion of Catholics making use of abortion services was equal to the proportion of Catholics in the population of that area. We respect Catholics who wish to adhere to the Church-approved method but want to indicate the hazards and sacrifices associated with it, and the fact that many depart from Church teachings on the matter, perhaps at the cost of a guilty conscience.

Q. If rhythm has such a high failure rate, why does anybody choose to use it?

A. Observant Catholics use it, and research may improve it. Rhythm is one method that need not be discussed with anyone—

boyfriend, parent, or gynecologist. Thus, many girls who are embarrassed about sexual activity feel that they have little choice but to fall back on rhythm. Then, too, any method is better than no method at all. If rhythm will result in as many as 35 pregnancies per 100 women per year—remember that no protection at all will result in about 80 pregnancies per 100 women per year.

Q. Can rhythm be used to *help* you have a baby when you want to?

A. Absolutely. Having intercourse during the fertile days is the way to get pregnant. Not everyone will in the first month because the cycles are not that precise. You can see how important it is, for getting pregnant or avoiding pregnancy, to understand the menstrual cycle.

Q. I read somewhere that the timing of intercourse has something to do with the sex of a baby that is conceived. How does that work?

A. The method of recording temperature may be useful in trying to choose the sex of a baby. The male infant is the result of a "Y" chromosome sperm entering the egg, and the girl baby results from an "X" sperm reaching the egg first. Theoretically, the "Y" sperm (boy babies) have a better chance of reaching the egg if intercourse takes place at the time of ovulation, because "Y" sperm travel fast but are short-lived. "X" sperm travel more slowly but survive longer; thus the chances are increased for a girl baby, by avoiding intercourse at the precise time of ovulation but having intercourse two or three days before the expected ovulation. Then the "Y" sperm will die off, leaving the "X" sperm to fertilize the egg. These principles are in the testing stages now, and one day they may provide a method that will enable parents to choose the sex of their offspring a large percentage of the time. Whether that ability will be a blessing or not remains to be seen. Like many other technical advances—and this is one of the technical fine points of family planning—it can be used unwisely. But we should consider the positive side: the joy it will bring to many families, and a reduction of the gambling with gametes—"trying again" for that girl or that boy—which has been the story for many couples.

Q. Is it dangerous to have intercourse during the menstrual cycle?

A. No. Some couples refrain because they find it less pleasant, and in some cultures the menstruating woman is "taboo." But menstrual blood is not unsanitary. If a woman's flow is light and she has no cramps, she may enjoy sex especially during her period, in part because of the increased desire which some women feel at this time and in part because it is the safe period from the standpoint of pregnancy.

Q. Isn't rhythm the only natural form of birth control?

A. We were inclined to give it credit for that, at least, until we read the following in the Catholic Alternatives booklet on contraception and abortion: This method "demands just as much human intentionality, control and deliberate planned *interruption* of the natural reproductive processes as 'artificial' methods of preventing conception.

"The rhythm method denies the one humanizing element in the sexual act, love, for the welfare of sperm and ova. It elevates the 'rights' of the sperm and ova to a position above the human dignity of their owners. . . .

"It is *psychologically* the least natural method because, more than any other method, it interferes with the sexual relationship as a human act that does not fit into biological rhythms."

5
The Condom

There is good news about the male contraceptive: It works, it has no side effects, and many satisfied couples are using it. A *Consumer Reports* study (October 1979) states that, properly used, condoms fail only once in 10,000 occasions. Pre-lubricated brands such as Nuform, Trojans Plus, and Conceptrol Shields were most preferred by users. The condom is the best starter method of contraception for most couples. It's a nonprescription item in drugstores and can even be ordered by mail.

The condom, prophylactic, "rubber," or "safe" is a very thin sheath of latex rubber which is rolled on the erect penis, leaving a little slack space at the closed end to catch the seminal fluid. A very effective means of contraception when properly used, it helps the male to improve his control as a lover and show concern for his partner. The condom stops germs as well as sperm: It is "prophylactic" (preventive) against venereal disease as well as pregnancy. VD can be transmitted in either direction during sex; the condom shields both partners against this risk—almost completely against gonorrhea and very well against syphilis. Rubber condoms cost twenty-five to fifty cents apiece, and must meet stringent federal standards. Some clinics sell them more cheaply or give them free.

Marla, a sixteen-year-old Phoenix, Arizona, student explained some of the typical reasons why many young couples choose condoms. She has not had intercourse before but is close to deciding to have sex with her boyfriend. "I feel it is up to him to use a condom," she said. "I don't think it's reasonable to expect me to make an appointment and go on the pill or something when he can get condoms with so much less effort. Besides, as things stand now, I, as a female, will be taking birth control responsibility for most of my reproductive life. I don't see why a guy can't assume the responsibility, at least at first." Marla's boyfriend agrees: "If we decide to have sex, it's up to me to make sure she doesn't get pregnant."

That makes good sense. Since the best female methods of birth control—the pill, the diaphragm, the IUD—require a considerable effort and commitment on the part of the girl, it seems too much for a boy to expect this of her from the start. Many couples will prefer a female method when sex becomes a regular part of a stable relationship. But if a boy is not willing to take initial responsibility for contraception, then probably he's not sufficiently mature to warrant the girl's confidence.

Linda, a Chicago student who is also sixteen, explained that she and her boyfriend decided to rely on the condom because they do not have sex that frequently. "We feel that sex shouldn't dominate our relationship. With some couples, whenever they see each other, all that's in their heads is 'Where can we go to screw?' But we don't have to make love in order to enjoy each other. So doesn't the condom make the best sense for us? Why should I have to take a pill twenty-eight times a month when we only have sex once or twice a month?"

Ralph, a somewhat older, sexually experienced boy who goes to Linda's school, prefers the condom to other means of birth control because he often dates several girls at once, and "I don't really know which girls are taking what. I'd sooner be in control of the situation anyway." He adds: "A lot of kids say using a rubber gets in the way of you being spontaneous. That's bull. I'll tell you what gets in the way of being spontaneous—when you and a chick decide to make it together and she says, 'Well, wait, we don't have any protection.' A condom doesn't hang you up from being spontaneous, except for maybe two seconds."

Ralph's use of the condom for casual sex is consistent with prevention of veneral disease. He also remarked: "Nothing brings a girl around faster than being able to say, 'See, I care about you, I'll see that nothing happens, you don't have to worry about a thing.' " Does he really care, or is he just interested in fast satisfaction? You decide, but don't blame the condom if you don't like his line, or his casual sex.

Does the availability of a condom really increase the likelihood of a sexual experience? We doubt it. Girls decide to make love for many reasons, psychological and physical—not because of condoms.

Sex-without-love that is safe—from pregnancy and VD—probably does less harm than sex-with-love that is unprotected. But we don't recommend either. If lovemaking is going to occur, it should occur safely; the absence of protection *always* ought to tip the scales against intercourse.

A condom is highly recommended if you have any reason to worry about VD—and unless you know your partner very well, you have reason to worry. Some girls who take the pill or have an IUD do not mention this fact to casual or "summer" lovers.

"On just a short acquaintance," said one seventeen-year-old, "you can be powerfully attracted to a boy but really not know him that well . . . so why do you have to tell him you're taking the pill? How do you know who he might have slept with within the last few months? Let him use a condom. I feel it's the only safe way to be sure I don't get the syph or something."

Purists may say that this practice does not meet standards of total truth, but she's not lying, either. If the relationship later develops into one of real trust, she can then tell him that she is taking birth control responsibility.

As for the supposed inconvenience of using a condom, creative couples, instead of grumbling, enjoy it. In Sweden and Japan placing the condom is regarded as an erotic part of foreplay. Unlike other methods, the condom can be shared contraception, or the closest thing to it. It takes the initiative of the male but allows the participation of the female, which can be reassuring to her. Early in foreplay she can help put it on—beware of sharp fingernails; the rubber is thin. (Some couples may take a while becoming this free and comfortable with each other.) The unlubricated or silicone (dry) lubricated condom is more suited than the moist condom to this approach, and with sufficient foreplay natural lubrication will be adequate.

There is a lot of prejudice against the condom, which we will try to dispel, since it is the *best first method of birth control for almost all couples.* Originally a popular method—most popular before the pill —the condom got a bad name earlier in this century. Contraception was so taboo that in many states condoms could be sold only for prevention of *disease.* For a long time soldiers and sailors were taught about them in crude "health" films about prostitutes and VD. Condoms were associated with veneral disease, casual sex, and prostitution (and they weren't as well made or tested then). It's true, condoms do protect against VD. That's an additional plus. But we're out of the Dark Ages now, so we can say that the condom is primarily a contraceptive. And a good one, fit for lovers.

A word is in order about the condom's history. For some time it was believed that a Doctor or Colonel Condom in England gave his name to the invention, but further research has cast doubt on this tale, and the origin of the name is a mystery. According to one story, the inventor became so famous that he had to change his name! Actually, condoms have probably been "invented" time after time by imaginative lovers throughout history. A thin membrane of sheep's intestine has long been used as an "envelope" for the penis and still is used in the high-priced "skin" condoms. (The "envelope" came to be known as the "French letter.") The "skins" are preferred by some men because they transmit heat more readily than rubber and seem to interfere less with sensation. But they cost more—four or five times more—and are always lubricated and very moist.

Linen or silk condoms were used in Europe and the Orient before the seventeenth century, primarily for control of venereal disease. Today's young men have fashioned condoms out of thin, transparent food wrap, and some have even used balloons!

These makeshift items may be better than nothing, but . . . You don't have to be that desperate! Thanks to the invention of a process called vulcanization in 1844, there was a revolution in the rubber industry. Until that time the bouncy, gummy stuff—which got its English name, "rubber," because little pieces of it were used to rub out pencil mistakes—could not be made as stretchy or as durable as it is now. The new, improved rubber revolutionized the condom business, among others, making the sheep-membrane sheath a relatively expensive specialty item. The latex process discovered in the 1930's further improved the product. In 1938 the United States government got into the act on behalf of the consumer, when the Food and Drug Administration took responsibility for setting standards for the quality of condoms, and enforcing the standards with reliable electronic tests.

Another few words about rubber. Petroleum products cause it to deteriorate. Your friendly service station attendant may have told you to avoid getting motor oil or gasoline on your tires if you want them to last. The same goes for the rubber condom—not that you're likely to lubricate it with motor oil, *but Vaseline and certain other lubricants are petroleum products and should not be used.* If the condoms you get are not pre-lubricated, you can use a spermicidal jelly or cream, surgical jelly (not cold cream) or plain saliva if the lubrication of sexual arousal is insufficient for easy entry.

Thanks to modern manufacturing techniques, the rubber condom today is extremely thin—.05 millimeters or 0.0025 inch—yet very effective in catching all the sperm if used properly. Experts rate it up to 97 percent effective, which means about 3 failures per 100 woman-years of proper use. It takes about one minute to learn to use, and a boy can practice by himself. Some boys say it blocks sensation, "like taking a shower with a raincoat on." Either they're looking for an excuse not to bother, or are too self-conscious to buy good condoms at the drugstore, or they just don't know what they are talking about. To the slight degree that a good condom lowers sensation prior to climax, it also increases male control.

Since condoms are the best first method of birth control, you ought to think ahead to which kind to buy. There are plain or lubricated latex "rubbers"—with or without reservoir ends—and "skins," made from animal membrane, which are heavily lubricated. One size fits all!

The reservoir end catches and holds the semen that is ejaculated. With the plain condom you make the reservoir by leaving a half-inch of slack at the tip. In either case the tip must be empty—no air in it —so that there is room enough for the seminal fluid. (The amount of semen produced varies, from individual to individual and from time to time, from less than a teaspoon to more like a tablespoonful. This has absolutely nothing to do with virility or fertility, by the way.)

After the male is aroused but before genital contact begins, put on the condom. Gently press the top half-inch between your thumb and forefinger as you unroll the condom down onto the erect penis with the other hand. The condom should be unrolled so that it covers the shaft of the penis all the way down to the base. Again, this should be done *before* there is any genital contact. Do not begin intercourse or penis-vulva contact unprotected, with the idea that the condom will be put on just before ejaculation. Ejaculation may occur sooner than expected. It's usual, too, for seminal fluid to be given off before the male's climax. Sometimes there are sperm in this fluid, and that's all it takes to result in pregnancy. Also, VD will not be prevented if contact occurs without the condom.

Lubricated condoms may be a favor to the girl involved. They make initial penetration easier, particularly if she is inexperienced. Some lubrication is necessary. But ideally her excitement and arousal will provide this naturally, through secretions of vaginal fluids. Contraceptive cream or jelly—NOT VASELINE—may also be used on an unlubricated condom. Pre-lubricated condoms are of two types, "wet" and "dry" (silicone). The latter is more satisfactory for extended foreplay, as it is not at all greasy. And some women find that *too much* lubrication decreases their pleasure.

The unlubricated condom is cheaper, and (like the "dry" lubricated condom) it can be worn throughout foreplay—as soon as the male has an erection. This also assures that it won't feel cold, which it may if you wait until the last minute. If lubrication is needed before entry, then contraceptive cream or saliva (warmer) may be used.

Those special condoms known as skins, which are made from natural animal membrane rather than latex, are supposedly for the connoisseur. Some users feel these are worth the extra cost, since they can barely be noticed when worn. Others feel there is little difference between a skin and a good brand of latex condom. Some males find the extreme thinness and sensitivity of the skins to be a disadvantage —they even prefer a thicker brand of latex condom, which, by slightly decreasing their sensitivity up to orgasm, helps their sexual performance to last longer. For this purpose, some extra-sensitive males even wear two condoms at once. Given good lubrication, the girl cannot tell the difference.

Occasionally, when entering the vagina the reservoir end of the condom may catch on the outside of the vagina; this is most apt to happen with an unlubricated condom and if the vagina is quite dry. If the male forces at this point, the penis may tear through the condom, and in any case forcing will be uncomfortable for his partner. A lubricant should be used, or foreplay should continue until the woman is more ready.

Another thing to watch out for is that the sheathed penis is withdrawn from the vagina before the erection has gone all the way down. When the man withdraws, he should hold the ring of the condom close to the base of the penis so that he is all the way out before the sheath comes off. Otherwise some of the seminal fluid can leak around the edge inside the vagina, and that can mean pregnancy. If a man loses his erection before climax—it sometimes happens—he must carefully withdraw, as described. The condom is secure only with a firm erection.

Being prepared with a condom presents something of a problem. While condoms will last for several years in their original packages, they can take a beating and be ruined if they are carried around in a pocket or wallet, or left in a car, where they may be damaged by overly high temperatures, especially if the car is left parked in the sun. Before using a condom, check to see that its foil wrapping or other packaging is unbroken. If the package is damaged, the condom may be also.

Another problem with being prepared is the possibility that at the time of first intercourse neither boy nor girl wants to seem to have planned the event in advance. Probably this was more a problem for past generations than for you today, although it is still an issue for many. Practical preparation for first intercourse need not be unromantic. Once a couple has experienced sexual arousal and seems to be heading toward intercourse, then they should think about it and discuss it. Our culture tends to support the idea that if you have intercourse before marriage, it's because you were swept off your feet, carried away with mindless passion—but that is an extremely foolish and hazardous idea. Sexual spontaneity does not require total surprise; sexual consideration—with contraception—is more deeply caring and so more truly romantic.

Once a couple has learned the use of the condom, they may then wish to consider other methods of contraception if the sexual relationship is well established and ongoing. The condom is ideal for the virgin on her honeymoon: The pill must be started ahead of time, and the IUD and diaphragm are more easily fitted after a woman has had intercourse over several months; the walls of the vagina and the opening to the vagina (the hymeneal ring) are stretched during this initial period of sexual relationships. So the condom is a natural "introductory" method for sexual initiation of the female.

It is good that the male partner can assume responsibility for birth control and VD control at the beginning of a sexual relationship, particularly since, even in the post-women's-liberation era, his interest in starting a sexual relationship, and his initiative toward that end, is usually greater than his partner's. If a girl has to provide the lead by going on the pill because the boy is too shy or stubborn to use a condom, then she may be in for disappointment. His reluctance to use the condom may signify failure to take some initiative and responsibility in the sexual relationship.

Questions Often Asked About Condoms

Q. Will a drugstore clerk sell condoms to you if you don't look eighteen?

A. Usually. Condoms are a nonprescription item; they are increasingly available—on display, in vending machines, or by mail. But some states still have certain restrictions. If you should get a shake of the head and a stern look from a drugstore owner or employee, try another drugstore. At larger drugstores, particularly, there should be no problem.

Q. Condoms never seem to be on display in drugstores. Where do you find them?

A. Go to the pharmacy department and ask the pharmacist. More and more drugstores are beginning to display condoms, particularly in the larger packages. If they are not displayed, the reason may be a practical consideration, not a moral one: Condoms on display seem to be popular items for pilfering.

Q. What do you say when you ask for them—do you call them condoms or rubbers?

A. You can ask for condoms, rubbers, or prophylactics; the pharmacist will know what you mean. Or simply have a brand name in mind and ask for "a package of Trojans (plain)" or some other brand name.

Q. Can a girl buy them?

A. Yes. Some girls do. A girl may want to share the expense or just take the initiative for a change. A condom in a purse is a legitimate item for responsible seduction, but some talk about it first might be wise.

Q. Can condoms be bought anyplace other than drugstores?

A. Yes. Planned Parenthood and similar clinics provide good brand names at very low prices, or even free. Condoms may also be ordered through the mail from Population Planning Associates, P. O. Box 400, Carrboro, NC 27510; phone (919) 929–2143. For $3 you get a special "Variety-Pack" of a dozen quality condoms, plus their catalog. Orders are filled on the day received and reach you in a plain package.

Condoms are available, in some states, in vending machines in men's rooms. If possible, though, these should be avoided. They are not as reliable as those carried by a good pharmacy.

Q. Why are condoms less than 100 percent effective? What happens the rest of the time?

A. To be effective, a condom has to be in good condition, and used properly. If the package is open a long time, or takes a beating in someone's pocket, or is in contact with a petroleum product, it will be weakened. A condom can break if the user neglects to leave about half an inch of slack space at the end to catch the semen. A condom can slip off if the penis is not withdrawn while it is still erect. *Very* rarely is a condom defective when bought. Theoretically, condoms should give almost perfect contraceptive protection. They are probably about 100 percent effective for 95 percent of the couples who use them; human error makes them ineffective for a few.

Q. Can a rubber be reused?

A. It's best not to. If you try to save a condom for use on another occasion, you can't package it perfectly and you increase the chances of its failure.

Q. Do some couples use foam or jelly along with condoms? Why?

A. That helps take care of the small percentage of occasions when condoms fail; combining contraceptives increases your protection. Foam plus condom is believed to be as good or better protection than the IUD.

Q. What if she doesn't trust a condom, or him?

A. If a girl is insecure, she should say so. He can quote the experts and then offer to show her the condom afterward. If it's all in one piece—that gives peace of mind. If there's an obvious break in the condom, or if it slipped off and does not contain semen, the girl should call Planned Parenthood or a sympathetic doctor within twenty-four hours. They can decide whether a "morning after" dose of hormone would help, or whether to wait and see.

Q. I've used condoms before, but the girl I'm going with now says she doesn't want to use a condom for our "first time."

A. You can try to convince her that your contraceptive won't really interfere with the closeness of your experience together—or she can visit her doctor or a clinic to get an IUD, a diaphragm, or contraceptive pills. Don't take a chance, though. If your first time is good, you'll have plenty of other times to use different methods. *Beware of girls who don't seem worried about pregnancy.* They—or you—may suddenly wake up the morning after in panic, when it's too late.

Q. Doesn't the use of condoms really interfere with sensations?

A. Physically, a little. Psychologically, condoms interfere with sensations such as panic and fear, which result from risk of a possible pregnancy and VD. To the extent that the condom filters skin sensation (slightly) during foreplay and vaginal thrusting, it gives the male more control. He will still reach the peak of excitement and pleasure, so he has nothing to complain about. True, in an established relationship, when he has good control during sex, when she is ready to assume responsibility for another method of birth control, and when the risk of venereal disease is zero, then it's nice to do without the condom.

6
The Pill

The oral contraceptive was the birth control breakthrough of the sixties. Two decades later we have smaller dose tablets, even "mini-pills," with fewer side effects. The pill is very popular, but suffers from a high dropout rate (discontinuation by the user). For this reason, every woman on the pill should have a second birth control method available which she knows how to use.

Dr. Gregory Pincus, with the encouragement of family planning pioneer Margaret Sanger, began work on synthetic hormones in 1950. By 1956 the research team was testing the oral contraceptive. The first contraceptive pill available commercially, Enovid, was marketed in 1960.

It all might not have happened without the work of a single-minded chemist who, early in the 1940's walked away from his university job and went looking for a plant that grew wild in the mountains of Mexico. His story is told in detail by Ernest Havemann in *Birth Control* (New York: Time-Life Books, 1967).

The chemist, Russell Marker, was seeking a source of progesterone, a female hormone produced by the ovary. At the time his search began, progesterone was rare and expensive selling for $200 a gram, $200,000 a kilogram. It could only be derived from the brains and spinal cords of animals.

Marker had an idea that a Mexican mountain plant, *cabeza de negro,* would yield progesterone in quantity. But research funds are always hard to come by, and he could find no one to finance research in remote regions of Mexico. So leaving his university job, he set off alone into the Mexican hill country.

At the end of the next summer he returned with two jars of progesterone—worth at that time somewhere between one-quarter and half a million dollars!

Other chemists then took over the job of uniting *progesterone* with another hormone, *estrogen,* to produce the modern birth control pill. And the mysterious Russell Marker simply vanished.

He left a few jobs, just as he had walked away from his university position at the beginning of his odyssey. Letters sent to his last known address in Mexico City are returned to senders stamped by the Mexican postal service with a phrase which translates, "He is not here."

By combining progesterone and estrogen the chemists create a chemical imitation of pregnancy in the woman taking the pill. Her bloodstream circulates the hormones to the pituitary (master gland) in the brain and the female organs (ovaries, uterus); since a pregnant state is signaled chemically, the woman's ovary stops producing and releasing eggs (ova). Since she does not ovulate, she cannot become pregnant even if sperm enter freely.

The contraceptive pill is now used by some 10 million girls and women in North America; it is far and away the most favored birth control method among teen-age girls who are given their choice.

The original brand, Enovid, has now been joined by more than thirty other brand names. Some brands combine hormones in a single pill, others provide them in sequence. Some are taken for twenty-one days per cycle, others for twenty-eight. They come in plastic cases, circular "dial-paks," or cameo compacts.

Why is the pill so popular?

Above all, it works. Taken properly, it is virtually a 100 percent guarantee against pregnancy. It is also convenient—taking something by mouth is easier for most girls than using genital methods. Fear of pregnancy is removed as an inhibiting factor; lovemaking is suddenly free of this worry. There is nothing to interfere with sensations, there is no interruption of sexual play before intercourse. The pill seems generally to suit today's life-styles. Its cost is about $75 a year, $40 of which is for the gynecological exam. But free or low-cost services are available.

For many girls, the pill offers benefits other than contraception. Girls whose periods have been unpredictable are pleased to find that the pill regulates their menstrual cycle; they are no longer caught by surprise. Quite a few girls are delighted with a slight increase in breast size that often results; some even report that their complexions clear up. (Clearer skin may result from the estrogens contained in the pill, or it may simply be due to the fact that a girl who is on the pill is no longer tense and anxious about pregnancy.)

Unfortunately, the pill also has some undesirable side effects in a few women—as is to be expected with any potent medication. These include nausea, fluid retention, vaginitis and discharge, and slight bleeding between periods. Serious complications such as blood clotting are very rare but do occur, and women who are susceptible—including all women over thirty-five—are advised against taking the pill. All women on the pill should have a yearly medical examination.

The pill is unique in the centuries-long story of contraception, like a spaceship compared with trains and airplanes. The condom and the diaphragm require application shortly before intercourse and act as barriers to the sperm. The pill does nothing about sperm released into the vagina but keeps the ripe egg from being released by the female ovary, so that no egg is *available* to be fertilized by a sperm cell. By mimicking a natural process, pregnancy, the pill tells the pituitary that this woman's ovaries are to take a rest. Chemically, that is quite a daring message to send to the pituitary gland—but it works very well.

The pill also works in two other ways to prevent pregnancy. It causes the cervix to produce a rather thick mucus which sperm cells find difficult to penetrate. And the pill keeps the lining of the uterus from becoming as thick as it usually does in the period between ovulation and menstruation. The thinner uterine lining would not be sufficient to nourish a fertilized egg, even if an egg should happen to be released and fertilized. (The relative thinness of the uterine lining offers what many girls consider to be a bonus: a lighter flow during menstrual periods.)

Since there are several ways in which the pill acts to prevent pregnancy, no wonder that it is virtually 100 percent successful.

Just about any girl who is looking for a method of birth control thinks about the pill. Two questions that are nearly always asked are *"How can I get it?"* and *"Is it safe?"*

The first question needs discussion, since the pill is a prescription item, and some girls hesitate to call their own physician or visit a new doctor or a clinic where they do not know anyone.

You might feel more comfortable calling a Planned Parenthood office or other clinic if you keep in mind that these services are there *for the very purpose* of helping you with birth control information and service. They tend to be friendly places, and the very fact that you probably won't know any of the staff doctors personally *may* make you feel more at ease than you would with your own doctor. ("I would have felt funny asking my family doctor for birth control pills," one girl told us, "but with a doctor I didn't know, I could talk more freely.")

Some girls, of course, *can* ask their own doctors about the pill. (Some even do so at their mothers' suggestion.) This depends on the doctor—and you will have to evaluate your own situation as best you can.

One girl who *thought* her doctor would be sympathetic told us, "When I went to my doctor last fall (I was seventeen) I asked him to prescribe birth control pills. He said to me, 'What for?' Well, what a dumb question for a gynecologist to ask! I went straight to another doctor."

Such experiences are becoming rarer, however. More and more state laws specifically recognize the right of unmarried teen-age girls to birth control services. A number of medical organizations have advised that teen-age girls should have the same access to birth control as older, married women. In 1971 the influential Executive Board of the American College of Obstetricians and Gynecologists issued an advisory statement urging that "the unmarried female of any age should have access to the most effective forms of contraception

. . . even in the case of the unemancipated minor who refuses to involve her parents." (An "unemancipated minor" is defined differently in different states, but generally it means a young person under the legal age of consent and not married, self-supporting, or in the Armed Services.)

Attitudes are changing.

One twenty-year-old college student told us recently, "When I was seventeen, I spent about $55 'shopping' for a gynecologist who would prescribe the pill for me. I first went to my mother's gynecologist, who told me flatly that he wouldn't prescribe the pill until I was married. I went to four different doctors, spending $15 or $20 each time along the way for a pelvic exam (I must have had the most thoroughly examined internal organs in the state!) before I found a doctor who said he would be glad to give me a prescription and approved of my decision. This year, however, that *same* old family doctor—the one I went to first—gave my younger sister a prescription with no hassle at all!"

If you prefer a private physician to a clinic doctor and want to be *sure* that the physician you choose will be helpful, there are two things you can do: You can ask a girl friend who takes the pill to recommend her doctor or you can simply phone a physician's office and ask the receptionist, "Does Dr. X. prescribe birth control methods, including the pill, for teenagers? If so, I'd like to make an appointment." This way you'll save time, trouble, and expense.

It should not be necessary to wear a wedding ring, lie about your age, or go through similar charades. In fact, you might do yourself a disservice if you pretend to be older than you are. *A doctor or gynecologist needs accurate information in order to decide if the pill is for you.*

The physician you see will give you a pelvic examination and ask you questions about your medical history. If everything is normal, he will probably agree to prescribe the pill. You are entitled to courteous and careful treatment, with full attention to your questions and problems.

The doctor may explain that there are several different types of pills. Some contain more hormones than others: Some are taken for twenty-one days each month, and others for twenty-eight days.

The first month you take the pill deserves special attention. You begin taking your pills on a particular day of your menstrual cycle—just as you finish your period. Counting the first day of the period as day 1, you will take your first pill on day 5. *You cannot begin taking the pills in the middle of the month!*

If you are given a prescription for a 21-day compact (such as Ovulen 21, Norlestrin 21, Ovral), you will follow a "three weeks on, one week off" pattern of pill taking. You will take a pill every day for twenty-one days; then, when the compact is finished you will *stop* taking the pill for seven days while you menstruate; then you will begin a new cycle with a new compact.

With the 28-day compacts, there is *no* skipping. You take *one pill* on *every day of the month.* However, you are actually taking birth control pills for only the first twenty-one days; during the seven days which include the time of your period the pills you take contain sugar or iron, not hormones. With 28-day compacts you need not stop and count days at the end of your cycle—you simply take a pill each and every day. The last seven pills are "blanks" (placebos), or iron supplements, which some women need.

The pill, whatever brand you use, must be taken for a full cycle, as directed! A few girls have had the idea that they could protect themselves from pregnancy by "snitching" just one pill from an older sister's compact and taking it on an evening when they thought they would have intercourse. Not only does this method fail as protection for the girl who steals just one pill; it messes up the older sister's schedule as well!

A final note is this: *An additional method of contraception (e.g., a condom plus foam) should be used during the first week of your very first pill cycle.* This will protect you in case you happened to ovulate very late in the month before you began taking pills.

After the first week no further protection is necessary. You will be safe as long as you just remember to take your pill on schedule: every day, or "three weeks on, one week off," whichever the case may be.

Your doctor may give you a prescription for six, eight, ten, or even twelve compacts, then advise you to come back for a checkup when you need a new pill supply. It's a good idea *not* to have the entire prescription filled at once, since you will want to make sure that the particular pill prescribed will work well for you.

Some girls find that a certain *type* of pill does not work well for them, and consequently switch to a different brand.

Sixteen-year-old Lorna, for example, was given a pill that contained only a "mini" dose of estrogen (Ortho-Novum 1). She worried about pregnancy when her periods practically disappeared. This is because she tended to have light periods in the first place, and, since the pill keeps the lining of the uterus from becoming very thick, her monthly discharges were lighter than ever. When Lorna phoned her gynecologist to report this, he explained that if she took the pill regularly, her light periods were not a sign of pregnancy. She could either enjoy the relative ease of a very light monthly flow or, if she felt more comfortable with a more normal flow, he would give her a new prescription for Ortho-Novum 2, which has a higher dose of estrogens. (She chose to change.)

Her experience, however, points up the importance of answering all questions carefully when you are examined by your doctor. When Lorna had been asked if her periods were normal, she had said Yes, not thinking to mention her characteristically light flow. Lorna's experience also points up the fact that a brand of the pill which is satisfactory for your best girl friend may *not* be the right brand for you. You should not "trade" compacts with a girl friend as an experiment—nor should you accept a supply of pills from anyone who is not a doctor!

Another girl's experience will demonstrate why:

Sue was not quite fifteen, but was sexually active and wanted the pill. Her boyfriend said "a friend" who worked at the Central Supply station of a Chicago hospital could get her some pills.

"Because I was only fourteen, I was fairly sure no doctor would actually prescribe the pill for me," Sue told us. "So I almost said OK to the plan. In fact, Larry (my boyfriend) got me two compacts of Ovulen from his friend. I was going to start taking them, but at the last minute I decided to take a chance and phone a doctor instead.

"I chose a woman gynecologist with a downtown address, just

figuring she might be more liberal. At the time of my appointment the doctor asked me about the regularity of my period, and I had to admit that it was extremely irregular. I told her that often it was over two weeks late, and that several days before it, I started feeling sick.

"The doctor seemed concerned. She said that she thought it might not be wise for me to go on the pill. Apparently I have an under-developed master gland. If I had gone on the pill, it might have kept the gland from developing all the way.

"She explained that I would probably be able to go on the pill later —but for the next year or two she recommended an IUD. I have been using that for several months, and it's no trouble. I'm glad I didn't take those pills on my own, without a doctor's advice. They're not like vitamins."

Although the pill is popular with sexually active teen-agers, most doctors have reservations about prescribing it for the younger girl— say, under seventeen—because her own hormonal patterns may not be well established.

Menstrual irregularity is not always a deterrent to taking the pill; the pill is sometimes used specifically to help make periods more regular. But if a girl is so young that her body has not yet established regular periods at all, most doctors, like Sue's, will suggest use of another method for a while.

Doctors will weigh many factors before prescribing the pill: tend-ency to form blood clots; varicose veins; family history of diabetes, liver trouble, heart disease, or glandular disease; eye problems; vaginal conditions; skin problems; migraine headaches; epilepsy; psychiatric problems.

That seems like a long list of factors to consider; however, it is because high medical standards are set that most girls are happy with the pill. Girls who might not respond well to the pill are advised to use other methods instead.

Is the pill safe? Yes, when properly prescribed, under good medical supervision. Over the past fifteen years millions of girls and women have taken billions of pills, with an excellent record of safety and satisfaction. Virtually all gynecologists prescribe it. Like *any other drug,* however, the pill is not advisable *for some individuals.*

The pill has been closely watched ever since it was introduced. And, partly because its action on body chemistry was unique in all the history of birth control—indeed, in the history of medicine—the pill was watched with some skepticism. Popular media as well as medical journals were quick to report side effects and alarms about the pill.

It is true that there often are side effects. That's why the pill is a prescription item—available to you only after examination by a doctor. But these side effects are generally temporary and minor.

About 25 percent of the girls and women who begin taking the pill will experience at least one of the following side effects: breast tenderness, weight gain, cramps, minor bleeding, or nausea. By the second month, however, the proportion of users who still experience side effects drops to only 2 percent.

The first women who used the pill did report more side effects. But the original birth control pills were about twenty times more powerful than those prescribed today.

Some doctors feel that side effects have more to do with a woman's psychology than with her body chemistry. With the exception of the change in breast size and sensitivity (almost inevitable), gynecologists have found that when they suggest to their patients that there may be side effects, the side effects are apt to be reported. When the side effects are not emphasized, they occur infrequently.

In one study, some women were given the pill and others given a simple placebo (blank). Some women in each group were told of possible side effects: headaches, breakthrough bleeding, nausea. About the same proportion of women in each group reported the side effects which had been mentioned to them! Some women who took the placebo even reported breakthrough bleeding.

Obviously, the relatively minor side effects just mentioned are no serious threat to health. But there has also been talk of cancer, blood clots, and other dangers as a result of the pill.

No connection with cancer has been found, although some researchers believe the pill may *reduce* the incidence of certain cancers in later life. It is well to be cautious, however, about the long-range effects of *any* potent chemical, and most doctors think women should take a rest from the pill every few years, using another birth control method for a year or two so their natural hormones can flow for a while.

And, while the risk of blood clotting problems due to the pill is a *real risk,* it is also a *small risk,* particularly when it is compared to the much greater risks of pregnancy. According to available studies, a girl or woman who takes the pill has more chance of being alive and well one year later than her sisters who choose to have a baby or who choose a less reliable form of birth control than the pill (assuming a "failure rate" and resulting pregnancy for the other methods).

The established serious complications are blood clotting (thromboembolism) and blood pressure increase (hypertension). Disability and death can result, but the likelihood is extremely small, and proper medical screening and supervision should make it even smaller. In England, in 1966, among 100,000 women aged twenty to thirty-four, deaths from embolism were 0.2; for women on the pill, the rate was 1.5 deaths per 100,000. That is an eightfold difference, but the rate is so low, even then, that it is a risk worth taking in view of death rates in the same age group from complications of pregnancy and delivery (22.8). For a better perspective, it is helpful to know that the death rate from automobile accidents in this group was 4.9, and that many other medications, including aspirin and penicillin, cause some deaths. (This study was published in the *British Medical Journal* 2:193, 1968.)

There is another side effect of the pill which is important to consider. It changes the chemistry of the vagina enough to favor the growth of certain microorganisms. Some women have annoying but not serious vaginal irritations from yeast or fungus growth. These respond to simple treatment. More serious is the problem of gonorrhea, the germ of which may have a greater chance of getting established in a woman on the pill than in a woman who is not—assuming both are exposed to an infected partner. Since most women do not have symptoms in the early stage of gonorrhea, they can harbor the disease and pass it on without knowing it, or getting treatment. To this side effect of the pill must be added the effect on pill users of less reliance on the condom, which prevents transmission of VD. (More on VD will come in a later chapter.)

Since 1967, however, the safety of the pill has improved. It was the estrogen component which seemed to produce bloodclotting problems; in the newer versions of the pill, the estrogen content has been greatly reduced (though the pill still works with the same effectiveness). Since the available forms of the pill differ in estrogen content, you may want to discuss this factor with your doctor. Especially if you notice side effects, you might be more comfortable with less estrogen.

Today alarms about the pill seem to have quieted down, and women who take the pill do so matter-of-factly and with confidence. Girls who take the pill tend to be far more enthusiastic about their choice than girls who use other methods. We have heard no extravagant phrases such as "It's fantastic!" or "I love it!" about other methods. We have heard such praise frequently about the pill. "Other methods you just *tolerate,*" one girl told us, "but the pill is an absolute pleasure. To me, that little compact represents absolute security!"

Anita, a student at the College of the Pacific who has done volunteer work for Planned Parenthood, summed up many often-expressed feelings as she told us why she advises the pill to girls who ask her personal opinion: "Keep in mind I don't say it's best for everyone. Whatever method you *want* is best for you. But I'm a real 'pill person.' My entire outlook improved when I began taking the pill two years ago. I also considered using the IUD, but it's not quite as effective. With the pill, I have control. Just by glancing at the day on the compact, I *know* my sexual activities are safe."

Many girls share Anita's enthusiasm (in fact, there is often a virtual "explosion" of pill use in many college dorms because of just such enthusiasm), but *not* all girls praise the pill without qualification. And not all girls find it quite so easy to remember *every day.* If you're going through a rough period with your lover, or you're separated for a while, taking the pill can become an emotionally charged event each day, and it can be forgotten, accidentally or on purpose. (See under "Questions" what to do when you forget a pill.) Failure (pregnancy) and discontinuance rates for the pill are considerable among teenagers—forgetfulness, guilt about sex, mood changes, and side effects all seem to be factors.

A friend of Anita's raised one of the Women's Liberation issues.

"As far as I'm concerned," she told us, "this is just another example of men experimenting on women's bodies. Probably it's safe, sure it works. But why not develop a pill for men? Because doctors are mainly men, that's why. If anybody's going to be taking chemicals for years on end, they'd prefer it to be the woman." (To this objection, some doctors reply that it is easier to try to control the production of one female egg cell per month than to try to control the continual production of billions of sperm cells.)

Other girls who consider themselves strong Women's Liberationists applaud the pill for the very reason that it is a female method—and leaves the girl herself in control of her own body. "I like the pill because it's my responsibility," said one. "I *know* I take it, and do not have to rely on men for my protection. With the pill, I am my own person, responsible for myself. The pill is really an aspect of my liberation."

Opinions about the pill may vary, but the central fact that makes the pill popular is unarguable: Taken on schedule, it is the most effective means of birth control ever developed. The effectiveness and freedom it provides put the pill in a contraceptive class by itself.

Questions Often Asked About the Pill

Q. What happens if you forget a pill?

A. That depends on how long you forget it. If you forget for only a few hours, or perhaps for half a day, there is no problem. Just take it as soon as you remember it. If you forget for an entire day (twenty-four hours), take two pills together. If you forget for *more than twenty-four hours,* take two pills together and continue to take the pills for the rest of your cycle, *but use another method of protection along with the pill until your next cycle!*

Q. Is it important to take the pill at exactly the same time each day?

A. It's a good idea. This will keep your body's hormone level constant. And if you always take it at a certain time, you're more apt to *remember* to take it than is a girl who takes it irregularly. (Sometimes, taking the pill at erratic hours—say, 8:00 A.M. on one day, 4:00 P.M. the next—is a cause of spotting or breakthrough bleeding.)

Many girls find it convenient to take the pill every morning, since they get up at about the same time every day, while bedtimes vary more. And if you miss a pill in the morning, you have all day to remember it.

Q. How much will the pill increase bust size? Can it change you from a 34A to a 36B?

A. The change in breast size is not that dramatic. It may be very slight; sometimes it may not be noticeable at all. You shouldn't buy a new supply of bras in anticipation of a big change, *nor* should you choose the pill solely because of a desire for this side effect.

Q. When my girl friend was taking her last pill of last month, she dropped it and then couldn't find it. She takes the 21-day kind, so this was a lost birth control pill, not just an iron tablet. She just decided to forget about it since she was about to have her period and figured it wouldn't make any difference. What should you do in a case like that?

A. Actually, every girl who takes the pill should set aside one *extra* compact of pills to use as "extras" if one is lost. If your girl friend had skipped a pill in the middle of the cycle, the results might have been serious. The last pill of the month is less crucial. But repeating what we've said before: Pills are meant to be taken *on schedule—every day.*

Q. Can you take the pill for two or three extra days at the end of a month to delay your period—for example, if you're going on a weekend trip?

A. Yes, you can, though it shouldn't be done as a matter of course. (This is another reason for keeping an extra compact of pills on hand.) *Caution,* however: If you are taking the 28-day pills, make sure you take the white or yellow *birth control pills* for the two or three extra days—not the peach-colored iron tablets.

It may surprise some of you, but most women seem to *want* their monthly periods. You could, with the pill, have a period less often— every six or eight weeks. (Longer intervals would lead to break-through bleeding.) But the monthly cycle is normal, and the body gets a break from the pill more often that way.

Q. Should I tell my mother I'm taking the pill?

A. One might similarly ask, "Should I tell my mother I use a diaphragm?" "Should I stop hiding that can of foam in the bathroom?" Etcetera. The real question is, "Should I tell my mother that I'm having sex?"

With parents we recommend as much openness and honesty as the relationship will allow. If you have good communication with your parents, and if it is consistent with tact and sensitivity, you may want to share this information with them. On the other hand, we also believe that teen-agers have a right to privacy in their sexual lives if they choose. Sensitivity is important here. *Opinions* about sex and contraception can be aired without telling personal details; this is as good policy for parents—whose sex life is *not* their children's business —as it is for teen-agers.

You can "tell" your parents, of course, by direct or indirect means. Quite a few girls seem to want their parents (particularly their mothers) to know, and they choose indirect means to convey the information. We've frequently been told, "My pills were in the top drawer and my mother found them."

It seems that more girls want to communicate their use of the pill than their use of other methods. For some, it's a way of announcing maturity to one's mom. Perhaps a girl wants her parents to know that she's having sex responsibly and using reliable birth control. Less frequently a girl may want her parents to know in order to rebel— to hurt or upset her parents.

Whether or not you share information about sex and contraception with your parents depends on your own individual family situation; it is your decision.

Q. Do girls and women who take the pill have sex more often than girls who use other birth control methods?

A. A survey of 1,000 women under twenty-five found that those who used the pill had intercourse an average of 11 times a month; those who used other birth control methods averaged 8.5 times per month.

There were several reasons given why girls on the pill might be more sexually active: (a) Anxiety about pregnancy is reduced; (b) The separation of the contraceptive act from the sex act increases spontaneity and enjoyment; (c) The chemical action of the hormones of the pill might increase a female's sexual desires. Professor Charles Westoff of Princeton University suggests that girls and women who have a higher interest in sex are the ones who choose the pill in the first place.

However, Dr. Westoff and the other investigators concluded that reasons (a) and (b) were most likely, since a small sample of women with IUD's also showed high frequency of intercourse, though no specific statistics were kept for the IUD users. It's logical that women having regular and frequent sex choose a method like the pill. It doesn't make as much sense for women whose sexual activity is slight or sporadic, as is the case for many teen-agers.

Q. Do Catholic women take the pill?

A. Yes. Numerous Catholics, including Dr. John Rock, whose research contributed to the development of the pill, hoped that the oral contraceptive would be approved by the Church, since it is neither a mechanical barrier nor a spermicide. This has not come to pass. But recent surveys indicate that more than 50 percent of Catholic wives use birth control methods other than rhythm, and the pill is a favorite.

Q. When a woman wants to have a baby, can she count on getting pregnant right away after she stops taking the pill?

A. Yes. Women who stop using the pill will, on the average, become pregnant within three months. Ninety percent become pregnant within a year. Babies born to women who have taken the pill are perfectly normal.

Q. What is the latest information about health risks to women on the pill?

A. About 40 percent of pill users report some side effects. A few are dangerous, and may be related to circulatory problems: Severe abdominal pain, chest pain, calf or thigh pain, headache or vision problems should be checked immediately. Older women and heavy cigarette smokers are especially vulnerable. The long-term effects of pill use are still being evaluated; a 1977 study from England reported an excess death rate of 20/100,000 among women who had used the pill over those who had not. If you are taking the pill, don't smoke, have a checkup at least once a year, and report any symptoms to your doctor promptly. If you see a doctor for any reason, mention that you are on the pill. Call your local medical society, health department, or Planned Parenthood for clarification of news reports which worry you (or interest you) about the pill or other contraceptives.

7

The Intrauterine Device (IUD)

The modern IUD looks like a delicate plastic earring and sometimes is worn that way, but not for birth control. As a birth control device, it is placed inside the uterus—thus its full name, "intrauterine device." The IUD provides near-perfect contraception until it is removed. And it may be left in place for years, if desired, without repeated expenses or daily routines such as pill taking or calendar watching.

Intrauterine devices come in a wide variety of shapes: tiny loops, coils, rings, shields, and spirals. The different IUD's are named for their shape or for the physician who first used or invented them (e.g., the Lippes loop, Copper "T" or "7," and Saf-T-Coil).

The IUD is often thought of as the newest of birth control devices. Yet, like many ideas that seem new and sophisticated, it has an ancient history. For example, Cleopatra reportedly experimented with using bits of hardened sea sponge and other materials as primitive intrauterine devices. For centuries in the Middle East, camel drivers have known that pregnancy in a female camel is prevented by inserting pebbles into the uterus (important if the camel is to be used in long trips across the desert). And in the Middle Ages Persian women used uterine plugs of tightly bound paper tied with thread.

The trouble with many of these early devices is that when inserted under unsanitary conditions they can lead to infection. Also, if the device is not inserted completely up into the uterus, it tends to carry infections from the vagina to the uterus. With the exception of an IUD developed by a Dr. Grafenberg in the 1920's, doctors had little success with this approach until about 1960.

A surprising thing about the IUD is that its action to prevent pregnancy is not fully understood. An IUD does not block the entrance to the womb or kill sperm. But somehow it either prevents the egg from being fertilized or from becoming implanted in the uterus.

Some physicians believe that the presence of the IUD causes minute vibrations of the Fallopian tubes that conduct the egg from the ovary to the uterus; this could speed the passage of an egg into the uterus prematurely, before the egg has reached the stage where it can become fertilized. Another theory has it that the IUD causes a tissue reaction which makes implantation of the egg impossible. One reason for the uncertainty is that the device works differently in different animal species. It is generally agreed that the IUD does not cause an abortion to occur, since implantation of the egg does not occur.

Regardless of the dynamics that make the IUD effective, it works well and is becoming increasingly popular.

Enthusiasts for the IUD point out that typically its insertion requires only one procedure, and thenceforth it stays happily in the uterus with no attention required, no interference in lovemaking, no chemical effects on the body in general (with the possible exception of some devices containing copper), and no continuing cost. It need not be refitted. As a contraceptive it is highly effective, second only to the pill, with a record of about 97 percent effectiveness—and that record is steadily improving.

As many as 2 million women in the United States now use the IUD. Though only about 3 percent of never-pregnant high school girls choose the IUD as their contraceptive, the figure rises sharply after age eighteen. On many college campuses, student health counselors say the IUD is next only to the pill in popularity.

A Tulane University sophomore told us, "My girl friends who began having sex during high school usually didn't know where to go for reliable contraception—or if they did, they lacked the nerve. So they used condoms or foam, or just crossed their fingers and hoped for luck. Lots of them got caught: pregnant. I'm very grateful that I didn't have to go through several years of trying methods that 'sometimes work.' I was not sexually active until this year, and I was old enough to know how to get a method that was statistically safe, and effortless.

"As a matter of fact," she added, "I got my IUD while I was still a virgin—so I've *never* had to worry!"

A University of Colorado coed used the IUD as her first method of birth control: "I wanted the IUD because it is the method that is effective, safe, and easy. And my life is complicated enough!"

"It suits my life-style," agreed an eighteen-year-old San Diego secretary. "I never considered a method other than the IUD. After all, who's going to bother to dash home to get the pill compact if you suddenly decide to spend the night someplace? It's too easy to miss a day or two. And who's going to take a diaphragm on a picnic?"

That secretary could manage a diaphragm or the pill if she made the effort, but she doesn't want to, and likes the IUD. Many other girls find the IUD the *only* suitable method for them; their life-styles are not compatible with remembering to take a pill or learning to use a diaphragm.

"We (my boyfriend and I) had tried every kind of nonprescription birth control: every type of foam, different kinds of rubbers, even rhythm. There was always some degree of inconvenience. With the IUD, there's not. . . ."

"Before I got my IUD, I had premenstrual tension that had nothing to do with menstruation. It was simply worry that my period, this month, would be late . . . because of pregnancy! I had to have something that would make me feel secure. The pill gave me side effects —so it had to be the IUD."

A lot of girls turn quickly from other methods to the pill or the IUD after a pregnancy scare—or a pregnancy!

Of those who limit their choice to the two surest methods, the pill or the IUD, those girls who choose the IUD sometimes mention worries about the long-term effects of the pill. One girl said, "Sure, the pill is probably safe, but why get a little dose of chemicals every day, year after year, when the IUD offers about the same protection, *non*-chemically?" Some experience side effects from the pill, and then switch.

An IUD can be obtained from a private physician (gynecologist) or family planning clinic. Since there are usually no chemical side effects to worry about, you may not have to give as complete a medical history as with the pill, but the doctor will ask whether you have ever been pregnant before, since women who have not may have difficulty retaining the regular IUD in the uterus. The type of IUD the doctor selects—if he does recommend this method—depends upon pregnancy history (childbirth or abortion), condition of the uterus, and problems of infection or menstruation.

The insertion of the IUD is a simple procedure that takes only a few minutes. Being quite elastic, the IUD fits into a special inserter: a thin sterile tube, about the size of a drinking straw. In this tube the flexible IUD is stretched out straight. The tube holding the IUD passes through the vagina and cervix—literally the *neck* of the womb —up into the uterus. The doctor gently pushes the IUD out of the tube, which is then withdrawn, and the IUD expands inside the uterus, resuming its original shape. Many IUD's have threads attached, which extend down through the cervix into the upper end of the vagina. These enable the woman to check that the IUD is in place.

Doctors generally prefer to insert the IUD during the menstrual period. There are several reasons: The cervix is slightly open at that time, making insertion easier; slight bleeding as a result of insertion will not be noticed; and the physician is sure that the patient is *not* in the early stages of a pregnancy. Some physicians insert the IUD when the woman wants it, rather than waiting for a menstrual cycle. It's advisable to phone first if you want to avoid making an extra visit —find out the policy of your doctor or clinic.

A nineteen-year-old political science major at Northwestern University chose the IUD after experiencing an unusual degree of breast swelling with the pill. Jenny phoned her gynecologist and explained that she wanted an IUD. "I had heard an IUD might be expelled if you'd never been pregnant, so I wasn't sure it could be done. But my doctor said there should be no problem, and asked me to make an appointment toward the end of my next menstrual period, when the cervix would be slightly dilated and insertion would be easiest.

"He explained that he was using a type of IUD called the Copper "7", since this was smaller than some other types and was retained well by never-pregnant women. He took some time to show me an IUD of the type he'd be using . . . told me that it was very effective . . . and said I could expect some bleeding for a couple of days, and possibly some cramps.

"The nurse gave me a local anesthetic. She said that without an anesthetic there was pain when the uterus opened up for the IUD to be put in. The inserter the doctor used was very skinny; I hardly felt anything at all. The nurse told me to take aspirin if I had any cramps, and showed me how to check (by feeling for the threads attached to the IUD) to see that it was still in place. If I had really severe cramps or bleeding, or if I could not feel the threads, I was to call the office.

"The insertion itself was absolutely painless and took only a few minutes. And after all that discussion I was really pleased that I had *no* problems with the IUD, none at all. There was no discomfort or pain from the cramps. I'm very pleased. The IUD is even more convenient than the pill, and I feel very secure now about my sex life."

Unfortunately, the IUD does not always work out as well as it did for Jenny. Some girls experience cramps during the first few months that the IUD is worn. These may be relatively mild (and can be treated with aspirin) or may be severe enough to warrant removing the IUD. Such cases, however, are becoming much rarer. According to Dr. Hugh Davis of Johns Hopkins University, the cramping "results from putting a large device into a small uterus—or putting a small device into a slightly wrong place." Dr. Davis and other gynecologists predict that these problems will become less and less frequent as physicians gain experience in working with IUD's and as more of the newer, smaller IUD's are used.

If that comes about, the IUD will be close to the ideal contraceptive. As it is, the IUD is gaining in popularity among both patients and doctors.

Some girls cannot use the IUD because it is not retained in the uterus (if it is expelled, this usually happens during the first menstrual

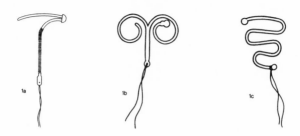

1. Different types of IUD's, about 1 inch in size: a) Copper
"7"; b) Saf-T-Coil; c) Lippes loop.

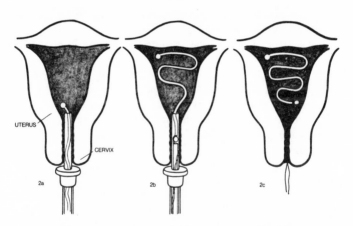

2. Insertion of an IUD: a) The IUD is stretched out straight
in the tiny inserter tube and the tube is gently pushed through
the cervix into the uterus; b) the IUD is pushed out of the
inserter tube into the uterus, where it springs back to its
original shape; c) when the IUD is in place in the uterus, the
inserter tube is withdrawn, leaving threads from the IUD
extending outside the cervix, where they can be checked by
hand.

period following insertion). Though rates of expulsion are becoming lower and lower, it *is* a possibility, especially among women who have never been pregnant, and it is that first unwanted pregnancy that most young IUD users are trying to avoid. Because the device may be expelled, a girl is shown how to check to make sure it is still in place —by feeling the tiny threads that extend down into the upper part of the vagina. (Right after her IUD was inserted, Jenny checked *daily* to see if the strings could still be felt, particularly before intercourse. Now that she has had the IUD for more than three months, she checks only occasionally. The chances are that an IUD that is retained for three months will stay there indefinitely.)

Just because the IUD sometimes is expelled naturally does not mean that you can remove it yourself, say if you have cramping. If you try to pull it out, you may very well injure yourself. *The IUD should be removed only by a doctor.*

If the IUD should be expelled, that does not necessarily mean that a girl cannot use the device. If it is reinserted, there is a greater chance of its "staying put" the second time. A 1970 report by a New York gynecologist, Dr. Robert E. Hall, indicates that "first expulsions" occurred with about 10 percent of his patients who tried the IUD, but among those women who had the same type of IUD put in again (in this case, the Lippes loop, one of the larger IUD's), the expulsion rate was only 3 percent.

Nevertheless, for one reason or another the device cannot be used by some women. But since the IUD has only been widely used for about ten years, strides forward are still being made in its technology, and every year the chances for successful use of the device become more favorable.

Improvements in IUD's are constantly under study. Different shapes and materials are being tested, especially in order to find a device that will be accepted comfortably by the never-pregnant uterus. Copper-wound IUD's are now attracting attention—good and bad. Copper itself seems to have contraceptive properties. For example, when Dr. Howard Tatum of the Population Council developed a very small "T" shaped polyethylene IUD, the device was accommodated well by childless patients, but about 18 percent of the first users became pregnant. Winding a single, thin strand of copper around the "T" caused pregnancy rates to drop to almost zero. But since it is possible that this copper is absorbed slowly into the body, further research had to be done to be sure the device is safe. Now both the Copper "T" and the Copper "7" have been approved by the FDA and are in widespread use.

In summary: While there are still some problems, and the search for the "perfect" IUD is still on, the IUD's now available are proving to be near-perfect for more and more girls and women.

Questions Often Asked About IUD's

Q. Why do you bleed for a day or two after the IUD is inserted?

A. Often, but not always, there is some bleeding immediately after an IUD insertion. This occurs because of unavoidable stretching and scratching of tissues during the insertion. The tissues heal promptly —like your gums after being worked on by a good dental hygienist.

Q. Can a girl's boyfriend tell if she has an IUD?

A. No. The IUD itself is located inside the uterus, not in the vagina, and the nylon strings are usually not detectable, except to the woman's careful touch.

Q. I always thought it didn't hurt when an IUD was inserted, but my girl friend had one put in and she said it "hurt like hell" at the moment of actual insertion.

A. Perhaps your friend was not having her period at the time. Usually doctors insert an IUD during menstruation because the cervix is slightly open then, and the procedure is easier. Some doctors give a local anesthetic routinely; others don't. Many make some attempt, at least, to judge whether an anesthetic will be necessary. (For example, if an IUD is inserted following childbirth or an abortion, no anesthetic is needed, since the cervical tissues are already stretched and insertion is painless.) You can certainly tell your doctor that you'd like to have a local anesthetic prior to having your IUD put in place.

Q. I've heard that if a girl has certain conditions (like varicose veins) a doctor will be reluctant to give her the pill. Are there some conditions which will make a doctor refuse to give a girl an IUD?

A. The presence of any pelvic infection. In such a case, the physician will postpone inserting the IUD until the infection is cleared up. Also, certain abnormalities of the uterus, which are not common, will prevent the use of an IUD.

Q. Can IUD's cause infections?

A. Extremely rarely today. In the case of earlier, cruder devices, which stayed partly in the uterus and partly in the cervix, this was a problem. These early devices could carry infection from the cervix or vagina (which are not free of bacteria) to the sterile territory of the uterus.

When a physician inserts an IUD today, it is under highly sterile conditions. The IUD and the inserter are sterilized.

Q. If a woman who is wearing an IUD wants to become pregnant, will she be immediately fertile after the IUD is removed?

A. Yes—the IUD provides birth control only while it is in the body. There is no "lingering" infertility afterward.

Q. I've heard that the IUD's sometimes haven't worked, that babies have been born with IUD's in their hands.

A. That last part is a fanciful story. It is true that there has been a small (3 percent) failure rate of IUD's in past years. Often (since an IUD wearer is obviously motivated not to become a mother) the resulting pregnancies are terminated by abortion. When such pregnancies have been carried to term, however, the IUD has been in the placental membranes which are expelled from the body following the birth of the child (the "afterbirth"). The children have been perfectly normal, unaffected by the IUD.

Q. Don't IUD's sometimes cause perforation of the uterus? Are there any other serious complications?

A. Perforation is extremely rare. Even with the "bow" type of IUD, which had the worst record, a maximum of 7 instances per 1,000 insertions was reported. All other types of IUD's taken together cause about one perforation per 1,000 to 2,500 insertions. But the newer types of IUD's seem to have a better record. Perforation is the most serious complication associated with IUD's, and it usually requires surgical treatment.

Q. If you are wearing an IUD, how can you be sure it's in the right place and has not been expelled?

A. It's easy enough to feel whether or not the device has been expelled: Follow the advice of most gynecologists and *check those threads.* It's a good idea to check especially carefully during menstruation. More expulsions occur during menstruation than at any other time; once in a while, girls have noticed their IUD on their pad or tampon. If you can feel the threads, you will know that the IUD is resting comfortably in its proper place.

Some IUD's will show up on an X-ray picture, which is one more way to check.

8

The Diaphragm, *Plus*

The diaphragm is the traditional standby of female birth control methods: a bit awkward to use at first, but very effective when properly used, and *absolutely safe*—no side effects, chemical or physical. The diaphragm is not strictly a modern invention. The "original" primitive diaphragm was probably the shell of half a lemon inserted in the upper end of the vagina to cover the cervix, the entrance to the uterus through which sperm travel to reach the egg. The citric acid in lemon juice was of some help in killing sperm.

A 1976 study of over 2,000 young, mostly unmarried women at the Sanger Bureau found a remarkable success rate: Only two pregnancies per 100 users per year. And 82 percent stayed with the diaphragm. (From 25 to 50 percent of pill-starters will discontinue within a year.)

As with any birth control method, if you choose the diaphragm you should understand it fully. And we think more couples would choose it if they knew more about it and had a doctor who taught its use enthusiastically.

When we speak of the diaphragm as a good contraceptive, we always mean the diaphragm *plus* a spermicidal cream or jelly. A "spermicide" is something that kills sperm, and this is the purpose of the cream or jelly which is put onto the diaphragm before it is inserted. Spermicides are available in any drugstore, usually displayed on an open shelf as tampons are. (Spermicides are *not* douches, deodorants, or disinfectants!)

The diaphragm itself is a soft rubber dome with a flexible or firm (arcing) spring around the rim. Since women come in different sizes, diaphragms do too, and if a diaphragm is to work, it must fit correctly. That is why diaphragms are not sold over the counter; a doctor must fit you and give you a prescription for a diaphragm of the correct size.

Diaphragms range in size from about two to four inches across but are measured in millimeters in the medical tradition. The larger sizes are generally for women who have had several children and whose vaginas are slightly stretched; generally the smaller sizes fit teen-age girls and childless women.

To determine the correct size a doctor has a series of flexible rings of different sizes which can be inserted into the vagina and checked for comfort and secure position. A diaphragm which is too small will move around too much and not provide an adequate barrier to the sperm. A diaphragm which is too large will not fit into place or will feel awkward.

A diaphragm with a very flexible rim is often used. It can be inserted by hand *or* with a plastic inserter designed for the purpose. The arcing-spring type of diaphragm (All-Flex, Koroflex, and Bendex) must be inserted by hand: it holds its shape better and is harder to dislodge. The arcing-spring was originally designed for women who have a weakness of the pelvic tissues. However, some obstetricians recommend it for *all women,* and so do we. The stronger support offered by the arcing diaphragm helps to stabilize it in proper position. It is easier to insert by hand, and it holds the jelly easily.

Dr. Jane Hodgson, a distinguished Minnesota obstetrician who served as medical director at Preterm in Washington, D.C., said that the diaphragms to be recommended are the arcing type. "We don't even have any of the other kind around, and so we don't bother with inserters. They were used more in the past when women were squeamish about putting something in the vagina. Now, with menstrual tampons being widely used, this doesn't seem to be a problem."

The arcing diaphragm has not been studied in surveys separate from the regular kind, but a number of authorities believe it is much better. *Faithful use of an arcing diaphragm with a contraceptive cream or gel may well be even better than 98 percent effective.*

The diaphragm fits over the cervix—covering it something like a hat (only put on upside-down from underneath). One edge of the rim is tucked back behind the cervix, and the opposite edge is tucked up in front behind the pubic bone.

Sperm cannot live in the vagina for very long. The secretions of the vagina are acidic, and sperm cannot survive in an acid environment. If the sperm reach the uterus, however, they find a more receptive environment. They survive longer, and may fertilize an egg. The result, of course, is pregnancy. That is why proper fit of a diaphragm is so important—since the entrance to the uterus must be protected.

A teaspoon of spermicidal cream or jelly is placed in the center of the diaphragm, and a little is rubbed around the rim. You don't have to measure with a teaspoon. The cream or jelly comes out of the tube in a column like toothpaste; squeeze out about three inches' worth. More is not necessarily better—in fact, too much may cause the diaphragm to slip around. When the diaphragm is in place, the spermicide is held in the cup of the diaphragm up against the cervix. (If you turn the diaphragm upside down the spermicide will tend to drop out, and this should warn you that you're putting the diaphragm in the wrong way.)

Should the movements of intercourse push the diaphragm slightly out of place (it occasionally happens), the cream or jelly still serves as an effective line of defense. In fact, some doctors believe that the diaphragm works mainly because it keeps the spermicide in place.

Perhaps the key to a happy experience with the diaphragm as a method of birth control is the initial fitting and explanation of how it should be inserted. Julie, who was *not* pleased with her diaphragm, was fitted in the office of a well-known (and expensive) New Orleans gynecologist who disapproved of diaphragm use. He took little time with the fitting itself. "If you decide to use a better method, like the IUD, let me know," he told Julie at the close of the appointment.

Karen got her diaphragm from a much less prestigious source: a New Orleans clinic which specializes in birth control. After a doctor had given her a pelvic exam and determined which size diaphragm Karen would need, a nurse showed Karen a life-sized model of the female internal organs, with a diaphragm in place.

1. Squeeze out about 3 inches of spermicidal cream or jelly into the diaphragm. Rub a little around the rim.

2. Press together the edges of the diaphragm, using your thumb and index finger. The brand of arcing diaphragm shown here is marked "press" where you should squeeze the edges together; then move your hand to the end of the diaphragm as shown. (Note, you may have to hold other brands of diaphragm more in the middle until partly inserted.)

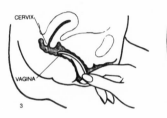 

3. With your other hand, open the lips of the vagina. Insert the diaphragm into the vagina, on an angle toward the back, as far as it will go.

4. When the diaphragm is in place, the back end will be tucked up behind the cervix and the front end should be pushed up behind the pubic bone. Check with your finger to be sure that the cervix is covered by the dome of the diaphragm.

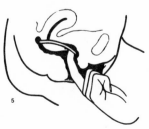

5. To remove the diaphragm, hook your finger under the rim and pull downward gently.

Next, under the nurse's supervision and with the model in front of her, Karen leaned forward on one elbow to examine herself and to learn a vital anatomy lesson: where her cervix was. Then the nurse explained how to insert the diaphragm, and Karen did this herself. The nurse checked to see that the diaphragm was correctly placed, and had Karen practice again until she felt confident that she herself could put it in and check to be sure she had done it correctly.

It does take a little time and practice to learn, but this is the correct method of inserting a diaphragm: Using the fingers of one hand, hold the rim of the diaphragm on either side and then pinch the sides together toward the middle. With the other hand, hold the labia slightly apart. It is best to do this in a sitting or squatting position, lying down with the knees raised, or standing up with one leg up on a chair, edge of the bathtub, or the like. The upper end of the diaphragm (the end nearest you) must be slipped far up into the vagina, up behind the cervix. When this is reached, the *other* end of the diaphragm is pushed up in front behind the pubic bone.

The diaphragm should then feel snugly in place to the finger. Also use your finger to check the position of the diaphragm. You should be able to feel the tip of the cervix under the rubber. (The cervix feels like the tip of your nose.) If the diaphragm is in properly, you—and your partner—won't be able to tell it is there, except by manual examination.

There are, certainly, many factors which will determine whether a girl can adjust to diaphragm use, but certainly a girl taught by a careful and understanding professional who is willing to *take some time* is more apt to learn quickly and comfortably how to use this method.

In this regard, doctors vary, and so do clinics. If you are not sure that you understand how to place the diaphragm, ask for more instruction!

Since the spermicide is so important in the effectiveness of this method, it is important to use new jelly or cream when a long interval goes by between insertion of the diaphragm and insertion of the penis. *Two hours* is the maximum interval. If more time than this elapses, a fresh application of jelly or cream should be made. It is not necessary to remove the diaphragm to do this; simply insert cream or jelly into the vagina with an applicator.

After intercourse, the diaphragm must remain in place for at least *six* hours, in order to be sure there are no sperm left active in the vagina. If intercourse is repeated, a new application of cream or jelly must be used between times. For this you will need an applicator, which is filled from the tube of cream or jelly. (However, one doctor, who claims 100 percent effectiveness for the diaphragm, recommends *always* inserting additional spermicide into the vagina *after* intercourse, to supplement what is on the diaphragm. It sounds like a good idea.)

To remove the diaphragm, hook your finger under the rim and gently pull it out, allowing it to bend as it did when you put it in. The arcing diaphragm may be a bit more difficult to remove than the regular kind—for the same reason that makes it better: It fits more snugly, as if by suction. Hook your finger under the rim, and be sure the suction is broken before you pull. If you just take hold of the diaphragm and start pulling, you may tear the rubber. Sometimes the arcing diaphragm rotates slightly inside, and you have to turn it a bit to find the spot where the rim bends to take it out: a small, occasional inconvenience in exchange for greater security.

After removal, the diaphragm should be washed with soap and warm water and carefully dried with a towel. You may sprinkle it with cornstarch (but not talcum or perfumed powder—they can harm rubber, as does Vaseline). Keep it in its protective case away from heat.

Girls who use the diaphragm should wear it whenever there is any possibility of intercourse. Wearing the diaphragm is not uncomfortable, nor will it interfere with normal activities. If you're wearing it, you don't have to find the diaphragm (or hide it), remember to put it in your bag, or say "Wait a minute—I've got to put my diaphragm in!" The only thing to be remembered is the addition of spermicidal cream or jelly before intercourse, if more than a few hours have passed since insertion.

Girls whose lovemaking is less frequent can insert the diaphragm any time before intercourse; *with practice, it takes only a few seconds.* It can be a bedtime routine—as natural and easy as washing your face or brushing your teeth. It's a good idea to wear the diaphragm whenever sex might occur. But take it out for washing at least every 24 to 36 hours.

A girl should check her diaphragm periodically for tears or holes by holding it up to the light, or by filling it with water and seeing if any drops form on the underside.

When well taken care of, a diaphragm will last for several years. It is a good idea, though, to be refitted and get a new one if necessary every year at the time of an annual checkup.

Diaphragm use sounds like a lot of trouble to many girls. Compared to the pill or an IUD, it *is* a rather complicated procedure; it takes some patience and skill to learn this method of birth control. But the diaphragm is chosen by some girls for the following reasons:

1. *It's free from complications or side effects.* If a girl (or her boyfriend) is concerned about possible side effects of some other methods —notably the pill—she should try the diaphragm. It's absolutely harmless. It is chemically inert: Neither the latex material of the diaphragm itself nor the various spermicidal chemicals interact at all with body tissues. (Some few people are sensitive or allergic to latex rubber or to certain brands of cream or jelly. Should this be the case, however, there are plastic diaphragms, and such a wide variety of creams and jellies are available that a satisfactory one can usually be found.)

2. *It's a local method.* That is, it operates only in the area where it is placed. It cannot affect any other body systems.

3. *You only have to use it when you need it.* If a girl knows she is not going to be having intercourse, she can set the diaphragm aside, unlike the situation with the IUD or the pill. On the other hand, if she is unable to anticipate when she will be having intercourse, this can be a drawback, especially if she is the forgetful type who, for example, leaves the diaphragm at home while away on visits.

4. *Once you learn how to do it, it just takes a few seconds.* Inserting the diaphragm can seem quite complicated at first; some girls, ini-

tially, spend five or ten minutes before they're *sure* it's in right. However, with practice, diaphragm insertion can become a quick and easy part of a personal regimen.

5. *It's not expensive.* Many clinics, such as the one Karen went to, will provide a diaphragm fitting at no charge. (Fitting by a private gynecologist, though, may run $15 to $25.) The diaphragm itself costs about $4, a tube of jelly or cream—sufficient for about twenty applications—about $2. (But whatever method of contraception is chosen—birth control is always a good bargain.)

6. *It works.* The diaphragm offers up to 98 percent protection from pregnancy when properly used. This means, above all, that it is not left in the dresser drawer during sex (because "we have to hurry, my roommate will be home any time") or used intermittently ("Well, I can't remember to carry it around with me *all* the time") or without the necessary cream or jelly. "You only have to use it when you need it" is true enough—but whenever you need it, use it!

Frankly, we feel that the diaphragm deserves to be more widely used. It is an excellent and safe contraceptive. Some authorities say that it's too complicated for young people. But young people drive cars, build stereo sets, and even write books. We suspect that in at least some cases the diaphragm has been made to seem more complicated than it is.

Dr. Joy Ozer, a biochemist, and a diaphragm enthusiast for years, made some sharp points very clearly in a recent discussion:

"The reason for my affectionate feeling for the diaphragm is that this is a method that has been used for fifty years, and the only statistics about its safety—in terms of health—show that women who are married to uncircumcised husbands have a significantly lower rate of cervical cancer if they use a diaphragm than those who do not. We have two generations of information. Women for the last ten years have been going to physicians who have not even tried to determine if they would be good diaphragm-users or poor diaphragm-users before dispensing a drug, a chemical. This practice has been completely irresponsible in my opinion."

Questions Often Asked About Diaphragms

Q. My diaphragm, which I've been using for only a few weeks, is changing color. Does that mean it's wearing out?

A. No. A diaphragm will change, with use and exposure to air, from its original white color to a shade of beige or tan. This is perfectly normal, and does not mean that the diaphragm is less effective.

Q. My mother suggested that I get a diaphragm. She knows that my boyfriend and I have been sleeping together, and explained to me that we had to take precautions. But I just can't bring myself to use it—I hate the idea of sticking it up inside myself. What should I do?

A. Some girls and women don't like the idea of touching and handling their genitals and internal organs. There is a special diaphragm inserter which you can get, but you still have to check the position of the diaphragm and take it out by hand. And we recommend the arcing diaphragm, which must be put in by hand.

You have two other choices: You can try to change your attitude and learn that there is nothing "unclean" or unhealthy about touching yourself, *or* you can choose another method of birth control.

We recommend the second choice until you feel that you will be comfortable with the diaphragm. A method of birth control which you don't feel at ease with is bad business; you're too apt to start skipping it. Rather than take chances with your body, choose a method of birth control that you *like*.

Q. I was told that a fresh application of cream or jelly should be made before a second act of intercourse. But my question is this: What if that second act of intercourse occurs right away? Is it necessary to interrupt the proceedings in order to insert more spermicide?

A. It would be wise at least to check the position of the diaphragm. If the first application of spermicide was hours rather than minutes before, then an interruption of the proceedings is a small price to pay for security.

Q. With repeated intercourse, and repeated insertions of contraceptive jelly, it gets very messy. Yet I understand I'm not supposed to douche. Is it at least OK to just wash with plain water or soap and water between acts of lovemaking?

A. Yes, certainly. You might also consider trying a contraceptive cream rather than a jelly. Creams are somewhat less lubricating, and just as effective. Wiping the vulva with facial tissue or a clean, soft towel will also be helpful.

Q. Why can't you use foam with a diaphragm instead of cream or jelly?

A. Foam is designed for use alone to spread out and fill up space around the cervix; it is supposed to hold itself in place. The diaphragm holds the concentrated cream or jelly in proper position. Foam may be used if there is no cream or jelly handy, but it is not convenient to apply to the diaphragm (foam is designed to spread all over; cream and jelly to stay put, more or less).

Q. My boyfriend strongly objects to the diaphragm. We have oral sex quite frequently before intercourse, and he says the odor and taste of the cream or jelly is offensive—and I've tried several brands.

A. It's a good idea if both partners agree on a satisfactory method of birth control. Since your present partner objects to this one, you might discuss other methods. However, have you tried washing the vulva with soap and water after inserting the diaphragm? This should wash off any of the spermicide that has rubbed off the diaphragm onto the vulva or entry to the vagina. Once the diaphragm is in place, the jelly in the cup and around the rim should not spread down to the lower vagina before intercourse; it will be held against the cervix higher up. What you describe also might follow from inserting spermicide after the diaphragm is in place.

Q. I'm going to have an abortion; will that mean I should get a diaphragm of a different size?

A. Maybe. Bring it along and ask the doctor to advise you.

Q. I find using the diaphragm very satisfactory, but I'm worried about its 10 to 15 percent failure rate. As I understand it, that means that after 100 women use it for one year, 10 to 15 of them will become pregnant anyway. I've been using my diaphragm for exactly one year, and I'm starting to worry that I might become part of those "failure statistics."

A. Keep in mind that when the rates of failure for various birth control methods are compiled, it isn't always easy to distinguish between *product* failure and *personal* failure. No doubt some of the failures in the statistics you quote resulted from improper use (or *non-use!*) of a diaphragm. Careful, constant use of an arcing diaphragm plus a spermicide is about 98 percent effective. And using it for a year does not mean "your number is up." Each time you use it, you have the same 98 percent protection. You could, of course, switch to a birth control method that has a 99 percent-plus success rate—the pill. If you prefer to keep using the diaphragm, you could increase your safety level by combining its use with another method, such as rhythm, or adding extra spermicide after sex. See Chapter 10, "Other Methods, Non-Methods, and Combinations."

Q. Can you be fitted for a diaphragm *before* you've ever had sex?

A. Yes. But it may require stretching of the hymen at the opening of the vagina, and after sex has begun, refitting may be necessary as the vaginal tissues stretch a bit. So we recommend starting with condoms.

Q. What if you start to menstruate while the diaphragm is in?

A. No problem. The initial flow usually is held in the cup of the diaphragm.

Q. If you are wearing a diaphragm, can you go ahead and use menstrual tampons, too?

A. Why? Since the risk of pregnancy is practically zero during the menstrual flow, the only reason to use a diaphragm then would be aesthetic—to temporarily catch the blood high up in the vagina—if you wanted to have intercourse during menstruation. Some girls like to use the diaphragm for this purpose. After intercourse the diaphragm can be removed (you don't have to wait six hours during your period) and the tampax can be inserted.

9

Vaginal Foams, Creams, and Jellies

The practice of putting something into the vagina to prevent conception is very old and widespread. It is known in primitive and scientifically sophisticated societies in all parts of the globe.

Prescriptions against pregnancy have been found in the papyrus fragments of Egyptian medical authorities, written four thousand years ago. The Greek physician Soranus in the second century A.D. and the ancient Hebrew Talmud described various techniques.

Of course, the ancients had no microscopes or chemistry laboratories in the modern sense, and they relied mainly on trial-and-error experiments. Aristotle suggested using oil of frankincense mixed with olive oil; other Greek sages advised peppermint juice mixed with honey. Ground pomegranate pulp or rind, lemon juice, alcohol, alum, and cedar gum were also popular.

Some of these early recipes were definitely on the right track. We know today that oil and honey are sticky enough to interfere with the travel efforts of sperm, and that acids such as lemon juice or vinegar are mildly spermicidal. Pomegranate pulp or alum would have an astringent effect on the cervix—causing the tissues to contract or shrink somewhat, and thus making passage of the sperm through the mouth of the cervix more difficult.

At some time or other, probably every herb, leaf, or potion imaginable must have been tried.

These ancient methods—even the most effective ones—did not

Using foam

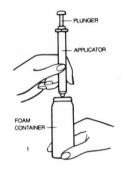

1. Fill the applicator with foam, until the plunger is pushed up.

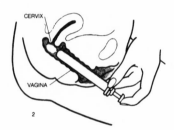

2. Insert the applicator up and back into the vagina until it touches the cervix; withdraw about half an inch, and push the plunger to release foam over the cervix.

work very well, however. If they had, there might be far fewer people around today!

Modern biology and chemistry have given us a much more effective array of such contraceptive substances. They come in different forms: cream, jelly or gel, and aerosol foam. *Cream, gel, and foam preparations are nonprescription items; they are available at any drugstore.* These products act to prevent pregnancy in two ways: Each contains a spermicidal ingredient which acts to kill the sperm, and the foam, cream, or gel base acts as a "barrier" to block the entrance of the sperm to the uterus.

Some of these products work better than others.

Foam is best—used alone, it is far more effective than cream or gel preparations, which are reliable protection only when used with a diaphragm. Two popular brands are Emko and Delfen. They contain a spermicidal ingredient in a foam base.

The foam base is really the secret of success of these preparations. Unlike cream or gel, the foam assures even distribution of the spermicide and is considered less messy to use.

Foams come in a pressurized can or vial, and are released into a clear lucite syringe-type applicator. To use, shake the can or vial and attach the end of the special applicator to the top of the container. The foam will push the plunger of the syringe upward until the applicator is full.

Remove the applicator from the container, and carefully glide the applicator into the vagina until it reaches the top. (You should feel it touch the cervix—the mouth of the uterus.) Withdraw the applicator slightly, about half an inch, and press the plunger so that the foam is left high up in the vagina. The idea is that the foam will thus coat and shield the cervix at the upper end of the vagina. To insure that the foam goes where it's supposed to, it's a good idea to insert it when you are lying down on your back.

Foam is easy to use, and it's also easy to buy. At most large drugstores Emko and Delfen will be on display, usually in the "feminine hygiene" section; you'll find the foam products somewhere among the Kotex, Carefree, Feminique, and Cupid's Quiver. Note: In some states it is still illegal to display contraceptives. From time to time this law is enforced and it is necessary to ask the pharmacist for the product.

The cost is under $5 for a container of Emko or Delfen *with special applicator;* refill cans of foam will cost a bit less.

Emko offers a "Pre-Fil" container, with applicators already filled and ready for use. Unless you are buying the "Pre-Fil" product, be sure—the first time—that you pick up a container *with* an applicator in the box too! The refill product alone won't do you a bit of good, because without the applicator you can't get it where it's supposed to be.

How effective are the foams? This is a much-debated question, and studies have yielded quite different answers.

One research project directed by Gerald Bernstein of the University of California School of Medicine involved 296 girls aged fifteen to twenty, who used foam for about ten months as their exclusive means of birth control. Of these 296 girls, 6 became pregnant (2 percent).

Of a total of 2,932 women of *all* ages involved in that same Bernstein study, 94 became pregnant (3.3 percent).

Of 130 women aged seventeen to fifty-one who used foam under the direction of Dr. Lowell Bushnell of Presbyterian Memorial Hospital in Los Angeles for an average of two years, 4 became pregnant (3 percent).

Of 142 women who used foam during a twenty-seven-month study in Puerto Rico, 35 became pregnant (a failure rate of almost 30 percent, contrasted to the very low failure rate of other studies).

Most pamphlets given out by Planned Parenthood and other clinics cite a figure of 80 percent effectiveness (20 percent failure) for the foam products. In their popular booklet *How to Take the Worry Out of Being Close,* Marian Johnson Gray and Roger Gray conclude: "The number of pregnant foam-users showing up at Planned Parenthood clinics and public health departments puts the effectiveness of foam well below a diaphragm."

However, the whole story is not in those statistics. Even a 20 percent failure rate (that is, a 20 percent chance to become pregnant) is four times better than an 80 percent chance to become pregnant—which is what you've got if you use no protection at all.

Also, even though a diaphragm may offer better protection (and such methods as the pill and the IUD certainly offer much better protection), the diaphragm, pill, and IUD are prescription methods of birth control and require a visit to a doctor or clinic. If you have hesitated to approach a doctor or clinic or for some other reason are without protection, *do* approach your nearest drugstore for a can of foam. The protection it offers is far better than none at all!

With regard to those statistics: One might wonder, since there is a wide range of failure rates shown from one study to another, whether the failure is due to the product or to the individual and her failure to use the foam correctly and consistently.

Dr. Jerome Siegel, general manager of the Emko company, stresses that "*consistent* use of foam—not just on occasions when you think you may be fertile, but used every time—will result in very good birth control. Very good, not perfect."

While foam is far from a perfect method of birth control (and while we do not advise it for girls unwilling to use abortion as a "backup" method), we agree with Dr. Siegel that it is a *good* method. You can maximize its effectiveness by following certain rules:

Use *two* applicators full, not one. The more foam, the more spermicidal protection.

Insert the foam *immediately* before intercourse—certainly no more than thirty minutes before. If more time than that elapses, insert more foam. The brochure which comes with your foam may tell you that it can be inserted one hour, or even several hours, before intercourse. We do not recommend this, however. The foam structure breaks down after a period of time, and the barrier effect is diminished.

Additional foam must also be inserted before *each* act of intercourse. (Both Emko and Delfen package the foam container and applicator with an attractive, purse-sized plastic carrying case included.)

Since the foam must be allowed to work for at least six hours *after* intercourse, DO NOT DOUCHE during that time or you will remove or dilute some of the spermicide. (Actually, douching is an unnecessary thing to do, anyway, and can even be harmful, since it destroys helpful, cleansing natural bacteria. Douching should only be done under a doctor's direction in cases of special problems. For the average girl or woman, natural secretions will take care of internal hygiene very satisfactorily.)

The foam must be deposited in the upper vagina, not close to the vaginal opening. For this reason, it's a good idea to insert the foam when lying down, rather than when sitting or standing. This gives the foam its best chance of getting where it's supposed to go.

Finally—*use it every time!*

Foam is a better contraceptive, used alone, than the spermicidal creams or gels. CREAMS AND GELS SHOULD BE USED ONLY WITH A DIAPHRAGM. Used with a diaphragm, they provide excellent protection. Used alone, they do *not.* Unlike foam, creams and gels do not disperse evenly; without a diaphragm, there is nothing to insure that they block the entrance to the uterus so that live sperm cannot enter. Used alone, creams and gels carry far too great a risk.

The creams and gels *can,* however, be used in combination with other methods to increase protection; they can supplement the use of condoms. And foam can be used with condoms or the IUD during fertile days. Condom plus foam combined—two nonprescription methods—offer protection that ranks with that of the pill. One woman who works for the Emko company favors foam plus a condom. "It's the method I've used for years," she says, "long before I was working for this company." She feels that this combination method offers three advantages: superior protection, no side effects, *and* shared birth control responsibility between two partners.

Dr. Hugh Davis of Johns Hopkins University, a leading advocate of the IUD, suggests that a girl who wears an IUD and also uses a puff of foam during her fertile period can raise her protection to virtually 100 percent.

Foam alone does not offer first-rate protection against pregnancy, except in combination with other methods. It is first-rate, however, in its almost complete lack of side effects. (It may even reduce the spread of certain vaginal infections, but studies on this are still inconclusive.)

It's a good idea to be familiar with the major brand names of the foams, creams, and gels, since they may be displayed near products which have nothing to do with contraception. K-Y Jelly, for instance, is a simple lubricant sometimes used with unlubricated condoms—it is *not* a spermicide. Some other vaginal jellies (Trimo-San Vaginal Jelly, as an example) are for treatment of certain infections but useless for birth control. A hasty glance at a drugstore display isn't always sufficient to tell you what will kill a sperm and what won't.

Information contained in product brochures (or slogans on boxes of these products) may not always be helpful, either. Several creams and gels, though intended for birth control, simply don't say so. Others indicate their limited effectiveness in language that is confusing: "When a pregnancy is medically contraindicated, the contraceptive program should be prescribed by a physician"—you don't realize that the product does not provide very good protection.

Some of the brochures which come with the contraceptive creams and gels advise you that these products are effective alone, without a diaphragm. The box of Koromex Jelly, for instance, says, "For use with a diaphragm"; the box of Koromex-A Jelly indicates, "For use alone." This is confusing, because experts agree that jelly alone is not advisable. We repeat our advice that creams and gels should not be used alone—only with a diaphragm.

A newer contraceptive is the vaginal tablet which melts at body temperature, creating a foam barrier with spermicidal action. Brands are Encare Oval and Semicid (do not mistake deodorants for spermicides!). Ten or twelve in a box, these are small and easy to carry. They get soft when warm; if that happens, hold one (wrapped) under cold running water for a few minutes. Insert it (unwrapped) high up in the vagina ten minutes before intercourse. Evaluations aren't in yet but, like other foams, this type should at least serve well as a combination or second method of protection.

Taking a trip? Girls who use diaphragms or cream-gel products might find it a good idea to take a supply of their usual brand with them when traveling abroad. An additional warning: In some countries, such as Ireland, contraceptive products are simply *not sold.* Take your own supply.

As with foams, it is important to remember the following when using creams or gels:

One application is only good for one exposure.

Two applicators offer more protection than one.

Cream or gel must be applied fairly soon before intercourse, or it loses effectiveness.

Cream or gel must not be douched out afterward.

Some girls and women like cream or gel products because they provide the least expensive means of birth control—as low as ten or fifteen cents per application for some gels, and only forty to sixty cents per application for the disposable Conceptrol tampon applicators.

However, penny-pinching where birth control is concerned is false economy! Cost amortization plans can go out the window when suddenly an abortion must be paid for, or a birth saved for. Use of a cream or gel in conjunction with a condom or diaphragm will really not raise the cost involved that much; use of these products *plus rhythm* adds no cost at all.

Think about it. Don't take chances where your protection is concerned.

Questions Often Asked About Vaginal Spermicides

Q. Can you use any of the three main types of vaginal products—foam, cream, or gel—with either a condom or diaphragm? Or do you have to use foam with a condom, and cream or gel with a diaphragm?

A. Foam can be used by itself but is more effective in combination with a condom. A diaphragm *requires* cream or gel to be effective, and cream or gel is only reliably effective when so used—not alone. It may also be used to supplement, or lubricate, the condom.

Q. Since you can get foam or cream without a prescription, they are what I tried at first. But by the time you insert it twice, and then reinsert it if you don't have intercourse immediately, it starts to feel too messy.

A. A facial tissue or clean cloth takes care of this annoyance. However, you should consider other forms of contraception if messiness is too much of a problem.

Q. What if, after inserting the foam, you have to urinate? Will this remove the foam or dilute it?

A. No. The opening of the urethra is outside the vagina, and the foam is high up inside. Having a bowel movement, however, might incidentally cause the foam to move down in the vagina, so a reapplication would be advisable then.

Q. When I lived communally with three other girls and some guys, the other girls and I shared the same tube of gel and also shared the applicator. I always wondered if you could transmit VD that way.

A. Not syphilis or gonorrhea, unless you transferred it from vagina to vagina in a matter of seconds. But trichomonas vaginitis, fungus, and other infections can be spread this way. The applicator should

Table IV
Summary of Major Spermicidal Products Now Available

BRAND NAME	COMMENTS
Foams Emko Emko Pre-Fil Delfen Koromex Because	These are the most effective spermicidal products. Foams are easy and pleasant to use; their presence is almost always undetectable. They provide first-rate protection if used in combination with a condom.
Creams Delfen Conceptrol Ortho-Creme Koromex	These white creams come with an applicator, as do the foams. (Conceptrol is actually Delfen Contraceptive Cream, specially packaged in an applicator that is like a tampon.) The creams are only really effective when used with a diaphragm. Combined with use of a condom, they give very good protection.
Gels (Jelly) Ortho-Gynol Koromex Koromex-A Ramses	These clear or blue-tinted gels also come with a special applicator. They are often used as lubricants for unlubricated condoms, offering the advantage of being spermicidal as well. If used for this purpose, a refill package (without an applicator) is all that is needed. Like the creams, they are best used with a diaphragm. They may also be effectively combined with a condom.
Foaming Tablets, **Suppositories** Encare Oval Semicid	Unwrap, place high in vagina at least ten minutes but not more than an hour before intercourse. *Take care not to mistake deodorants for birth control!*

always be washed with warm water and soap after use. However, there are some personal things you share with others only at the risk of contagion: your toothbrush, towel, vaginal applicator . . . and most of all, your lover.

Q. What if you feel burning or irritation or some other allergic reaction to some of these products?

A. This is unusual, since the products are relatively mild. However, ingredients do vary somewhat, and if you or your partner have any reaction, you can simply switch brands or switch methods of birth control entirely.

Q. Don't some men find it a bother to have a girl use these vaginal products?

A. Yes; this is one reason why many girls choose another method, one that does not interrupt the sex act. However, some men do not mind at all.

Q. If you use foam—or vaginal gel or cream without a diaphragm —as your method of birth control and get pregnant, can you sue the company?

A. No; the companies make no guarantees. In fact, some brochures have careful disclaimers: "No product will protect you from pregnancy 100 percent of the time." Only abstinence is guaranteed! So if you decide to use foam, please read carefully the section of this chapter which gives tips for maximum effectiveness.

10
Other Methods, Non-Methods, and Combinations

As you know by now, there are several different good methods of contraception. None are perfect, but most people can find at least one method that is both convenient and effective. The best choice depends upon the person's circumstances and preferences. And what is right for you at one time may not be the best choice later on. For example, the condom is a good beginning method, but if a couple is having sex regularly, they may prefer to try another approach.

The more you know about how reproduction works and what birth control methods are available, the better the chance that you will be satisfied with sex, contraception, and family planning. If you do your studying ahead of time, there's less worry and more freedom later.

Some people will never try anything new, and others will jump on any bandwagon just for the ride. The newest popular methods may not be right for you. For example, the pill is spaceage contraception; by comparison the diaphragm is as old-fashioned as the bicycle. But the bicycle is being rediscovered by a lot of people, and so is the diaphragm. As we've mentioned before, obstetricians' wives use diaphragms more than women in general do. So although your first concern is to know about at least one method that works, for the long run it's worthwhile to be familiar with other choices. If for any reason you must or want to use a new method, the change can be made without panic.

In this chapter we talk about a few new and old methods you may have heard about, a few you should forget about, and some good combination methods.

Some Methods

Withdrawal (coitus interruptus). This technique requires the male to withdraw his penis from the vagina prior to ejaculation, so that the sperm are not deposited inside the female genital tract. Withdrawal must be timely—that is, before ejaculation begins, a matter which some men either cannot precisely determine or cannot control. Also, sperm do appear in the fluid emitted before climax from the penis about 25 percent of the time. So even withdrawing at the point when ejaculation is coming may be too late.

Withdrawal must be complete so that the semen is not deposited too near the vagina. Sperm can travel up into the vagina from its outer edge, and a few women who are virgins—who have never had penetration of the penis into the vagina—have become pregnant by petting in the nude, when the male has ejaculated very close to the vaginal opening. Apart from these physical risks, withdrawal is psychologically unpleasant for most couples, since it interrupts the closeness which is emotionally fitting to the height of sexual passion.

Nevertheless, withdrawal has been used by many couples with considerable effectiveness. In the nineteenth century the French birth rate fell significantly, apparently because of the widespread practice of coitus interruptus. Some men take pride in their ability to control sexual arousal and climax so as to be very effective with this method. A boy in England who used withdrawal said, "It's like the British Railways—always pull out on time." He had good control (and luck) on his side. But most young people cannot practice withdrawal with any reasonable hope of success. The relative newness of sexual experience and the lack of ability to control feelings and physical actions at the peak of sexual excitement lead to accidents.

A small percentage of men may have excellent control over ejaculation and a few men even have a problem of achieving climax while in the vagina and can continue intercourse indefinitely. This minority of men may indeed be able to "take care," but women should be wary of male confidence on this subject unless they know their partners very well. In this day and age of easily available and good-quality contraception, there seems little reason to rely on a method as frustrating and unreliable as withdrawal.

The cervical cap. This is a contraceptive device rarely used in the United States, although some doctors and patients are enthusiastic about it. The device is a little cup which fits over the cervix and stays on all month, preventing entrance of sperm into the uterus. It must be taken off in order for the products of menstruation to flow out of the uterus. The fit of cap to cervix must be good, and the cervix is not that easy for many women to reach when inserting the device, so the method has its problems. You should know about it, though, in case there are future improvements.

The morning-after pill. A form of estrogen known as diethylstilbestrol (DES), or just stilbestrol, will interrupt pregnancy if taken within forty-eight hours of fertilization. The usual dose is twenty-five milligrams a day for five days; the drug is not new, having been used by gynecologists for many years for a number of medical conditions. Recently a controversy arose because the drug has been shown to cause cancer in some animals when used over a long period of time. And few, if any, experts would allow a woman to use it repeatedly or regularly. However, the defenders of DES as a morning-after pill insist that a short period of use is not risky, and that the alternative risks have to be considered—pregnancy or abortion.

Dr. Sadja Goldsmith of the Planned Parenthood Teen Clinic in San Francisco says there is a place for DES in the birth control spectrum. "The girl who is raped, or who got drunk at a party and later realizes she had intercourse, doesn't want to wait two weeks to find out if she is pregnant. She wants something done right now." For the girl who doesn't mind waiting, menstrual extraction (discussed in the chapter on abortion) is available if needed. But DES is useful for the girl who is desperate, for whom two weeks' wait would be terrible. She must, however, begin treatment within forty-eight hours of fertilization. Unfortunately a girl may miscalculate her cycle (see the chapter on rhythm) and think that last night was the high-risk time, when in fact it was last week. If she had intercourse last week also, thinking she was safe from getting pregnant, then DES will *not* bring on the period; it may create a deformed fetus instead. Therefore, if a woman takes DES and finds herself pregnant anyway, it means she took it too late and will need an abortion (or risk having a malformed baby).

Non-Methods

The folklore of birth control is full of fanciful but worthless suggestions about avoiding (and terminating) unwanted pregnancy. Norman Himes's *Medical History of Contraception* (1936; reissued 1963) is the key reference and well worth looking into. All kinds of potions, motions, and notions—like sneezing by the woman and breath holding by the man—have been tried and recommended by somebody at some time. Of course, there were no careful evaluations of results. Since pregnancy does not always result from intercourse—statistically it happens only once in twenty-five exposures—you can see that almost anything will *appear* to work for a while, simply on the basis of chance. Be very skeptical of "research" based on one or two cases; people will sometimes swear by a method that worked for them or a friend, but beware! Either they've been lucky or they may be subfertile or infertile without knowing it.

Douching (washing out the vagina). This is not a method of birth control, because some sperm will probably move from the upper vagina into the cervix (where they are safe from the douche) within a matter of seconds. It may be that a douche, even with plain tap water, is better than nothing, for example in the unlikely event a condom has broken during intercourse. The sperm are very fragile and vulnerable to tap water. But douching can't be counted on. Furthermore, douching in general does more harm than good to the vaginal tissues and is regarded as an undesirable procedure for "feminine hygiene" by many gynecologists. Women who think they have to "pretty-up" their vagina and external genitals with douches and chemical spray have apparently been sold a bill of goods. Not only are those "intimate, feminine" deodorants useless—they can cause real damage to delicate vaginal tissues. Gynecologist Bernard M. Kaye reports in *Medical Aspects of Human Sexuality* (July 1971) that potential hazards of such products include: genital itching, vulvitis, contact dermatitis, and genital irritations in *males* whose girl friends use these "gyne-cosmetics." The penis can be just as sensitive as the female genitals to the chemicals contained in these products. Soap and water for the external genitals and nothing inside is a good rule. Women who think they need something inside should consult a gynecologist in case there is a mild infection or some other problem creating a discharge or irritation. Douching should be used only as a medical procedure with medical advice, and not for birth control. It just doesn't work.

Other non-methods. These include relying on breast feeding as a method of birth control. While breast feeding does tend to suppress ovulation in some women for some time after childbirth, it is not possible to predict when ovulation will resume. Your first menstrual period after childbirth indicates that ovulation *has* resumed, but that period may never come, for in the meantime you may have become pregnant again.

A non-method that is even less reliable is based on the true fact that the production of healthy sperm depends upon the testicles being at the right temperature, among other things. An undescended testicle that is maintained at a warm temperature inside the body does not produce sperm. Unfortunately there is no practical way for men to take advantage of this fact. Wearing jockey shorts, taking a hot bath before intercourse, or any other method used to heat the testicles won't work. A hot bath, for example, may slow down the process of sperm production, but there still will be millions of sperm available.

Some young girls are aware that menarche (the start of menstruation) precedes ovulation and feel that they do not have to worry for a while. But the onset of ovulation is not predictable. If your periods have begun, you should consider yourself a risk for pregnancy if you have sex.

Combinations

We present a summary table on page 121 to provide easy reference to family planning methods. As you can see, the most effective methods require a visit to the doctor or clinic (pill, IUD, diaphragm, abortion, sterilization); and the methods that are effective and free from side effects (diaphragm, condom) are somewhat less convenient. Perfect contraception doesn't exist yet, except for abstinence, of course—and we emphasize again that good sex is worth waiting for and thinking about.

To increase protection to 100 percent—or nearly—you can combine methods of contraception. Some methods can be used together, and even should be. For others it would be pointless. For example, it makes no sense to combine anything with the pill, once you are taking it regularly, except the condom if there is any risk of VD (the condom is not needed as contraception if the pill is being properly used). Of course, if you forget to take the pill a few times, then you *must* add another method such as a condom until the next monthly cycle begins, as explained earlier. The IUD is not quite as effective as the pill. It can be improved by, in effect, combining it with rhythm—keeping track of the safe and fertile times of the month and practicing abstinence around mid-cycle—or by using foam or a condom at mid-cycle. Again, the condom is always advisable if either partner has been exposed to VD.

The diaphragm and jelly is slightly less effective than the IUD or pill, but is free from side effects and hazards. For this reason Dr. Christopher Tietze, an expert on contraceptive evaluation, has found that the best combination for effectiveness and safety is the diaphragm (or condom) backed up by early abortion in those instances when contraception fails. Abortion is not an acceptable last resort for everyone, but if it is acceptable, those individuals who don't find the pill or the IUD suitable should consider the diaphragm, with abortion as a fail-safe measure. The combination of other contraceptive methods with the diaphragm is also worthwhile—for example, practicing periodic abstinence or using a condom in mid-cycle. Remember, the *arcing* diaphragm with spermicide may be even better than 98 percent effective.

The condom can be combined with other methods, as mentioned.

Table V
Summary of Contraception, Abortion, and Sterilization

METHOD	EFFECTIVENESS	SAFETY	CONVENIENCE	COMMENT
Abstinence	100%	Perfect	It all depends . . .	No purchase necessary
Pill	99%+	Very good	Taken daily by mouth	Rx. needed
IUD	95%+	Very good	Ideal, if it stays in	Rx. needed
Diaphragm and spermicide (arcing type gives highest protection)	90–98%	Perfect	Insert before intercourse	Rx. needed
Condom	90–97%	Perfect	Put on before intercourse	No Rx. Also protects against VD
Foam	Good—but less than above	Perfect	Put in shortly before intercourse	Rx. not needed
Rhythm	30–40%	Perfect	Requires charts, abstinence	Catholic Church approves

METHOD	EFFECTIVENESS	SAFETY	CONVENIENCE	COMMENT
Withdrawal	Low	Perfect	Difficult and frustrating	No purchase or preparation necessary
Douche	Very poor	May irritate vagina	Poor	Inconvenient as well as ineffective
Abortion	100%	Good	No hospitalization needed in first 10–12 weeks of pregnancy	Hard to obtain in some areas, especially for poor women
Sterilization	Virtually 100%	Very good	For males, great; for females, fair	Mainly for people with children

Alone it is not perfectly effective, and it is well to keep in mind the mid-cycle high-risk time and use a vaginal foam in addition.

Vaginal foam is rather less effective than the above methods but can be used to back up all other methods (except the diaphragm). If foam is the basic method you use, it should be supplemented, at least during the fertile mid-cycle days, with abstinence or a condom.

Rhythm is a very weak method of contraception. However, it is important to understand how it works so that other methods can be made more effective, and so that you can achieve pregnancy without undue delay when you want to.

Withdrawal is a very unsatisfactory method that no couple should use when anything else is available. It doesn't combine well with anything, except possibly with rhythm, if that is your basic method. Don't rely on withdrawal. If you have no other contraceptives, you can abstain. Sex is worth waiting for, especially since the alternative

—sex now, pay later—may bring weeks of anxiety followed all too often by the misery of unwanted pregnancy. Keep in mind Dr. Elaine Pierson's title for her guide for college students: *Sex Is Never an Emergency.*

In looking at the reliability figures you might wonder whether, when a method is 98 percent effective, it will fail the ninety-ninth time you use it. The answer is No. *Every* time you use it, the chances of success are 98 percent. That figure is an average based on research done with many people over the years. The results, then and now, depend on the *theoretical* effectiveness of the method and its effectiveness in *actual* use. Some of the failures of condom and diaphragm, for example, are due to human error—*carelessness.* For many couples these methods have been 100 percent effective over a lifetime of use. For other couples there have been failures. The 98 percent statistic expresses many different experiences in one figure, which is a *very solid* level of confidence.

11
Abortion

Shui yin tastes bitter, is of cold nature, and contains poison. It is a specific for ulcers, white itching sores on the scalp, will kill parasitical worms in the skin and flesh, cause abortions, and cure fevers. . . .

Earliest known prescription for abortion,
China, about 2700 B.C.

Abortion is an ancient and still widespread means of limiting births. Not a form of contraception, abortion is the technique of birth control which is applied when unwanted pregnancy already exists. Experts believe that abortion is the most common form of birth control practiced in the world today, even though in many places it is still illegal.

Our discussion concerns intentional or induced abortion. (Sometimes pregnancies end spontaneously in abortion, for which the word "miscarriage" is often used.) Until recent times there was no truly safe method of inducing abortion. The ancient Chinese prescription quoted above and similar folk remedies either did not work reliably or risked killing the woman as well as the fetus. The same is true of quinine pills or any other medicine or substance that you may hear can cause an abortion. The most likely result of trying such a remedy is that you will make yourself sick. And anything taken in large enough doses to cause abortion may kill you as well. Too many girls have died still pregnant. The only exception is the "morning after" pill which was discussed in Ch. 10, and even this works only under certain conditions.

Primitive abortion methods using herbs are still being studied in the hope that a medically safe substance will be found, but so far there have been no helpful discoveries. We do know that in the past more pregnant women who did not want children had them anyway. Infant abandonment, or infanticide, was common and even condoned in some societies.

There is, however, a safe, modern obstetrical technique of abortion using a thin, sterile, flexible tube that is inserted gently through the vagina into the womb. This is the vacuum aspiration or suction method. Before the fourth month of pregnancy this method of abortion can be performed in an office or clinic, with local anesthesia only, in a matter of about fifteen minutes. The patient can go home after an hour's rest, and the risk of harmful effects is very slight—less than if the same woman continued on to childbirth.

In the 1970's, medically safe, legal abortion became widely available in the United States. The Public Health Service reported over 1 million abortions were performed in 1977; 92 percent of these were in the first trimester (first twelve weeks) of gestation. Three-fourths of the women were unmarried; about 31 percent were teen-agers, another 34 percent were twenty to twenty-four years old. Overall, there was one abortion for every three babies born that year. Because teen-agers have more unwanted pregnancies than older women, the teen abortion rate is high: Girls under fifteen had slightly more abortions than births, while young women age fifteen to nineteen had about one abortion for every two live births.

The vast majority of these younger women were single, pregnant for the first time, and had not been using any reliable form of contraception. Medically safe, legal abortion at reasonable cost enabled them and their partners to postpone parenthood and marriage, which were unwanted at the time. Considering the statistics on illegal abortion and on normal-term pregnancy, safe early abortion is, for some women, a lifesaving operation. Considering the psychological and social consequences of teen-age parenthood—with or without marriage—in today's society, abortion is a lifesaving procedure in a broader sense: Young women and men have a second chance for self-determination of their personal lives, a chance they could not have had otherwise.

The same self-determination is possible through the use of contraception, which is safer and less costly than early abortion. The problem has been the lack of contraception education and services for young people. We hope that abortion rates go down rapidly as more people learn to use effective contraception. Meanwhile, one place where they will learn is the abortion clinic. This type of clinic, which nearly always provides contraceptive counseling, has become a de facto school for family planning. Until the rest of the schools catch up with this important aspect of health and mental health education, abortions will be numerous.

Abortion is a matter of controversy because some people regard the fetus as a human being. This view has essentially no medical or legal authority; according to law—confirmed by the U.S. Supreme Court in 1973—the fetus does not have the status of a person. Believing that the fetus is a human being is a personal, usually religious view deserving of respect. But this belief should not, in a free society, restrict the rights of others to safe medical abortion.

We believe that the fetus is only a *possible* human being, like the sperm and egg it comes from. Further, we believe that to be *wanted,* loved, and cared for is a child's most important birthright, and that the determination of whether or not a child is wanted can only be made by the pregnant woman. The abortion decision should be between her and her physician, with additional counsel if she chooses. A woman's constitutional right to make this decision, at least during the first three months of pregnancy, was established by the Supreme Court on January 22, 1973.

There is hardly anything more disruptive and restrictive of a young girl's life and future than an accidental pregnancy. Abortion guarantees the right of every child to be a wanted child, and the right of every woman to determine her own destiny.

These views relate to the stories of Joyce and Linda which follow. Had Joyce been more conscientious about other birth control, her abortion probably would not have been necessary. For Linda, the fact that a safe medical abortion was not available when she needed one made all the difference in the world.

Joyce and Joe

"I must have conceived in December of 1971. I should have gotten my period about New Year's Eve. I didn't. So I had to start the New Year with some unhappy problems.

"Joe and I had been going together for a long time. We had talked about getting married, but there were so many things we wanted to do first, before we even thought about a baby. We agreed when we heard a Planned Parenthood announcement that said, 'Leave a lot of time for the two of you—before you become the three of you.'

"The second Monday in January I was at the doctor's office for a pregnancy test. It came back positive. Maybe I should explain how this accidental pregnancy happened. It was due to a diaphragm which understandably failed—*since it wasn't used.*

"Thank God I live in California. I had a private doctor who arranged for me to have an abortion as an outpatient: I would be at the hospital clinic for a few hours. My doctor explained the abortion procedure the day I got my pregnancy test. He told me that he would be using the suction method, which works like a tiny vacuum cleaner. I was only concerned about whether or not it was safe and could be done almost immediately.

"Joe knew about it; my parents didn't. I wanted to keep my mom and dad unaware, if possible.

"I arrived at the hospital promptly on the appointed morning, only to wait what seemed to be a long time. There were about twelve women there for abortions that morning; four or five of us looked young, like students.

"Friends have told me that they've talked and made new friends while waiting to have their abortion. But there was not much talking in this particular group of women. We were all too preoccupied, I guess. Nearly everybody seemed very intent on reading the magazines in the lounge. I did a few math problems.

"Another thing I'd heard was that some nurses were very uptight, and might make you feel like 'abortions are nasty business, and you are nasty girls.' But the nurses and aides here were kind, sympathetic, and warm.

"At 9:30 it was my turn. I was helped into a hospital gown and had to remove my rings, jewelry, contact lenses, and anything else extraneous. Then a little cap was stuck on my head to hold my hair back; and I was wheeled into the operating room on a stretcher, feeling very relieved that it was finally happening.

"I was given an injection to help me relax, because I would be awake during the procedure. They sponged my pelvis with an antiseptic solution (but did *not* shave the pubic hair—this isn't considered necessary). My feet were placed in special stirrups at each side of the table, and the doctor said I would feel a pinch inside, on my cervix, and then a needle. I did. That was the local anesthetic (a lot safer, he told me, than being put to sleep with a general anesthetic, and no after effects of drowsiness or headache). Then, I felt just a little pulling sensation, and heard the whirring of the vacuum pump. Before I knew it he said, 'You are no longer pregnant.' I thanked him, and they wheeled me out. I had been in the operating room about fifteen minutes in all.

"In the recovery room there were four other women: two quite young, one probably twenty-five, and another who looked about thirty-five. The tension of the other waiting room was gone. We chatted about how relieved we were, and how hungry. Shortly after that we were allowed to get dressed and have something to eat. Then it was time to have a post-abortion counseling session, although my doctor had talked with me beforehand about the procedure, and my feelings about it.

"I had already decided to go on the pill. My doctor had offered to insert an IUD at the time of the abortion, but I thought I'd go with the method that had absolutely the least risk of pregnancy. I didn't see why counseling was really necessary, but I changed my mind. Mrs. Jensen, the woman I talked with, had just counseled a girl who couldn't have been more than thirteen! There was no question in my mind about whether *that* girl needed all the good advice she could get. And it dawned on me that *I* didn't know it all either.

"Mrs. Jensen asked how the procedure had gone and how I felt. Then she asked about worries or problems, associated with the abortion or otherwise. The only thing I wanted to talk about was how grateful I was to have been able to have my abortion. I had made a mistake, I had slipped up, but my life could be my own again now. And whatever plans Joe and I might make for the future wouldn't be forced.

"We talked about contraception, and went over my reasons for wanting the pill, and the slight risks and side effects associated with it. She explained how it works and gave me the first month's compact and the doctor's prescription. She also gave me a package of sanitary napkins and said if I was feeling fine—which I was—I could go directly back to school for the afternoon but should take things easy. She gave me a sheet of written instructions about what to do in case of bleeding, pain, discharge, or fever. Mainly, she said, call up if anything is bothering me, emotional or physical. It was very comforting to feel that they really cared about you. She also asked me to take a questionnaire form and mail it back after two weeks, as part of a follow-up survey of abortion results. It would be kept anonymous, and I was glad to cooperate.

"How did I feel afterward? Well, the bleeding lasted for about two days. It was about like a normal period. I had no other problems at all—no pain, no cramps, nothing. Nothing but a feeling of relief that it was all over, and a determination not to let it happen again. The abortion was not a bad experience. It's not an experience I want to repeat, but it was infinitely better than going through an unwanted pregnancy and having a baby when I wasn't ready."

Linda

Joyce was lucky. She lives in a state where teen-agers can make their own decisions about abortion, and she had a sympathetic doctor to help her make arrangements and advise her on contraception, too. Another girl, whom we shall call Linda, was not so lucky. She lived in Wisconsin. In 1971 she, like Joyce, was pregnant. But the laws of her state, unlike those of California, were restrictive.

Linda cannot tell her own story, so it will be told by someone else: Mrs. Anne Gaylor, a counselor who testified before the Judiciary Committee of the Wisconsin Assembly after a Madison, Wisconsin, abortion clinic had been "raided" (illegally, it turned out) and closed.

"What happens when an abortion clinic closes?" Mrs. Gaylor began before the Assembly. "When the Midwest Medical Center of Madison was ruthlessly closed . . . a tragic chain of events began whose total effect may never be known. Lawmakers, so prone to investigate everything, could be investigating these tragedies, but of course they are not. At least they can listen: They can listen to what happened to one Wisconsin girl.

"This girl had an appointment at the Midwest Medical Center the week it was closed. She and her boyfriend had read about the clinic in the papers, and although they had only a little money they were able to arrange an appointment for a partial fee. When the clinic was raided, they were all but paralyzed because they had no knowledge of where else to turn. At first they procrastinated, then the boy made several calls to hospitals and doctors, but they were all abrupt with him. Those who talked to him at all talked about the high cost of a hospital abortion, the need for parental consent, the legal uncertainties. They suggested no other alternatives of places to go, and the young couple's despair deepened.

"The boy and girl had come to each other from backgrounds of parental rejection; the girl had run away from her home. They had both been hurt, they had been unhappy in their home life. In each other they seemed to find some measure of security and acceptance, of uncritical love, something they had never had.

"Although the boy had no thought of abandoning the girl, she became terribly depressed. She could only think that each day she was getting farther and farther along into this unwanted pregnancy and what a terrible burden she was becoming to the boy. He was the only one she had to cling to and she was afraid.

"So . . . without the boy's knowledge, she took a last desperate way out of her problem. She took a coat hanger and jabbed it into her uterus. Toward morning, when the pain became too much to bear, she told the boy what she had done and he went to get help for her.

"Now because he was very young and frightened, he did not call the logical people to call in an emergency—a doctor or a hospital. You will remember they had rejected him before. He did not call the police because he actually feared he and his girl would be arrested. He phoned collect to a clergyman in a town one hundred miles away who was the only person he felt he could trust, and this man put him in touch with a counselor in his own city.

"The counselor came out and convinced the boy that his fears of legal retribution were overblown, and that the girl was in very serious condition. She helped him take her to a hospital.

"But they were too late. The girl had punctured her uterus with the hanger, she had bled excessively, and she died in the hospital a few hours later.

"Last night I talked to that counselor who was with the girl when she died, and she asked me to convey a message to you.

" 'Tell the legislators,' she said, 'that it is a terrible thing to watch a young girl die, and to know that her death was unnecessary, a total waste. Tell them how terrible it is that anyone should have to lose her life because of fear, because everyone who could help her was too intimidated by our law to give her the help she needed. Let them know about this girl's family who last saw her warm and alive and now will see her always as something dead to be carried out and disposed of. Tell them about the boy who had to be physically restrained from destroying himself when he realized his girl was

dying. Don't let them sit there and debate abortion without knowing the tragedies that occur when abortion is not available. Let
them know about this girl. One girl's death is one too
many. . . ."

The New Era of Safe Abortion

We cannot tell Joyce's story without telling Linda's. It would not be
fair to tell the story of a safe and easy abortion without pointing out
that up until now, abortion was most often neither easy nor safe.

Over the past decade legal, medically safe abortion services have
developed tremendously. But recently, public funding of abortions for
poor women has been cut back. And there will be more attempts to
roll back or restrict the rights established by the Supreme Court
decision. It is important not to take one's rights too much for granted,
but to be familiar with laws and procedures in your own community.
In particular you should understand that the decision only guarantees
complete freedom of choice for the first three months of pregnancy,
and that some states still require parental consent for minors to obtain
medical treatment. Therefore, it is very important to act quickly if you
know or suspect that you are pregnant and you do not wish to continue the pregnancy.

Probably the best source of information about where to turn for
help is the nearest office of Planned Parenthood. No matter what your
age, you can ask for confidential advice there. We have also listed on
pages 149–150 other sources of information and some of the outstand-
ing clinics. As time goes on, some of the information services may be
discontinued as no longer necessary, and more and more good clinics
will be available in all parts of the country. Also, you can turn for help
to a doctor whom you trust to protect your right to privacy.

Any girl who is sexually active should know as much as possible
about abortion. Strictly speaking, a girl who uses methods other than
the pill should be prepared—emotionally and financially—for the
possibility of abortion. This is not to imply that she can afford to be

careless—but a slight pregnancy risk does exist with most contraception. Safe medical abortion is a reasonable last resort in those few
instances when even properly used contraceptive methods fail.

There is a difference, however, between using abortion as a backup
method of birth control and relying on it as a *substitute* for birth
control. Having unprotected sex because "I can always get an abortion" is rather like eating food that may be tainted because "I can
always get my stomach pumped" or walking barefoot around broken
glass because "I can always take the splinters out." Having unprotected sex is being careless with your body, and wasting medical
resources which are in short supply.

A seventeen-year-old Boston teen-ager named Rita has a point of
view that seems to us both responsible and realistic. "I have decided
to use a diaphragm for birth control for several reasons," she told us.
"Though the pill and the IUD are 'safe and sure,' I don't like the idea
of having something in my body all the time—like synthetic hormones
as in the case of the pill, or a piece of plastic as with the IUD. But
I know I'm taking a small chance of pregnancy, and I don't want to
have a baby. So I 'supplement' my use of the diaphragm with two
things: the New York City phone number of the National Abortion
Federation hotline and a special savings account of $275. If I become
pregnant, that is more than enough to pay for the cost of my transportation and my abortion. I use my diaphragm for maximum safety so
that I *won't* get pregnant. But I've got to be prepared in case it
happens."

The savings account Rita mentioned is not unique. Other girls we
have interviewed have taken similar precautions. In some cases a
steady boyfriend has contributed. In other cases girls simply have a
general idea of where they could borrow the amount of money necessary for an abortion.

Diagnosing Pregnancy

The need to consider abortion begins, of course, with the knowledge
that you are pregnant. If you think you may be pregnant, the first
thing to do is to find out for sure. Early signs may include a slight

swelling of the breasts, feelings of nausea (particularly in the morning), swollen ankles, and a tendency to urinate more frequently than usual. However, the most dramatic signal of pregnancy is a missed menstrual period.

If you have had intercourse since your last period, and if your next period is late, you may be pregnant. *Don't wait* very long to find out. The difficulty and cost of an abortion increase rapidly as time passes, and many clinics will not accept patients who are more than ten or twelve weeks pregnant. When your period is ten days overdue, a pregnancy test will probably be reliable, and you should get this simple test done without delay.

Since early diagnosis of pregnancy is so important, you should be aware that sometimes, after conception has occurred, a girl will have one or two *very light* periods—and will not know that she is pregnant. If you have had intercourse and experience an unusually light period (for example, slight "spotting"), you should take the precaution of a pregnancy test.

Your own doctor or gynecologist can examine and test you, or you may go to a free clinic or public health service clinic. Planned Parenthood clinics will nearly always test you without charge. On many campuses student health centers offer pregnancy testing. Wherever you go for your test, you can be assured that the results will be confidential. If your family doctor is not someone you can confide in, you may wish to choose another doctor or clinic for your test.

The pregnancy test itself is simple. You bring a morning urine specimen in any type of bottle to your gynecologist or to a clinic. (Some clinics will accept a urine sample taken at any time of day. It's a good idea to phone a clinic first to find out just what its procedures are.) Your specimen may be tested immediately, and you will know in about ten minutes whether the results are "positive" or "negative." Or, if your specimen is sent from a doctor's office to a laboratory, you can telephone to know the results later that day or the next morning.

If the test is "negative," it is probable that fatigue, illness, change of activity, or emotional stress (even worrying about pregnancy) has delayed your period. But a small percentage of "false negatives" do occur in early urine tests. If your period does not occur within another ten days, you should return for another test.

In 1978 home pregnancy testing kits became available in drugstores without prescription. The "e.p.t." brand costs about $10; its reliability is 97 percent if positive, but only 80 to 90 percent if negative. Don't try it too soon—it takes about nine days after a missed period to develop detectable hormone changes.

Incidentally, when false negatives occur, they are usually the result of a urine specimen that is too dilute for key components to be identified. You can help avoid a false-negative result by limiting your intake of fluids for about twelve hours before the test is made.

While false negative tests can occur, "false positives" almost never do. If your lab report says "positive," you are almost certainly pregnant.

Obtaining an Abortion

If you have money and are over age eighteen, you should be able to arrange an abortion on request from a doctor or clinic in your area, if you are less than three months pregnant. Two hundred dollars should cover the cost, and with some of the newer techniques the cost may become much lower. If you are under age eighteen (in some places, seventeen), parental consent may be necessary. If this is impossible in your case, you may be able to travel to an area that has a more liberal law. (This will be more expensive.) At present, California has no age or residency requirements for abortion. More information can be obtained from Planned Parenthood or the information services listed on pages 149–150.

Of course, it may not be possible for you to travel, and therefore it may be necessary to get your parents' consent. If so, do not spend weeks agonizing over this. Your parents are going to find out sooner or later. In most cases parents are far more understanding in this sort of crisis than their children expect. They are deeply concerned with your future, and despite being understandably upset, do not want to see your chances harmed. Many parents do more than just accept the situation—they offer valuable understanding and comfort.

If you are going to tell your parents, either because you want to or have to, it is best to do this quickly. Delays can mean difficulty in getting an abortion later. However, it is often best first to find out the details of where an abortion can be performed and what the cost will be. Your parents will see that you have made a decision and taken responsible and practical steps toward solving your problem. If you feel that your parents will be very upset, you may be able to arrange for the doctor or a counselor at a clinic to talk with them. Sometimes it is particularly helpful to talk to a sympathetic clergyman/woman, since then you'll be able to tell your parents, "I've discussed it with a minister." And doctors, nurses, and counselors in abortion services have spoken personally with distraught parents more than a few times.

In the same way, it may help to have a few facts in hand before discussing the matter with your boyfriend. Ordinarily the boy involved should share some financial responsibility for an abortion. If you can give him some idea of the cost this may aid practical planning without panic.

Abortion clinics have multiplied around the country since 1973, and now provide two-thirds of all abortions. They have also broadened their scope to become comprehensive women's or reproductive health centers, providing such services as gynecological care, venereal disease screening and treatment, male and female sterilization, and prenatal and postnatal care. In 1977 the National Abortion Federation was founded to develop standards and guidelines for the use of service providers and consumers. (There have been a few clinics which take advantage of patients and/or give poor service.) Affiliation with the NAF means the member agency subscribes to a code of standards and ethics which guarantees patients a high level of care.

The nonprofit Preterm clinics, among the earliest and best, offer pregnancy testing (free), marital blood tests, contraceptive prescription, abortion (now $175) and sex counseling, as well as vasectomy, gynecology, and VD services.

These clinics (and most others) offer sensitive and helpful guidance, including birth control advice. One girl from Atlanta, Georgia, told us, "They didn't just tell me to be there at noon on August 15 and then leave me hanging. Lynn, who answered the phone when I called Preterm, told me what flight would be best to take from Atlanta, and how to get my parental consent form notarized without charge at a local Women's Lib office. She said she or another girl from Preterm would meet me at the airport, and also return to the airport with me to get my flight home. (My mom was reassured about that—she thought I'd probably faint afterward or something.) Lynn said I should expect to be at the clinic about three hours, but that the operation itself would take only ten minutes. She was very helpful, and I felt very reassured after only a few minutes on the phone with her. . . ."

Girls who have been to Preterm praise that clinic and its staff very highly. "I've never been so relaxed with strangers in my life," one girl wrote. "The atmosphere was so friendly that I wasn't nervous for long." Another girl wrote simply, "I can never thank you enough for helping me out of one of life's most difficult situations: an unwanted pregnancy."

One girl said, "I was grateful for one tiny detail. I had had visions that some loudspeaker would announce my full name in front of the other girls when it was my turn. Instead, my own counselor just came into the waiting room and just said my first name. She said, 'Judy, you can come with me now.' Afterwards, about six of us were resting on couches in another room. She (the counselor) came in to check on me and said, 'Just settle down under that blanket and rest for about an hour. How do you feel?' I felt wonderful. I felt more at peace than I'd been for two months, since I'd first realized I was pregnant. . . ."

Again, remember that it is very important to have your pregnancy test early—soon after you have missed your first period. Good clinics have crowded schedules, and you will need to make your appointment as soon as possible—before your pregnancy is so advanced that more complicated and expensive treatment will be needed.

The advisory services listed on pages 149–150 will be able to tell you about the nearest good clinic in any area. They are valuable sources of information and support.

We have been told over and over, "Calling an abortion counseling service was the best thing I could have done . . . It's good to know that somebody cares . . . just knowing that helps you to face everybody else with the facts." And many, many girls have said, "Without the counseling service, I would never have known how to go about making all the arrangements."

A counseling service can advise you of the total cost of an abortion at various facilities, *including* the cost of special medications if required (such as Rhogam, used for Rh-negative patients). Not all doctors and clinics volunteer such details.

Beware of commercial counseling services; some charge $30 to $50 for giving you a phone number you could have obtained free from Planned Parenthood or the National Abortion Federation. Some states outlaw profiteering referral services—a good policy. Cashing in on someone else's misery and desperation is bad business.

The counseling services can also guide you through such details as:

Terms of payment (cash, check, money order, credit card)

Whether a signed, notarized letter from a clergyman or guardian can substitute for parental consent

In what circumstances it is possible to claim emancipated-minor status instead of receiving parental consent

Specific travel arrangements, if necessary

Whether there are state residence requirements that might affect your case, either because of your age or the length of pregnancy

Whether you can obtain a loan to pay for your abortion, or whether you can obtain one at no cost. If you *really cannot pay,* even on a deferred basis, a counseling service may still be able to help you. Many abortions are done gratis, and the referral agencies will know which doctors or clinics to contact. Some doctors and clinics like Preterm cooperate with referral agencies by taking about 10 percent of patients free of charge. The referral agencies can get the procedure done at reduced or no cost even when a girl on her own could not. *But this benefit should not be abused!* Don't say you "can't pay" if it is merely inconvenient or embarrassing for you to borrow the money— or you will be depriving some woman who is more truly in need of a free abortion. Family, friends, your boyfriend, or his parents may be more willing to help you financially than you think.

Whether a certain hospital or clinic facility offers post-abortion counseling, particularly as regards birth control. Most do.

Those are a lot of benefits to be derived from one phone call—even if the phone call is a long-distance one which must be made at a pay phone with a handful of quarters!

The Procedure

The abortion operation itself is a relatively simple surgical procedure. Abortion is the removal of the embryo or fetus prior to the time of viability—ability to live on its own—usually within the first twelve weeks, when the fetus is approximately three inches long and weighs about one ounce.

Two types of abortion operation are common in pregnancies of under twelve weeks' duration. One is *dilatation and curettage (D & C)*. Although newer methods are now in use, this is a standard method and is still favored by some doctors. The patient lies on her back on a table with her knees up, as in a pelvic examination. A local anesthetic is used (in hospitals sometimes general anesthesia is used). The doctor gently and gradually widens the opening of the cervix— the neck of the uterus—by passing a series of increasingly larger dilators into the cervix. That's the dilatation part of the operation; it is done so that a cylinder about the width of a pencil can enter the uterus. Then, with a curette (which resembles a very small spoon) the uterine lining that contains the embryo is loosened and removed. The instruments used are sterile, and the operation involves no cutting of any body tissues. Usually a D & C takes less than fifteen minutes. Some cramping may be felt and there is a little soreness after the anesthetic wears off.

Vacuum aspiration is the more modern and now most common procedure used for early abortions. It is sometimes called *vacuum D. & C.* or suction method. The position of the patient is the same as just described. Little dilatation is necessary. The doctor inserts, through the cervix, a very narrow, sterile, hollow tube with a single opening near its tip. This tube is connected to a suction bottle. A small suction pump operates as the aspirator tube is moved inside the uterus, withdrawing the contents in a few minutes. This operation is simple and rapid, as described in Joyce's case. With the vacuum aspiration method, a general anesthetic is *not* needed. Just before the operation the patient may be given a mild tranquilizer, and a local anesthetic is injected in the cervical area to prevent pain.

With either a D & C or a vacuum aspiration abortion, you are free to leave the clinic or hospital within a few hours, depending on how drowsy you become from the sedative. Many girls sleep for about an hour, then feel fully alert.

The IUD is gaining favor with young women and the medical profession. Since it can easily be inserted at the time of an abortion, it is often the contraceptive method of choice in this situation. For this reason the better abortion clinics have counseling sessions on contraception *before* the abortion is done.

For later pregnancies (the fourteenth through the twentieth weeks, rarely later) a *saline injection* is used to cause an abortion. A small area of skin below the navel is anesthetized. Then a needle is inserted through the abdominal wall into the cavity of the uterus. The amniotic fluid surrounding the fetus is withdrawn and is replaced with a solution which will induce a spontaneous abortion within about twenty-four hours. This method is more complicated and more expensive than the D & C or vacuum aspiration methods, and requires that you spend a day or more in a hospital.

Other surgical methods may occasionally be used, particularly for pregnancies advanced beyond the twentieth week, but the three methods outlined above are by far the most common.

Late abortion is sometimes done to protect the health of the mother. Sometimes it is done because, with new techniques, geneticists can tell parents whether a particular fetus is abnormal (mongoloid, for example), but only after about sixteen weeks. If a woman is already six months pregnant, she is carrying a fetus which could survive outside with special medical attention. Although some people feel she has a right to terminate pregnancy even at this stage, most doctors would not do so, and it may be illegal in your state.

The main aftereffect of an abortion will be menstrual-like bleeding which may last one, two, or three days. Almost immediately after an early abortion, you may resume normal activities, but many doctors advise you to refrain from sexual intercourse for several weeks—or until after your next menstrual period. Until the cervix tightens up again, infection of the womb is a slight hazard.

Medical abortion is now so safe when properly performed that the risk of undergoing it in the first twelve weeks is less than the risk of carrying a pregnancy to term over nine months and delivering a baby. In the first year of the New York law, abortion proved eight times safer than normal childbirth.

Illegal Abortion

We have been discussing legal abortion. Illegal abortion works differently:

"You drive up to the border at a certain spot between Laredo and Nuevo Laredo, has to be exactly at eleven at night, guy has to do it, not a girl. Ask where you can find a souvenir shop open late, and flash a $5 bill. If the right guy's on duty, he'll give you an address . . ."

". . . There's this farm out Route X—the wife sells eggs but she used to be a nurse, she does it real cheap; she won't say anything on the phone, you've got to drive out there and . . ."

"I have a friend who . . ."

"Just call this number . . ."

Hopefully, there should no longer be any need for anyone to risk the consequences of an illegal abortion. If you are thinking of it for whatever reason—*forget it.*

Usually abortionists who don't have an M.D. use a crude version of the D & C procedure. But lacking the precise instruments and sterile technique of the licensed physician, the illegal operators may use knitting needles, coat hangers, a length of curtain rod or rubber hose, or even chopsticks. These are all dangerous. Even if actual surgical curettes are used, they may be used improperly—*and the walls of the uterus may be punctured.* You may find yourself with long-lasting injury and pain. Infections (from nonsterile instruments) and excessive bleeding are common. Sometimes the excessive bleeding is enough to put you into a state of shock. *Sometimes women die.*

There may be someone at your school who will tell you, "I had an abortion from this woman last year, and so did half a dozen girls I could name" (she may even name them); "I mean, she's *safe,* and she's *inexpensive.* And you *know* your parents won't find out. A doctor might tell—but *she* won't, or she'd get in trouble herself. Honest, it'd be better than going to that clinic . . ."

Your friend may sincerely think she is helping you. But don't be swayed by arguments of cost: Illegal abortion is no bargain. And don't be swayed by the idea that your parents won't find out: Many bungled abortions by amateur operators end up in an emergency room. Most of all, don't be swayed by "friendship," thinking that your best friend who's trying to fix you up with an illegal job couldn't possibly lead you wrong. You can find friendly help and support that will be far safer—from a legitimate counseling service or licensed clinic. *You do not have to go to an illegal abortionist!*

Please reflect on this: The many legislators and doctors who have worked to liberalize laws and establish clinics wish to save you from the risks of illegal abortion; the many clergymen who take time from busy parish schedules to advise you want to help you find safe, legal procedures—as do the many concerned men, women, doctors, nurses, and counselors who often *donate* their time in order to work at referral offices or clinics. And you, personally, should want to avoid the risks of illegal abortion. Your body deserves to be treated by professionals—not amateurs.

"Do-It-Yourself" Abortion

Don't try it.

You cannot end a pregnancy with hot baths, herb teas, starvation, stomach punches, quinine, long-distance jogging, castor oil, laxatives, quarts of rum, handfuls of birth control pills, psychic energy, hypnosis, or falling down stairs.

Nor can you end a pregnancy with a coat hanger. (Well, you might end a pregnancy that way, and your life, too. In the early stages of pregnancy the developing embryo is very tiny—your chances of locating and dislodging the embryo are less than your chances of puncturing the walls of the uterus, which are soft and have a rich blood supply during pregnancy.)

You *can* end a pregnancy. But end it with a telephone call for help —not a coat hanger. See the advisory services listed on pages 149–150.

The Public Debate

In very recent years abortion has become a major issue in the United States. Even prior to the Supreme Court decision, several states passed laws making it possible for a woman and her doctor to make the decision whether to carry through her pregnancy or terminate it in the early months. Before this, abortion was permitted only under extreme circumstances: when pregnancy was a threat to the life, health, or mental health of the woman, or when rape, incest, genetic defects, or disease was at issue. New York, Washington State, Hawaii, Colorado, and the District of Columbia were among the first to provide for medically safe abortion to be decided by a woman and her doctor.

Sometimes this is referred to as "abortion on request," but it requires that a doctor join in the decision and not simply act as a technician, which he can never ethically do: He is bound to do only that which is in the interest of his patient's health and never to do that which harms the patient. If a doctor finds the abortion operation morally repugnant, he cannot be required to do it, but as an ethical professional he must refer the patient to a competent doctor who can judge the procedure on its health merits alone.

When the liberalized abortion law went into effect in New York, that state and several others providing safe medical abortions were able to keep reliable abortion statistics for the first time. (Underground abortionists didn't report to the Public Health Service.) The typical patients obtaining an abortion in the first year of large-scale clinic services were young, single women *pregnant for the first time.* These girls and women had not used contraception effectively before, but more than 90 percent of them accepted contraceptive advice at the time of the abortion.

Since good birth control counseling is an integral part of a good abortion service, the abortion facilities also serve as schools for family planning, where many girls and women receive their first competent instruction about contraceptive methods. Abortion clinics, therefore, are important services functioning to *prevent abortions* in the future.

The importance of the right to delay parenthood cannot be overemphasized. Parenthood is the most complex and demanding task most individuals will ever undertake. While it can be a wonderful experience, its negative effects—particularly on the young—have long been recognized.

Simone de Beauvoir has written in *The Second Sex:* "The first twenty years of a woman's life are extraordinarily rich; she discovers the world . . . at twenty or thereabouts, mistress of a home, a child in her arms, she stands with her life virtually finished. . . ."

That may be overstating the case for some, but for others, not. Despite Women's Liberation and the opportunities for young mothers to work or continue their education, the birth of a child means that certain options in a woman's life will be very restricted. If marriage results from an untimely pregnancy, and a young man shares the new parental responsibilities with the girl, the situation may be no better than that of an out-of-wedlock birth. Forced marriages often produce conflict, guilt, and blame. And the presence of a child in the first *two years* of marriage often detracts from marital adjustment.

A young, single woman may sense these implications of parenthood only after she becomes pregnant. She should have complete freedom to end her pregnancy. She may become a happier mother some years later. Or she may make a decision not to have children at all—a decision most women never have time to consider.

As a New York teen-ager told us, "I am not ashamed that I had an abortion. I *am* ashamed that I became pregnant. But I am proud that I decided to terminate the pregnancy. For me, the abortion was an act of responsibility—in fact, an act of love. If I ever become a parent, it must be much later, and under much, much different circumstances."

The fact that she was able to have a safe and legal abortion had a profoundly positive effect on this girl's outlook and her future.

Of course none of these considerations are of interest to those who believe that abortion is wrong no matter what suffering is caused by unwanted pregnancy. They feel that there is a "higher law" that overrides this misery. Practically speaking, it is often useless to argue about this, because people aren't talking about facts that can be proved or disproved. They are talking about what they *feel,* and such feelings usually change gradually through experience.

However, since you will continue to hear arguments on both sides, some points may be of interest.

Those opposed to abortion cite stories about abortions done very late in pregnancy (after about six months), when the fetus can survive outside the womb, at least temporarily. This occurrence is very rare. It is usually illegal, unwise, and even impossible to get an abortion in the last months of pregnancy, and there are and probably will continue to be restrictions applied after the first three months of pregnancy in some states. The Supreme Court ruled that since abortion after three months is more of a health risk than early abortion, the states may pass laws regulating the health aspects of the operation— such a law might say that an abortion can only be done in a hospital and under certain conditions, and it could be used to make it difficult for women to obtain abortions. Abortion can be outlawed in the last months of pregnancy.

In the recent past, when late abortions have been done, this has usually been because of the restrictive laws that forced women to go seeking an abortion from place to place, as they dealt with hospital red tape, screening committees, psychiatric examinations, and so on —all of which delayed the abortion.

Some people feel that we should still have these laws against abortion, but the strict laws to prevent abortions never worked. They didn't prevent abortions—they prevented safe, fairly priced abortions. And if the purpose of such laws was to protect fetuses and future children, this is impossible without the willing cooperation of the pregnant woman. No law can force a woman to take care of her fetus by eating well, not smoking, or not taking drugs. No law can force a woman to love and care for her baby.

Most legal scholars agree that there are personal moral decisions that are outside the range of the law. The term "bad law" doesn't necessarily mean that what the law is trying to do is bad, but that the results of the law are bad. The Prohibition laws against drinking were bad in this sense: They caused crime and corruption and didn't stop people from drinking. Even people who personally oppose abortion have argued that the abortion laws were bad in the same way. They feel that the decision to terminate or carry through pregnancy must be made privately, and that the law should stay out of the picture.

It should be noted that many of those who oppose abortion on religious grounds, primarily Catholics, are not aware that the Church's present position is relatively new. Catholic law did not always oppose abortion.

St. Thomas Aquinas was one of the most important philosophers and theologians of the Catholic Church; it was his belief that the soul was not present until the fetus had attained human shape and human organs. He believed, therefore, that early abortions should be permitted. And that was the prevailing Catholic opinion for centuries.

As Leslie Aldrich Westoff and Charles Westoff point out in their book *From Now to Zero: Fertility, Contraception, and Abortion in America* (Boston: Little, Brown, 1971):

> Papal, as well as theological, opinion varied with the times. Pope Gregory IX (1227–1241) declared that abortion was acceptable if performed before the fetus had moved, usually during the first forty days. But more than six hundred years later, in 1588, Pope Sixtus V announced that all abortions were murder. And three years later in 1591 a new pope, Gregory XIV, revoked all penalties except for abortion after the forty-day period. This Church law lasted until 1869 when Pope Pius IX returned to the sanctions of Sixtus V and eliminated the distinction between an animated and a non-animated fetus and disallowed abortion at any time. This makes the present Church attitude condemning abortion only one hundred years old. A good Catholic woman living in the six hundred years between the thirteenth and the nineteenth centuries (except during the three years of Pope Sixtus' pronouncement) could have had an abortion during the first forty days of her pregnancy and remained a good Catholic.

Many Catholics today favor the liberalized abortion laws, even though they personally may remain opposed to abortion.

In 1968 Father Robert F. Drinan, then dean of the Boston College Law School, suggested to the Catholic Theological Society of America that there might be nothing binding on Catholics to prevent them from accepting liberalized abortion laws as part of civil law in a pluralistic society.

Father Drinan reminded the Society of the "Declaration on Religious Freedom" of Vatican II, which stated: "The usages of society are to be the usages of freedom in their full range. These require that the freedom of man be respected as far as possible, and curtailed only when and in so far as necessary." Father Drinan concluded: "This new accent on freedom surely contains a new and profound principle which is capable of bringing about the most profound shifts in Catholic thinking about legal-moral problems."

The late Richard Cardinal Cushing of Boston said in 1970: "Catholics do not need the support of civil law to be faithful to their religious convictions, and they do not seek to impose by law their moral views on other members of society."

Father Joseph Donceel, professor of philosophy at Fordham University, stated in 1968 at the International Conference of the Association for the Study of Abortion: "There is a minority Catholic opinion, which has good standing in the Church, which was the opinion of her greatest theologian, Thomas Aquinas, and which is now slowly gaining favor. . . . This minority opinion holds that there is certainly no human being during the early stages of pregnancy."

Many girls and women who have abortions are Catholic. Some Catholic abortion patients are unquestionably devout—a few have found support for their decision from their parish priests. Some feel that having had an abortion was wrong, but many do not.

Catholic Alternatives, a nonprofit educational organization of laypeople, supports Catholics in their thoughtful and free choice of birth control methods, including abortion. "We wish to remove the entire area of sexuality from the confessional and place it back in the hands of the Catholic laity, where it belongs. . . . A pregnancy should not be undertaken, or should be quickly terminated, when there is not the means (psychological or material) to raise the child with some adequacy." These statements appear in their excellent booklet on contraception and abortion. They also have a teen hotline, with counseling in English and Spanish, in New York (212-921-9111).

Some blacks have interpreted liberalized abortion (and family planning generally) as an effort to keep minority groups small. On the other hand, Representative Shirley Chisholm, the black Congresswoman and crusader for women's and minority rights, is an outspoken supporter of abortion as a choice women are entitled to make. It has always been available to the privileged few. Now it is legally available to all.

Of course, no one should be pressured to have an abortion. Responsible doctors and counselors will not recommend an abortion if the patient is opposed or even uncertain; they will recommend further counseling, psychiatric or pastoral, until the issues are clearer. But imposing religious constraints on people of other faiths is wrong. Christian Scientists may oppose vaccination, but they do not deny it to the rest of us; Jehovah's Witnesses oppose blood transfusions for themselves but not for others. We see the abortion controversy—religious or racial—in analogous terms.

For some teen-age girls the abortion question seems more related to Women's Liberation than to religion. An Evanston, Illinois, high school girl wrote in a term paper: "anti-abortion feeling has more to do with male chauvinism than with 'morality.' What better way to keep women away from good jobs than to keep them chained to children whenever their birth control fails?" She went on to point out that, among her friends who had become prégnant, most of the girls had been eager to seek abortions—it was their *boyfriends* who had often objected.

Many older women agree. Maurine Neuberger, former United States senator from Oregon and chairwoman of the 1968 Citizens' Advisory Council on the Status of Women, declared in *Abortion and the Unwanted Child* (1971): "Men make the laws. Do they still believe that women are chattels? Do they subconsciously feel that women are not virtuous?"

Finally, it should be remembered that abortion is a matter of importance not only to a girl or woman but to her children already born, or to the children she may one day have, under better circumstances —and, for that matter, it is of utmost importance to all children to be born in the future. In a world which daily becomes more crowded, an unwanted or unplanned-for birth is a planetary burden, as well as a personal one.

Where to Go for Help

We list below names, addresses, and telephone numbers of agencies that will help you obtain a safe, reasonably priced abortion. Most will also provide some personal counseling and help with contraception for the future. More listings are also given in the Appendix to this book.

We give here only selected names that will be convenient for the parts of the country with the largest populations. If you want to try first in your own area, remember that the most likely source of information will be a birth control or family planning clinic, such as a branch of Planned Parenthood. There may also be a teen health center or clinic in your area. But do not hesitate to call long-distance if you don't know where to turn. These agencies will tell you if there are good clinics closer to your home.

Addresses and phone numbers do change, so if you have difficulty ask for Information in the area you are calling.

> National Abortion Federation
> 110 E. 59th St.
> New York, NY 10022
> Phone: 212-688-8516
> Hotline, all U.S. except New York State: 800-223-0618
> Hotline, New York State: 800-442-8178
> In New York City use local number

The Hotline provides callers with guidelines which are spelled out in a brochure called "How to Choose an Abortion Facility" (free on request). It can refer callers to reputable facilities around the country, and is interested in hearing from women about their experiences in regard to abortion services.

Abortion clinics and abortion referral services are listed in both the white and yellow pages of telephone directories. Most women who are anxious about an unwanted pregnancy do not have the background or the patience to determine which of these is suitable. Even assuming most are good, you will benefit by avoiding the bad ones, so take the time to call and ask. Besides the National Abortion Federation, remember your local public health department, crisis hotline, medical society, or the organizations listed below.

> Religious Coalition for Abortion Rights
> 100 Maryland Ave., N.E.
> Washington, D.C. 20002
> 202-543-7032

Here are the names and numbers of a few reputable clinics across the United States. Wherever you are, remember that the closest Planned Parenthood or local public health department should be able to help you find the nearest resource.

> Preterm, Boston: 617-738-6210
> Preterm, Cleveland: 216-368-1006
> Mayfair Women's Clinic, Denver: 303-355-3551
> Feminist Women's Health Center, Hollywood: 213-469-4844
> Women's Health Services, Pittsburgh: 412-562-1900
> Reproductive Health Services, St. Louis: 314-367-0300
> Preterm, Washington, D.C.: 202-452-1700

Questions Often Asked About Abortion

Q. How do most teen-agers feel about abortion?

A. Let's begin with a look at attitudes of Americans eighteen and older—the nationally representative samples chosen by major polling organizations. *Redbook* (June 1979) published a Gallup survey indicating that 80 percent think abortion should be legal under all or some circumstances. Seventy percent feel Medicaid should pay costs of at least some abortions for women who cannot afford private medical care. Among Catholics, 21 percent favor legal abortion in all, and

52 percent in some, circumstances. The Harris survey (February 1979) found that 73 percent believe decisions about abortion in the first trimester rest entirely with the pregnant woman and her physician; 25 percent disagreed.

Where teen-agers specifically are concerned there are few scientific surveys. In one conducted in San Francisco and Oakland, California, in 1970, several hundred girls aged seventeen and under were asked their attitudes about abortion. The girls were divided into three groups: those who were using contraception, those who were getting an abortion, and those who were carrying through a pregnancy in a maternity home. The large majority of all three groups understood that abortion is safe if done in a good hospital or clinic, and the majority also felt that abortion should be legally available to anyone who desires it. This was true even for the girls in the maternity home, who had not, themselves, decided on abortion.

Acceptance of abortion increased with age in each of the three groups. Catholic girls were not significantly different in their approval than non-Catholics. (One girl quoted this statement she had heard from a doctor: "Abortion provides, for an irresponsible act, a responsible outcome.") Only a few of the girls agreed with the harsh view: "If a girl fools around and gets pregnant, it's her own fault and she should not be able to get an abortion." (What should the boy's "punishment" be?)

Q. Do most girls feel guilty after having an abortion? I've heard that this is true.

A. For many years, articles appeared in medical journals implying that women would experience severe guilt if they had abortions.

Legal or illegal, abortions were thought to intensify normal post-delivery depressions or even cause long-lasting depression based on guilt. In the absence of good research on the question, this belief continued.

When scientific investigation was done, the supposed guilt and other ill effects of abortion were found to be very rare. In an article entitled "Post-Abortion Psychiatric Illness—A Myth?" published in a 1963 issue of the *American Journal of Psychiatry,* Dr. J. M. Kummer found, after surveying thirty-two psychiatrists who had an average of twelve years' experience and practice, that 75 percent of them had *never* seen a patient with any moderate or severe psychiatric aftereffects from an induced abortion, whether legal or illegal. The other 25 percent encountered aftereffects only rarely.

In 1970 the American Psychoanalytic Association said there was no evidence that psychological aftereffects of abortion were necessarily negative or enduring. Freely available abortions, it seemed, even constituted sound preventive psychiatry.

However, many women feel some guilt or depression following an abortion. Some feel ashamed at being pregnant; others want a baby, yet know this is not the time; for some it marks the end of a carefree, or careless, romance.

When excessive guilt occurs, what is the reason? In the view of Garrett Hardin, professor of human ecology at the University of California, Santa Barbara, reactions to abortion depend on social context. "Society can make the experience a traumatic one or a psychologically negligible one," he writes. "If society thoroughly approves of abortion, the reasons for trauma virtually disappear."

Counselors do attempt to identify those girls for whom an abortion might cause guilt. Even in such cases, however, the guilt following an abortion may not compare with the guilt and shame of following through with an unwanted pregnancy and bearing an unwanted child. A critical factor, of course, is the actual setup of the clinical situation, and a sympathetic counseling attitude toward the girl.

In her fine book, *Sex and the Teenage Girl* (1972), Carol Botwin discusses the question of guilt feelings and abortion. After stating that she has known many, many girls and women who have had abortions, Carol writes: "Do you know what all of them said their reaction was to the abortion? Tremendous relief that the unwanted pregnancy was over and they could resume their normal lives. None of them are haunted, traumatized, or regret for one minute their decision." Carol adds that many of these girls came from conservative backgrounds, where abortion was disapproved of. "It makes sense to let yourself live out your young life without burdens and responsibilities you aren't prepared for," she concludes.

Q. Those who favor abortion say, "If a woman does not want to have a child, she isn't apt to raise it well and love it." Those opposed to abortion say, "Even if a woman doesn't want her child at first, she'll learn to love it." Which is true?

A. In Sweden a few years ago, two doctors completed a study called "One Hundred and Twenty Children Born After Application for Abortion was Refused."

The 120 children studied, born to mothers who had wanted abortions, had more problems throughout their lives than a companion group. At twenty-one years the overall health of the study group was below the norm. They were more apt to be antisocial, destructive, and self-destructive. Boys were likely not to meet physical or mental requirements for armed service; girls were apt to repeat the cycle of early or unplanned childbearing. Use of alcohol was above average.

Studies in the United States, too, have shown that unwanted children have problems and may fail to thrive. For example, a three-year investigation carried out at St. Vincent's Hospital and Medical Center in New York City led Dr. J. Patrick Lavery to conclude: "The product of an unwanted and rejected pregnancy, born only because of moral or social reasons, may be in as great jeopardy as the product of a medical high-risk pregnancy."

Our own feeling is that "compulsory pregnancy" due to restrictive abortion laws is potentially harmful—to both mother and child.

Q. I've heard of something called "menstrual extraction" which is similar to abortion. How is this performed?

A. Menstrual extraction (or induction) is much like vacuum-aspiration abortion, but it is simpler. It can be performed shortly after you have missed a period, and before you are sure you are pregnant, even if you are *not* pregnant. With menstrual extraction no dilation of the cervix is required. A *very thin* plastic tube (about four millimeters in diameter) is inserted through the cervix to the uterus. The contents of the uterus (which may or may not include a microscopic embryo) are then removed by suction or syringe. No pregnancy test is necessary; a girl or woman whose period is late requests her gynecologist to perform the procedure. This saves anxiety, waiting time, and even knowing whether a pregnancy existed. For many girls this earlier, simpler procedure causes less psychological conflict. And the cost is less (perhaps $30 to $55), since menstrual extraction is simpler even than early abortion of the usual type. However, not all gynecologists and clinics offer this procedure. As time goes on, menstrual extraction may become a frequent practice, but it may not escape the religious controversy associated with more traditional abortion procedures.

Q. After a girl has an abortion, does she have her next regular period on schedule?

A. Since an abortion removes the uterine lining (just as menstruation does), it will be about four to six weeks before the lining builds up again, and is then shed by menstruation.

Q. If you have an abortion, are there any physical marks left which would indicate it?

A. Not if one of the usual methods is employed. *Very* rarely, surgery similar to a Caesarean section is done—in which case there will be a scar on the abdomen. Early abortions leave no signs at all.

Q. Do you think teen-agers should be able to get abortions without parental consent?

A. It's better when parents know and consent, but there shouldn't be a law. It forces some kids to lie and some to die attempting do-it-yourself abortions. If a girl is old enough to be pregnant, she should have the same legal rights as other pregnant women. In 1971 the American Academy of Pediatrics and the American College of Obstetricians and Gynecologists recommended that doctors be empowered to prescribe contraceptives to girls who request them without parents' knowledge. Abortion is a logical extension of this principle, but, especially with the very young teen-ager, the possibility exists of establishing better rapport by counseling her parents: Some girls are surprised to find how supportive and understanding their parents can be. Nevertheless, youngsters can have sex without parents' consent, and they can become pregnant without asking. Why shouldn't they have a choice when the problem is unwanted pregnancy? Happily, we report that in 1979 the U.S. Supreme Court struck down a Massachusetts law requiring parental consent for abortion. The Court upheld the right of a mature minor to her privacy if she so chooses in seeking a safe medical abortion.

Q. I am liberal in my opinion of abortions, but I have a friend who keeps having them over and over again. She's had four—two within the last year. I can't quite approve of that, somehow, and wonder why she doesn't learn to use birth control.

A. One abortion will not hurt you, nor will two or even more over the course of a long period of time. But repeated and closely spaced abortions place a strain on the body—and may indicate a problem with the mind.

You've asked a good question: Why *doesn't* your friend get serious about birth control? Does she enjoy the "drama" of being pregnant and going through tense discussions with parents, counselors, boy-friends? Does she want attention? Is this self-punishment? Any girl who needs repeated abortions should discuss the above questions with a competent counselor, psychiatrist, or psychologist.

Q. I know all the arguments, but I personally could never bring myself to have an abortion. I just don't believe in it. If I become pregnant, what should I do?

A. What you should do is *not* become pregnant! With abstinence, the pill, or the IUD, you should not have to worry about pregnancy. Since they are the most reliable, these methods are best for someone whose conscience would not allow the possibility of an abortion. If you have an unwanted pregnancy, you may contact an adoption agency and arrange to place the child.

Q. Do some religions favor liberalized abortion?

A. Yes, and the Clergy Consultation Service was a great boon to women when legal abortion first became available. For detailed infor-mation consult the Religious Coalition for Abortion Rights (p. 150).

Many ministers have been in the forefront of the fight to liberalize abortion laws. As early as 1918 the Unitarian-Universalists urged that existing anti-abortion laws be abolished and the decision regarding abortion be left to a woman and her doctor. The Union of American Hebrew Congregations, the Board of Christian Social Concerns of the United Methodist Church, the Lutheran Church in America, the United Presbyterian Church in the U.S.A., and the United Church of Christ have all taken positions favoring legalized abortion in the last few years.

The Convention of the American Baptist Churches of America

offers a good example of a major faith which moved rather rapidly from a cautionary position to a favorable position on abortion. In May 1967 the American Baptist Convention requested "thorough study of this issue." One year later, in June 1968, an American Baptist Convention statement read: ". . . we as American Baptists urge that legislation be enacted to provide that the termination of a pregnancy prior to the end of the twelfth week (first trimester) be at the request of the individual(s) concerned and be regarded as an elective medical procedure . . . further we encourage our churches to provide sympathetic and realistic counseling on family planning and abortion."

The National Board of the Young Women's Christian Association, the American Friends' Service Committee, the American Ethical Union, the American Jewish Congress, and B'nai B'rith Women are also on record as favoring repeal of restrictive abortion laws; and the Federation of Protestant Welfare Agencies believes "that every woman should have the right to decide for herself whether or not to secure the termination of her pregnancy."

Q. Is there any danger that a woman's right to have an abortion might be taken away or restricted?

A. There may be. As we mentioned earlier, it is never wise to take freedoms for granted. New York's early liberal abortion law was almost repealed two years after it was passed. Only a veto by Governor Nelson Rockefeller saved the law. A Supreme Court decision, however, is much stronger and more permanent than a state law.

An active and energetic political minority group would like to overturn the 1973 Supreme Court ruling which legalized early abortion. Some even propose a constitutional amendment stating that a human being exists when sperm and egg unite! Unfortunately, these anti-abortion efforts have succeeded in one area: Restriction of public funds for abortion services. As a result, women who can least afford to raise a child are the ones denied free choice in case of an accidental pregnancy. But not all the news is bad. Not only does the Supreme Court ruling of 1973 still stand, but additional rulings in 1976 and 1979 hold that a married woman does not need the consent of her husband, nor does a minor require the consent of a parent, to obtain an abortion.

The area in which there may be many restrictions is abortion done after the third month of pregnancy. Such restrictions are possible under the Court's ruling; they will probably vary from state to state and keep changing for many years to come. Some may be motivated by strictly medical concerns, but others may be primarily intended simply to stop abortions. This points up the importance of reaching a decision about whether you want an abortion and making arrangements *early* in pregnancy.

12
Permanent Birth Control

What's done is done.
Shakespeare

Although few teen-agers will even consider sterilization as a form of birth control until they are much older, important and interesting issues are raised by the few who insist on their *right* to permanent infertility.

This chapter deals with vasectomy, the male sterilization procedure. But first let us mention that there is a female operation, tubal ligation, in which the Fallopian tubes, or oviducts, are tied off and cut, so that the egg released from the ovary cannot travel the usual route to meet a sperm. The egg is absorbed in the body, and everything else goes on normally. Female sterilization is a more complicated operation than vasectomy because the organs involved are inside the abdomen, but new techniques are being devised to make it a simpler procedure (a tiny incision, with special instruments, leaving no visible scar; operation with local anesthetic, in a clinic rather than a hospital). Meanwhile, in most places it requires hospitalization, considerable expense, and risks very much greater than vasectomy. Tubal ligation is logically done at the time of delivery of a woman's last child: She is in the hospital anyway, and has conferred with her doctor about the procedure during the course of the pregnancy. Nevertheless, a few teen-age girls, or never-pregnant older women, have asked and will ask for tubal ligation. The arguments for and against it are similar to those we relate in regard to vasectomy.

Infertility, or sterility, means inability to conceive a child. Permanent birth control, or sterilization, is the intentional creation of such a state in the male or female. It has nothing to do with *potency,* which is the male ability to have an erection and to ejaculate during sexual intercourse.

Vasectomy

The male sterilization operation is called *vasectomy.* The method consists of tying and cutting the small tubelike *vasa deferentia* on each side of the scrotum that transmit sperm from the testes to the urethra. Thus, during sex sperm are not present in the semen which is ejaculated. The operation takes about twenty minutes in a clinic or doctor's office. In 1978 about 500,000 vasectomies were performed in the United States; its popularity is increasing as people seek an effective, safe, and permanent method of birth control.

Most men having vasectomies are over thirty and have two or more children. By 1970, however, the Association for Voluntary Sterilization in New York City (a clearinghouse for information about sterilization operations which maintains a roster of about 2,000 cooperating physicians) had received 10 percent of its referral requests from men in their early twenties. Many of these men had no children. Some were not even married. AVS also began to receive numbers of inquiries about vasectomy from college and high school students.

Here is what a few of these letters said:

Martin B., Dallas: "Vasectomy is ideally suited to my beliefs and ideology. I believe in having a good sex life, but I think there are enough people in the world now. I am nineteen and would like to prevent any accidental births brought on by other methods of birth prevention."

Dick R. and Patrick C., Grand Rapids, Michigan: "We are two college students very concerned about the ecological crisis that has resulted from overpopulation. To insure that we never unintentionally add to the problem, we would very much like to receive vasectomies."

John D., Oberlin, Ohio: "Even though I am just eighteen, I have no hesitation about this permanent means of birth control. Should I or my future wife ever want children, we would adopt."

Van Y., Spokane, Washington: "I am eighteen and have already fathered one illegitimate child. I do not wish to father another."

T. N., Denver: "Having kids is something I do not want to do, now or ever. But I am nineteen and will be having sex relations for about forty years. If I follow the pattern of my last few years, I will have four or five serious girl friends a year and have sex with all of them. That means I will expose several hundred girls to the danger of pregnancy. I do not use condoms."

Most teen-agers requesting vasectomies have been turned down, but a few have persisted and obtained them. The issue of voluntary sterilization for teen-agers may be seen as part of the larger social trend toward recognition of the rights of minors. Minors have always been allowed to fight—kill and be killed—for their country. Now they have gained the right to vote and, in some cases, to hold office. They have the right to drive cars, smoke cigarettes, choose a vocation, get married, and make religious commitments including celibacy. Minors are gaining the right to control their own fertility by such temporary methods as the condom or pill. The legal situation is not entirely clear, but they may also have the right to reject fertility permanently, by sterilization, should they choose.

Sterilization does not make sense for most teen-agers. But should anyone be denied the choice? Harriet Pilpel, a New York lawyer who is a consultant for AVS, says, "No, there is no legal basis for refusing to recognize the choice of an adolescent—age eighteen or over—who desires a sterilization operation."

There may be no good legal basis for refusing teen-agers the right to choose sterilization, but there are laws which do so. Some states require that an eligible minor be married; others require the consent of a parent or guardian; or there may simply be an age limit of twenty-one. Legal restrictions reflect the concern that teen-agers who make such a decision may later change their minds. True. But no one seems equally concerned that teen-age *parents* may later change *their* minds.

Chuck B., who is nineteen, called twenty physicians who perform vasectomies. Most refused even to discuss it. The most usual thing he heard, however, was, "You're nineteen. What if you change your mind at twenty-five?"

Chuck pointed out that an older brother, who had volunteered for

duty in Vietnam at nineteen, returned home severely disabled, probably unable to have children *or* enjoy sex or make many of life's great
choices. "*He* changed his mind at twenty-five and wishes he hadn't
gone to Vietnam. Yet they let him make that decision—isn't vasectomy a much simpler decision, really?"

Chuck offers a new twist on the "old enough to fight, old enough
to vote" argument: it may seem illogical to allow minors to make some
final decisions and not others. Nevertheless, it can be argued that
vasectomy is a luxury that can wait.

John N. Erlenborn, a member of the Commission on Population
Growth and the American Future, states:

A particular fear haunts me with regard to the lack of a recommendation that
teen-agers be exempted from laws permitting voluntary sterilization beyond
the assumption that usual and accepted medical judgment will be exercised.
. . . I do not know of any age a human being passes through that is more
susceptible to suggestion than the teen years. To couple this impressionability
with access to sterilization without parental guidance can mean that many
youngsters, in their zeal to be patriotic, to do something for mankind, will
know more than a few moments of torment and regret. . . .

John Erlenborn's concern is also echoed among the generation
we're talking about. A senior honor student at a California high
school puts it this way:

Right now, I somewhat feel that I'd like to have a vasectomy. I'm concerned
about overpopulation—and it would also simplify my present and future sex
relationships. But how do I know for sure I'll feel the same way in ten years?
I'm not going to make any permanent decisions any sooner than I have to,
because permanent decisions limit your choices later on. I have to say I'd be
no more willing to have a vasectomy right now than I would be to have a
child.

In view of these concerns you can understand why many physicians
are reluctant to do vasectomies for men who are under twenty-one.
After age twenty-one, the operation is not difficult to obtain, although
a discussion of the procedure and its meaning is always in order, to
make sure a person's decision is well considered and fulfills the criterion of informed consent.

A single male between eighteen and twenty-one years of age usually cannot obtain a vasectomy simply by calling a private physician or urologist. The following are typical responses:

"I only do vasectomies for men over twenty-six who have two children."

"It goes against my personal policy to perform a vasectomy on anyone who isn't married. The wife should be involved in the decision."

"You don't know your own mind at your age."

Or even, "At your age, you shouldn't be having sex. Behave yourself. Or leave birth control up to the girl."

The doctors on the roster of the Association for Voluntary Sterilization, 708 Third Avenue, New York, N.Y. 10017, are likely to regard the idea more sensitively than would the average urologist in the telephone book. And there are about two hundred vasectomy clinics nationwide. These clinics invariably set a minimum age limit (twenty-one or even twenty-five) as a matter of general policy, but some may make exceptions. We think twenty-one is soon enough— even too soon—for most, but allow that there might be a few convincing exceptions.

When Steve A. of Chicago decided that he wanted a vasectomy, he was nineteen. The following year, he phoned a vasectomy clinic with his request for the operation. He was asked to write a letter explaining his reasons to the clinic director, then have a personal interview.

This is the letter Steve wrote:

My name is Steve A_____. I am twenty years of age, single, and for various reasons, which you will find enumerated below, I desire a vasectomy operation.

I am aware that the Midwest Population Center does not, as a rule, perform this operation for single males under twenty-five, because of a justified fear on your part that the applicant may be immature in his judgment.

This letter is an attempt on my part to assure you that I regard this operation with the proper gravity.

To begin with, I fully understand that I should consider vasectomy to be irreversible.

Whether or not I am personally mature, I leave to your judgment. I have desired the operation for the past twelve months. During this period my conviction has become ever stronger. In studying the literature on the operation I have developed an understanding of what is entailed. Further, I strongly believe that if I am old enough to die in a foreign war and old enough to elect my government, I am old enough to make decisions regarding my reproductive system. I am old enough, already, to make a decision about other people's reproductive systems that is at least of equal consequence: I am old enough to make a woman pregnant with a child.

Why do I want a vasectomy? I do not have the desire to bring a child into this world. There are reasons which underlie this attitude. Having raised my brother since his infancy, I understand the problems involved in raising a child.

I understand how much time I would have to allocate, how much labor, how much money. I understand the problems of urban education and of the urban environment. I do not think that I can provide the time, money, or labor involved in raising a child. I do not think that I can raise him to be happy and well-adjusted in our problem-filled society. It can be argued that this is not my decision only, but the woman's decision also, and of course, this is true. But I object strongly to the notion that men have always held: that the man can decide to have a child, whether or not he can comply with the conditions of raising it.

The couple then has a baby, and the woman is usually subjected to the task of raising it, a task that the man has not even thought about, in most cases. I believe that if I seriously want a child, I should be prepared to raise it, irrespective of my relations with one or another woman.

This is not a complete answer, though. I want the operation because I believe that the supplying of contraceptive measures is at least as much a man's duty as it is a woman's.

Of all the male contraceptive measures, vasectomy is the only really effective one. Furthermore, I have had some experience with female contraceptives and thus know that, for the woman, they are not always completely effective or safe.

I do not want to force any woman to have children, pay for New York abortions, or go to a local butcher due to my not providing an *effective* contraceptive.

The most common crotchet that I hear is this: "When you grow older and wiser you will regret not being able to raise children." Even if this were to come true, I do not understand why the children I raise have to be the result of my insemination. If I could not raise an adopted child with the same affection and success that I would have with a child of my own insemination, then how could I be a good and proper parent anyway? If I ever do grow old and wise enough to consider raising a child, I believe that I will be wise enough and mature enough to be able to raise an adoptive one.

These, then, are my reasons for requesting a vasectomy operation. I cannot tell if they will be sufficient to meet your criteria, but I can assert that they are sufficient for mine.

Sincerely,
Steve A._____

The same week his letter was received, Steve was interviewed by the medical director and head of the clinic. The vasectomy was performed three weeks later, at a cost of $150.

The case for early vasectomy is not always so convincing. The letter just quoted is thoughtful and persuasive, but if counselors or doctors at a clinic feel that an applicant has *not* thought the decision through sufficiently—if it seems an impulse or whim—the applicant will be turned down. Screening procedures at least serve the purpose of guaranteeing that an applicant will think over his choice carefully.

Though procedures vary, these or similar questions will be asked of applicants eighteen to twenty-one years old:

Are you aware vasectomy is permanent? (Reversals are not to be counted on, nor are sperm banks, given present knowledge and technology.)

What is your intended life-style, and what are your reasons for feeling you will not want to be a parent?

Should you change your mind, what are your feelings about adoption? What if there are no children available for adoption then?

Have you considered the possibility of falling in love with a woman who desperately wants to get pregnant and have children of her own? How would you react to this situation?

For how long have you wanted a vasectomy? (Often, counselors say, sudden panic over an accidental pregnancy, or a "pregnancy scare," will prompt someone to think he wants a vasectomy. Counselors put more credence in long-range motivations.)

Will you be able to accept this decision which you are now making in good faith, even on the outside chance that you later change your mind?

Counselors look for any indications that the decision has been arrived at impulsively. They are also alert for indications that an applicant does not have a strong masculine identity. "Vasectomy is not for the insecure," said one counselor. "It's not for anybody who confuses *fertility* with *virility.*" The former is, of course, the ability to produce children; the latter is the ability to produce sexual satisfaction for self and partner. They have nothing to do with each other, except in the unenlightened mind. Any applicant for vasectomy needs to understand this well. Vasectomy leaves the testes untouched, and sperm production (not *delivery*) continues, along with normal male hormone production and sexual function. Nevertheless, some men cannot accept the idea of vasectomy at all: For them, the idea of masculinity has been closely tied with the ability to produce children.

The operation itself, while not the easy snip-snip some would have you believe, is definitely within the bounds of minor surgery. It is usually a twenty-minute office procedure, and the term *vasectomy* means just what it says (from the Latin *vas,* "vessel"; *ec,* "out"; *tomy,* "cut").

The surgeon feels the upper area on each side of the scrotum to locate both *vasa deferentia* (which carry the sperm from the testicles). He then injects a local anesthetic; the patient feels a momentary pinprick. Next a small incision is made in one side of the scrotum; the *vas* is located, tied, and cut. The incision is closed with two or three stitches. The procedure is then repeated on the other side—and the vasectomy is complete. The penis is not involved in the procedure at all. The patient is awake but feels no pain.

After the operation a gauze dressing is applied. The patient is usually advised to rest for about half an hour before leaving the clinic or doctor's office. He is also usually advised to wear an athletic supporter and refrain from heavy work for about twenty-four hours. Aspirin should be taken if there is any pain or soreness within the next few days. Complications (infection or bleeding) are rare but sometimes occur and must be treated promptly. For this reason a patient is advised not to be alone for any extended period the first day.

A man who has had a vasectomy may have intercourse again almost immediately—one doctor says, "Wait till you get home, please!"—but *contraception will be needed until the vasectomy is checked after six weeks. A vasectomy is not effective immediately.* Since the *vas deferens* is a rather long tube (twenty-four inches, but all curled up), there are many millions of sperm present in the part of the *vas* that leads to the penis from above the site of the operation. These will be expelled during the next twelve or fifteen ejaculations. *Another form of contraception must be used until a sample of semen (usually taken six weeks later) shows complete absence of sperm.*

The risks of vasectomy are low. The satisfaction rate is high: Over 95 percent of patients report being pleased with the result. According to follow-up studies done by AVS, many men report an increase in both frequency and quality of intercourse. The explanation for the improvement is psychological, of course. There is no biological cause for change in post-vasectomy sexual feeling or performance.

Questions Often Asked About Vasectomy

Q. When a man has had a vasectomy, does he ejaculate the same amount of semen as before?

A. Virtually the same. The difference will not be apparent to the man or his partner. This is because sperm cells make up only 5 to 10 percent of a man's seminal fluid.

Q. If the sperm are not ejaculated, what happens to the sperm cells a man's body produces?

A. They are absorbed by the body.

Q. Can the operation ever fail—and pregnancy result?

A. Rarely, but you should know about it. There are a few cases recorded when men had vasectomies—properly checked out after six weeks—and later their partners became pregnant. In such cases a further test of seminal fluid may or may not show sperm. If it does, a new operation is needed. If the ejaculation if free of sperm, there are two possibilities: Either another man impregnated the woman or a temporary reappearance of sperm occurred. Because it is very serious to implicate another man, physicians have been alerted to the fact that sperm can (rarely!) reappear after successful vasectomy; probably the sperm were hidden in a portion of the *vas* that was kinked or otherwise blocked temporarily. The vasectomized man cannot tell whether he is ejaculating live sperm, dead sperm, or no sperm. Nor can anyone else, except with a microscope.

Q. Can a woman notice any difference when having sex with a man who has had this operation?

A. No. Neither she nor he can tell whether he is "shooting blanks or bullets." The only way to tell is by a sperm test—or a pregnancy.

Q. I had sex with a boy who told me he had had a vasectomy. He even had a vasectomy pin: a small gold circle with an arrow that he said was only given to men who had had the operation. However, as a result of having intercourse with him for about three weeks, I became pregnant. How can I be sure this won't happen again?

A. The best thing we can do is use your experience as a warning, particularly to high school and college-age girls. *Very few* high school and college-age men have had vasectomies. Some people are unscrupulous; if you are not a good judge of character, watch out! Vasectomy is hard to prove: The small incisions made during the operation generally leave no scars. A receipted bill from a vasectomy clinic is much better evidence than a vasectomy pin; pins are available through several sources and you have no way of knowing if a man is wearing one legitimately. You have to know your sexual partner very well—well enough to trust him. The "vasectomy" story is a variation of the old pitch to girls: "I'm sterile, you don't have to worry." A girl may even feel sorry for the person who feeds her this line until the cruel awakening. Any male who thinks he's sterile can prove it with a series of sperm counts performed by a fertility specialist.

Q. I've heard that vasectomies are widely used in densely populated countries. What is the role of this operation in population control?

A. Campaigns encouraging vasectomies have taken place in India and Pakistan, where thousands of men have been sterilized at convenient locations such as train stations. Incentives of money or gifts have been offered by the governments of these countries.

Vasectomy is an important part of the family planning "inventory" and as such is relevant to population control. It is a safe, economical, permanent way to control fertility.

Q. Can vasectomies be reversed?

A. Sometimes, but don't count on it. A skilled urologist can often reunite the sections of the severed *vas deferens.* Occasionally it "takes," but not always (this is much more complicated surgery than vasectomy). Even if it does work, the body *may* have produced antibodies against the sperm protein which was absorbed, and normal sperm delivery cannot be guaranteed. *The fact that some men have changed their minds after vasectomy should be a further warning:* Don't rush into it. If you choose it, consider it final. If you change your mind after a vasectomy, consult a good urologist and cross your fingers (if you think that will help).

Q. What about sperm banks?

A. Sperm banks work primarily to help infertile couples (with artificial insemination) and to preserve sperm specimens for men who must undergo procedures (radiation, surgery) which could render them sterile. Normal babies have been born as a result of insemination with sperm stored (frozen) for as long as ten years. Of course, sperm banks cannot guarantee results, and, if you choose permanent birth control (sterilization), it must be with the expectation of not having children afterward.

Still, some men may choose to store their sperm. That will require $55 per sample initially, plus $25 per year for storage. Several samples are advised, since more than one try at insemination may be needed before pregnancy results. For information on fertility problems from a reputable source, contact the American Fertility Society, 1608 13th Ave. S., Birmingham, Alabama 35205.

Some experts, and the Association for Voluntary Sterilization, have raised questions about the length of time sperm can be stored and used, and warned that there are other questions requiring further research. *If you want "fertility insurance," don't have a vasectomy*—use contraception. The experience with sperm banks is still much too limited.

Q. Is vasectomy castration?

A. No. Castration means removing the gonads (the testes in a man, the ovaries in a woman). These organs produce sex cells (sperm, ova) *and* sex hormones. They are not affected by vasectomy, which only blocks sperm transfer.

Q. Is sterilization always voluntary? I've heard that sometimes it is done without somebody's consent.

A. In certain instances of severe mental retardation an individual cannot give informed consent and a guardian may arrange for sterilization—a reasonable procedure in cases where the patient could never raise a child, since such a child would have slim chance of being adopted. There are other cases, however, where sterilization is done or suggested under duress—e.g., a judge offers a lenient sentence if a sex offender agrees to the operation. This is unethical, in our opinion. If a person with sexual-impulse problems requests such a procedure, that is one thing. Coercion is quite another.

In the case of the average citizen, however, the man being sterilized must consent to the operation. At some clinics this consent is sufficient. Some clinics and physicians require, in addition, the consent of the spouse, if any, but this can be a nuisance, especially in cases of separation.

Although there are some circumstances (such as a long-standing separation) in which the individual should have the prerogative of deciding whether to request the spouse's consent, it is generally very important for a couple to *discuss* sterilization together, even if the consent of the spouse should not be required. A counselor should always ask if the patient's wife knows and approves. If she does not, the reasons are explored. Sometimes the wife approves but cannot be part of the decision for religious (Catholic) reasons, and prefers not to know if and when sterilization takes place.

Q. Do Catholic men ever receive vasectomies?

A. Yes. As early as 1963, in a study of 330 couples who chose vasectomy as a form of birth control, professors Judson T. Landis and Thomas Poffenberger reported that 19 percent of the men and 24 percent of their wives were Catholic—not much different from the proportion in the United States population. John Rague, former executive director of AVS, says that the percentage of inquiries from Catholics has remained at about that level, and may even be starting to rise somewhat.

An interesting sidelight was shown by one study, which indicated that more Catholic men than non-Catholic men (52 percent versus 35 percent) reported increased sexual enjoyment following vasectomy. This suggests that more Catholics had been burdened with fears of pregnancy due to poor contraception (rhythm) or guilt about better contraceptives repeatedly used.

Q. I've heard that a vasectomy can make your sex life more satisfying. Can it help correct sex problems?

A. As we've mentioned, many men report that sex is more enjoyable following a vasectomy. This is a psychological reaction, probably due to there being no more worry about pregnancy. But a vasectomy cannot cure a sex problem.

For most men, vasectomy will have no spectacular effect. Any man with self-doubts who seeks a vasectomy as a solution for his sexual problems will be disappointed—and may even find those problems aggravated. This was the case with three men (out of seventy-three reported on in *Psychosomatic Medicine,* July–August 1967) who were interviewed extensively and who had had potency problems *before* their vasectomies.

Counselors try to be on the alert for men who expect miracle cures of sex problems. They will also discourage men who have a long history of unsatisfactory surgery, e.g., "hypochondriacs," and also those men who seem to want vasectomy as a weapon in a marital dispute, or to punish themselves, or to express low self-esteem. Such men *may* qualify for vasectomy, but they need psychiatry first.

Q. How much does a vasectomy cost?

A. From $90 to $150, generally. The price may be somewhat higher with a private urologist, or somewhat lower at some clinics. Several insurance plans will pay all or part of this cost for policyholders.

13
Venereal Disease

You catch syphilis by screwing a girl you aren't married to.
                                        Max (age twelve)

Max was talking to Ed Brecher (age ten) who didn't quite believe what he was hearing! The boys were in a rowboat on a Minnesota lake one sunny August day in 1921, and Max's announcement sparked Ed's interest in the scientific study of sex. In his book *The Sex Researchers* (1969), Edward M. Brecher recalled his reaction to that boyhood conversation:

I didn't argue, but I didn't believe him, either. I just couldn't see how a marriage license or the words of a wedding ceremony could prevent the spread of a venereal disease. How can you catch syphilis, I asked myself, from a girl who doesn't have syphilis, even if she isn't your wife? Such doubts led me to the library, and to the solution of a number of other sex mysteries. . . .

Ed was right. The germs of venereal disease (VD) do not pay attention to marriage licenses, skin color, age, or station in life; these particular germs simply go along the highways and byways of human sexual intimacy. The diseases they cause take their name from Venus, the Roman goddess of love. They are still widespread today, although they are well understood by medical science and can be cured.

The great Canadian physician, teacher, and scholar, Sir William Osler, said, "He who knows syphilis, knows medicine." He was referring to the many forms which syphilis takes and the fact that it attacks practically all organs, all age groups. Knowing its course, one knows practically all the vulnerabilities and responses of the body. Furthermore, he who knows venereal disease knows human behavior. VD is a mirror of social and sexual patterns; its history and treatment is a reflection of the attitudes and science of the times.

Today, a scientifically informed attitude toward *all* Sexually Transmissible Diseases (STDs) can be stated quite clearly: these diseases are painful, destructive, and often very, *very* difficult to get rid of.

Since the 1940's it has been known that the microbes which cause both syphilis and gonorrhea succumb to penicillin. But these infections still plague us: There are always some untreated carriers spreading them around. There is no vaccine, and no immunity against them. You can get them one at a time or both at once; you can be cured and then be reinfected. Condoms protect somewhat against these and other STD's except the viral ones—most notably, herpes.

Venereal diseases are infections that spread by intimate, usually sexual, contact between human beings. The germs involved are very fragile outside the human body, and cannot be transmitted through air or by contact with inanimate objects like toilet seats, doorknobs, or towels. But when inside the body, the germs multiply and spread, and in a complicated way, so that only in the past century have gonorrhea and syphilis been understood by scientists.

Many young people have the impression that VD is not all that serious, and that they've been fed a lot of scare stories to keep them away from sex. Unfortunately you may be right about being fed scare stories. But VD is serious. The trouble with scare stories about VD is that they're not believed, or that they cause so much fear and embarrassment that the disease is driven further underground and does even more damage.

How can you protect yourself from VD? Well, how do people protect themselves from tuberculosis, hepatitis, pneumonia, and other serious diseases? Not usually by avoiding all other people. It is almost equally extreme to avoid all sex because of worry about VD.

Young people are a high-risk population for sexually transmissible diseases: About 25 percent of STD's occur among teen-agers (40 percent in the age group from twenty to twenty-four). The American Social Health Association estimates (1979) that there are 10 million cases of STD's annually in the U.S., and that teen-agers account for 2.5 million of these. This is one case for every eight teen-agers! The epidemic goes on in part because people don't know enough about STD's—including many doctors—and embarrassment keeps people from asking questions and seeking help early.

Take the same precautions with STD's that you would with any threat to your health. 1. Learn the symptoms; if you have any, see a doctor or call the hotline (800-227-8922). 2. Avoid likely sources of infection; don't take chances—as with pregnancy, the moments of pleasure must be balanced with concern for the long-term consequences of sex. 3. If you have possibly been exposed to a carrier of STD, watch for symptoms and don't expose anyone else until you've been medically cleared. 4. Follow the letter and spirit of public health practice: If there's a chance you have transmitted an infection, let the other person or persons know about it. VD is not a crime; the only "crime" is not telling someone who could be infected and may infect others.

In this chapter we focus on syphilis and gonorrhea, but summarize other forms of STD's in Table VI (p. 184–85).

Prevention can only be assured by sexual abstinence or by fidelity between two partners who are free of STD's. Note that males transmit more readily than they catch STD's, and they can tell more easily than females when an infection is present. Females have less pronounced symptoms initially, but suffer more long-term damage as the disease progresses silently within the pelvis.

Learning you have VD can be a shock, but having it and not knowing is a lot worse. At least if you know, you can get treatment and perhaps also do some thinking. In the case of one girl we spoke to—Donna—learning was a double shock: She thought she was her boyfriend's one-and-only. A few weeks after they first had intercourse, she received a call from him: "I have something to tell you . . . I've been with a girl who just called me and said that I ought to get a shot." The other girl—a bad enough surprise for Donna—had come down with symptoms (or suspicions) of VD, or had been notified by another male partner that he was contagious. Both Donna and her boyfriend got their penicillin shots.

One moral of the story: If you want to have an exclusive sex relationship with your partner, don't just think it, discuss it. Know the facts: You *can* get VD from a single intimate contact with someone who has it, whether that person realizes he is infected or not. Conversely, two people who are not infected with VD can have all the sex they want with each other and never come down with syphilis or gonorrhea. If your partner has never had sex with an infected person, you don't have to worry about VD.

Although nine out of ten sexually active people do *not* have VD, there's no way of guessing for sure which *one* has it. A doctor, with the help of laboratory tests, can make an accurate diagnosis and thereby reassure an individual or couple about it. Obviously, VD is more common among more promiscuous individuals, but they do not only have sex with each other.

Casanova, writing in 1793, quotes a surgeon telling him how VD patients came along:

You had a connection with Don Jerome's housekeeper, and you left her a certain souvenir which she communicated to a certain friend of hers who, in perfect good faith, made a present of it to his wife. This lady did not wish, I suppose, to be selfish and she gave her souvenir to a libertine, who in his turn was so generous with it that in less than a month I had fifty clients.

Casanova's doctor does not mention any homosexual transmission, but otherwise the progress of the disease is very much what public health experts find in America today.

Gonorrhea

This ancient disease has many nicknames: clap, g.c., male whites, and gleet, among others. The most familiar term, "clap," was the standard English word in the middle of the sixteenth century and became slang around 1840. It comes from the old French *claboir,* which originally meant "rabbit hole" and later a brothel.

The gonococcus (plural, gonococci) bacterium that causes gonorrhea measures about one micron across—that's a millionth of a meter. It was first discovered in 1879 by Albert Neisser, a German scientist.

The gonococcus, like the syphilis germ, inhabits mucous membrane. Thus it can be passed to or from the penis, vagina, mouth, anus. If you have been infected it may take as long as two weeks for symptoms to appear, but three to five days is the average.

Among males, 80 percent have very obvious symptoms if the penis is affected. There is usually a discharge containing pus from the penis; it usually is thin at first but becomes thicker. There is usually pain or burning during urination. The mucus and pus seen in the urine is called "clap threads," and the burning is sometimes described as "pissing pins and needles." Other symptoms to watch out for in case the first signs are not so obvious are irritation under the foreskin of the penis; pain or swelling in the testicles, groin, or lower abdomen; pain while moving the bowels; fever.

Infection of the vagina is much less obvious, and 80 percent of the women who are infected do *not* know it. There may be an irritating discharge from the vagina, yellowish or greenish in color. This could be caused by a relatively harmless trichomonal infection, but get treatment. Don't put up with discomfort and possible danger. You have a right to considerate medical care. There may be pain or burning during urination or a swollen spot in the genital region. A month, two months, or more after infection there may be tenderness or a dull pain in the lower abdomen, groin, or lower back. You may run a low fever, or just tend to feel tired and rundown. Again, there might be another or many other causes for these symptoms, but find out what's wrong. Don't fool with your health. Symptoms of serious complications also include problems with menstruation (longer or irregular and more painful periods, pain after one's periods), high fever, headache, nausea.

Infection of the anus may not be noticed by either women or men (in women the infection may spread from the vagina to the anus). Be alert for any discharge from the anus, blood in the bowel movements, pain on moving the bowels, or pain in the anus or rectum.

Whether the patient is male or female, the disease can be transmitted to others from the first contact until it is cured. If gonorrhea goes untreated, it may cause sterility in the male by damaging the delicate little tubes surrounding his testicles and may also cause a narrowing of the urethra that will produce permanent difficulty in urinating. In the female the disease may cause sterility by producing scarring and adhesions which block the Fallopian tubes leading from the ovaries to the uterus. The disease is initially confined to the reproductive system, but it can spread through the bloodstream, causing a form of heart disease and/or arthritis. The gonococcus causes blindness if it grows in the eye, and for this reason newborn babies are always given drops of silver nitrate or penicillin to kill any gonococci which might be picked up in passage through the mother's birth canal.

Diagnosis of gonorrhea can be made by finding the specific germ in a stained preparation under the microscope, or more reliably by growing the organism from a culture taken from the patient and placed in a special medium which is favorable to the germ. After a few days the germ, if present, will multiply to such an extent that it can easily be detected. Treatment is by antibiotics—usually penicillin. Recently there has appeared a new type of gonorrhea that requires quite massive doses of antibiotics.

There are problems controlling gonorrhea because, first, there is no prevention except avoiding contact with a diseased individual; there is as yet no vaccine. Second, the disease may be present and yet not recognized by the infected individual, or "carrier," particularly a woman. There is little time to find and treat a patient's sexual contacts before they have passed the disease on to others. For this reason, and because some patients do not cooperate in case-finding, the detection of contacts as a means of VD control becomes a very difficult business.

There are 2 to 3 million cases of gonorrhea in the U.S. annually, and at least that number of cases of the similar conditions called nongonococcal urethritis/cervicitis (NGU/NGC). Dr. Paul Wiesner, Chief of the VD Control Division, Center for Disease Control (U.S. Public Health Service), has warned: "If unchecked, the consequence of today's gonorrhea problem will be an epidemic of infertility in the future." The USPHS reports cases by age, and in 1978 there were more than 10,000 youngsters under fifteen with gonorrhea—almost three times the number reported in 1960.

Not everyone exposed to gonorrhea is automatically infected, but a major new development has occurred which helps the spread of this

disease. The birth control pill has a side effect of increasing the al-
kalinity and moisture of the vagina, which favors the growth of the
gonococcus bacteria. If a girl on the pill has sex with an unprotected
partner, the chances of contracting VD may be increased. Furthermore, the availability of the pill has reduced the use of condoms,
which is an effective prophylactic against gonorrhea. Therefore, with
the condom being used less and the pill more, it is not too surprising
that the disease spreads rapidly these days.

About one in fifty young people in the fifteen-to-nineteen age
group contracts gonorrhea, according to the American Social
Health Association. In a recent report on teen birth control clinics,
it was said that 5 to 10 percent of the sexually active teen-age clients
had the disease.

Syphilis

A less common disease than gonorrhea, syphilis is more terrible. The
spirochete bacterium that causes it can invade practically any tissue
of the body, and in its late phases the disease attacks the nervous
system, causing paralysis and deterioration of the brain. The origins
of syphilis are still somewhat of a mystery, for the disease as we know
it appeared suddenly in Europe at the end of the fifteenth century.
Since then geniuses and dullards, kings and footmen, queens and
scullery maids have lost their sanity and their lives to syphilis. It was
not until 1905 that the specific syphilis bacterium, *Treponema pal-
lidum,* was discovered by F. R. Schaudinn and Erich Hoffmann.

There is an incubation period of from ten to ninety days with
syphilis—the time between contact and appearance of the first sign,
usually a chancre (pronounced "shanker"). The chancre is a painless,
small, swollen spot, like a bump, that becomes an open sore which is
full of the spirochetes. It is therefore highly infectious. It ranges in size
from very tiny to the size of a dime. When it appears on the penis,
it is a clear sign of syphilis. In the woman, however, it is likely to be
high up in the vagina and therefore go unnoticed; even in the male
it can be inside the urethra. If the chancre is noticed by an unsuspect-

ing individual, he or she may just ignore it (it doesn't hurt) or put some ordinary lotion on it, and it will go away. It *always* goes away, with or without medical treatment. Sometimes it does not appear at all.

Chancres can appear on or in the mouth, the anus, or anywhere the spirochete takes hold, usually where there is a mucous membrane or a cut or scraped area of skin (a dentist can get syphilis from a patient's mouth—if the patient has a chancre and the dentist has a tiny cut on his finger). Washing with soap and water may be helpful in preventing syphilis, as the germ can enter small cuts anywhere on the body.

The chancre goes away within a week or a few weeks. But the spirochetes are multiplying in the body, and within a matter of weeks (but sometimes up to six months) after the chancre disappears the next set of symptoms comes along. During this secondary stage the victim may have a skin rash made up of many small hard bumps, a rash-like growth in the area of the genitals or anus, sore throat, mild fever, or headache. Highly contagious sores may develop; hair may fall out. And then after a few weeks, even without treatment, the disease may seem to fade away again. The person remains infectious for about a year, however, and pregnant women may transmit the disease to the fetus for up to five years.

Certainly, in the second stage, syphilis is a good deal more obvious in women and men than many cases of gonorrhea. However, some people manage to ignore even the most obvious symptoms, and others overlook mild but important symptoms. One reason may be that too many young people have been given the impression that the onset of venereal disease is sudden and dramatic (it may be, but it may not be). An awareness of this problem was cleverly expressed by Carrie M., a thirteen-year-old girl, in a classroom test on venereal disease: "VD is growing too because many people have it unawarely. You don't get syphilis and fifteen minutes later you're banging your head on the wall, your sanity completely vanished."

Your sanity may vanish, but this occurs in the third and final stage, years later and when the person is no longer infectious to others. The spirochetes, like termites in an old house, make themselves known by signs that the innermost structures have been damaged: brain, heart, and spinal cord.

In one respect syphilis is easier to diagnose than gonorrhea: There is a blood test, first discovered by August von Wassermann in 1906. The Wassermann blood test becomes positive, however, only three months after initial infection. A positive diagnosis can be made before then if material from a chancre shows up spirochetes under a specially lit microscope, in what is called a darkfield examination.

Many compounds were used, not too successfully, in the treatment of syphilis prior to the discovery that penicillin cures it. It can be treated at any stage, but of course the damage that is done in later stages cannot be repaired. Remember that a blood test may be negative soon after infection and then turn positive later. Also, although there are many different blood tests done during routine physical examinations, the Wassermann may not be done automatically, so be sure to ask about it if there is any possibility that you have been infected.

Prevention and Control

Health departments have increasingly recognized that control of gonorrhea and syphilis requires respect for privacy, with a fully confidential doctor-patient relationship. Many young people will not consult a doctor if they feel their private life will be exposed to their parents or anyone else. As a result, an increasing number of medical clinics are now willing to treat young people without parents' consent and to keep all medical details confidential, including diagnosis, treatment, and the source of the disease. When VD investigators ask for contacts, the patient is encouraged to give names because otherwise these individuals may be (a) suffering from the disease without knowing it and (b) giving it to others who are in contact with them. The disease can be treated as early as it is suspected, even if you don't have symptoms but are concerned that you may have had sexual contact with a carrier. By going to a doctor or clinic you may save yourself considerable suffering later and may prevent the same happening to others.

In the past decade most states have passed laws permitting doctors to treat minors without parental consent. This is a development supported by the American Public Health Association and most physicians. A requirement for parental consent would deter many young people from seeking help.

There is a new VD National Hotline, a service of the American Social Health Association, supported in part by United Way and the Center for Disease Control. It operates daily, fourteen hours a day, and is staffed by trained volunteers—mostly high school and college students—from the Palo Alto area. This service is the successor to Operation Venus, provided by the Archdiocese of Philadelphia for eight years beginning in 1972.

VD NATIONAL HOTLINE

800-227-8922
800-982-5883 in California (except 327-5301 within 415 area code)

The VD National Hotline has a referral list of over 5,000 public and private medical facilities which offer free or low-cost diagnosis and treatment of STD's. Calls are toll-free in the continental U.S. The service is geared to receive 300 calls daily, or 120,000 annually. It not only helps callers with sound advice, but gives ASHA an idea of the extent of STD problems nationwide.

In the past few years articles on VD have appeared in *Seventeen Magazine, Senior Scholastic, Science News, Parents' Magazine, PTA Magazine,* and many others, including most of the leading news magazines. These are all respectable magazines, and not so many years ago the topic of venereal disease was unmentionable in such places. In 1972 Dick Cavett hosted a National Educational Television network show on VD. Of course, VD itself has always been found in many respectable places, including the "best" families.

A summary table of nine sexually transmitted diseases appears on pages 184-185. There are a few other, rather exotic members of the VD family, but they are less common than the nonvenereal diseases which affect the genitals but have no connection with sex. For example, pain and burning with urination can be due to various kinds of bladder and urethral infections or irritations. Itching, a rash, a sore, or a pimple on or around the genitals can be due to any number of causes, most of them unrelated to venereal disease. If you have had sexual contact with anyone who might have VD, then you must consider that as a possibility. If not, then the ailment is definitely due to something else, but it still should have a doctor's attention.

Occasionally a doctor will jump to the conclusion that a symptom is the result of sexual activity when it isn't. If he comes on with remarks such as "OK, who have you been sleeping with?" and you haven't been sleeping with anyone, tell him firmly he's off the mark. It's his job to reach a correct diagnosis and prescribe correct treatment, and it's bad medicine and bad psychology to be rude. As a matter of fact, even if you have been sexually careless, you definitely have a right to courteous and careful treatment. If the doctor seems to be treating your problem too lightly, you might consider changing doctors. On the other hand, the doctor does have the responsibility to try to reduce the spread of a disease, and this may mean asking some personal questions. In such cases it's important to answer his questions honestly and fully.

Detailed information on venereal diseases is becoming widely available (the *VD Handbook* published by and for students is a good example; it is available from the Students' Society of McGill University). Treatment is available from your physician, student health service, free clinic, or public health department.

Those who want to read a fascinating study of VD from ancient times to the present will find it in *Microbes and Morals,* by the late distinguished microbiologist Theodor Rosebury.

We began this chapter with a twelve-year-old's pronouncement on syphilis, and we close with a poet's view of a twelve-year-old with gonorrhea. The poem, by E. E. Cummings, is first in a series titled "Portraits." It was first published in 1925.*

being
twelve
who hast merely
gonorrhea

    Oldeyed

child, to
ambitious weeness
of boots

tiny
add
death
what

shall?

Cummings wrote many poems on love, sex, and youth. One critic's response to the theme, and this poem in particular:

Morality does not depend on where and when a sexual experience occurs; it depends on whether there is participation in a genuine giving. Cummings heaped scorn on those who cannot express themselves sexually because of their preoccupation with social customs; but he had no more use for those who indulge themselves sexually as a badge of achievement. One of his most viciously satirical poems, for example, is directed at a boy of twelve who proudly bases a claim to manhood upon a case of gonorrhea. . . . Cummings would have been utterly contemptuous of the sexual competition that characterizes so much of adolescent dating.*

Other readers have pointed out that in the poem the sex of the child is not given. Could it be a girl? The word "Oldeyed" suggests a child who has "seen it all"; it also suggests the blindness gonorrhea causes in newborns. Whether Cummings knew about this or not we don't know; surely he saw sexually precocious youngsters and widespread VD during World War I in Europe. (Does the poem's shape remind you of anything?)

*E. E. Cummings by Barry Marks. New York: Twayne Publishers, 1964, p. 86.

Disease	First Symptoms Usually Appear	Usual Symptoms
GONORRHEA (called dose, clap, drip) Cause: bacterial	2 - 10 days (up to 30 days)	White or yellow discharge from genitals or anus. Pain on urination or defecation. Pharyngeal infections are usually without symptoms. WOMEN: Low abdominal pain especially after period. May have no symptoms. MEN: May have no symptoms.
SYPHILIS (called syph, pox, bad blood) Cause: spirochete	10 - 90 days (usually 3 weeks)	1st STAGE: Chancre (painless pimple, blister or sore) where germs entered body-i.e. genitals, anus, lips, breast, etc. 2nd STAGE: Rash or mucous patches (most are highly infectious), spotty hair loss, sore throat, swollen glands. Symptoms may reoccur for up to 2 years.
HERPES SIMPLEX II (called herpes) Cause: viral	Highly variable	Cluster of tender, painful blisters in the genital area. Painful urination. Swollen glands and fever.
NON-SPECIFIC URETHRITIS (called NGU, NSU) Cause: bacteria, chlamydia	1 - 3 weeks	Slight white, yellow or clear discharge from genitals, often only noticed in the morning. WOMEN: Usually no symptoms. MEN: Mild discomfort upon urination.
TRICHOMONAS VAGINALIS (called trich, TV, vaginitis) Cause: protozoan	1 - 4 weeks	WOMEN: Heavy, frothy discharge, intense itching, burning and redness of genitals. MEN: Slight, clear discharge from genitals and itching after urination. Usually no symptoms.
MONILIAL VAGINITIS (called moniliasis, vaginal thrush, yeast, candidiasis) Cause: fungal	Varies	WOMEN: Thick, cheesy discharge and intense itching of genitals, also skin irritation. MEN: Usually no symptoms.
VENEREAL WARTS (called genital warts, condylomata acuminata) Cause: viral	1 - 3 months	Local irritation, itching and wart like growths usually on the genitals, anus or throat.
PEDICULOSIS PUBIS (called crabs, cooties) Cause: 6-legged louse	4 - 5 weeks	Intense itching, pinhead blood spots on underwear, nits in hair.
SCABIES (called the itch) Cause: itch mite	4 - 6 weeks	Severe itching at night, raised gray lines on skin where mites burrow - hands, genitals, breast, stomach, buttocks.

Transmission	Diagnosis	Complications
...rect contact of infected ...ucous membrane with the ...ethra, cervix, anus, ...roat or eyes	WOMEN: Culture MEN: Smear or culture	Sterility, arthritis, endocarditis, perihepatitis, meningitis, blindness WOMEN: Pelvic inflammatory disease MEN: Urethral stricture - erection problems NEWBORN: Blindness
...irect contact with infec-...ous sores, rashes or ...ucous patches	VDRL blood test, or microscopic examination of organisms from sores.	Brain damage, insanity, paralysis, heart disease, death. Also, damage to skin, bones, eyes, teeth and liver of the fetus and newborn.
...rect contact with blisters ...open sores	Pap smear, culture taken when the blisters or sores are present	May be linked with cervical cancer; severe central nervous system damage or death in infants infected during birth.
...rect contact with infec-...ous area	Smear or culture usually to rule out gonorrhea	WOMEN: Pelvic inflammatory disease NEWBORN: Pneumonia and conjunctivitis
...rect contact with infec-...ous area	Pap smear, microscopic identification	WOMEN: Gland infection
...e organism is frequently pre-...nt in the mouth, vagina and ...ctum without symptoms. Act-...e infection may follow anti-...otic therapy or direct contact ...th infectious person.	Microscopic identification	WOMEN: Secondary infections by bacteria NEWBORN: Mouth and throat infections
...rect contact with warts	Examination	Highly contagious; can spread enough to block vaginal, rectal or throat openings
...rect contact with infes-...d area or clothes and ...dding which contain lice ...nits	Examination	Secondary infections as a result of scratching
...rect contact with infes-...d area or clothes and ...dding containing mites	Examination	Secondary infections as a result of scratching

Venereal disease is a miserable part of the human story. It is uniquely human, and it is still with us. It needs to be understood, and literature provides a means of understanding which is as important in its way as the understanding of facts we get from biology, medicine, and the social sciences.

Questions Often Asked About VD

Q. Is there any way to determine ahead of time whether a potential sex partner has VD?

A. The only way to get an answer to that question is to ask it. Hopefully, you and your partner have built a close enough emotional relationship (*before* the advent of a sexual relationship) to permit an honest exchange of such information.

Of course, such checking should be done well in advance of the actual moment of intercourse. It's a bit unromantic to murmur, "By any chance, do you have VD?" just as you're about to make love.

For your physical (and emotional) protection, you may want to ask, "Are you sleeping with anyone else?" or, "Have you been with anyone else recently?" "How's your health?" or, "I'm not contagious; are you?"

You don't have to fire these questions off as though you were an interrogation officer, but you should make it your business to know as much about your partner as you possibly can.

Guard against rip-offs of your health and heart.

Q. Is it true that a girl is less likely to get VD when she is having her period?

A. No. If anything, the opposite holds true. As the menstrual flow is shed, the endometrium (the lining of the uterus) becomes a bit tender and more susceptible to the growth of bacteria. Thus a girl who's exposed to VD can become infected *more* easily at this time than at any other.

Q. If girls who use the pill are more likely to get VD, should I stop using it for that reason?

A. No. So far, the studies which link the pill to a higher susceptibility to VD are not conclusive. And remember that the pill is the most highly effective method of birth control.

Remember, too, that you *are* very likely to get VD if you sleep with a person who has VD—something over which *you,* not the pill, have control.

Q. I've heard that there is a strain of gonorrhea which cannot be cured. Is this true?

A. There are some strains of the disease which have become resistant to the usual dosage of penicillin. And there are some strains of the disease—notably those imported from Mexico, Korea, and Southeast Asia—which do not respond to penicillin at all.

In such types of cases, however, increased dosages of penicillin, *or* use of alternative antibiotics, have been effective. Research is continuing into the development of new drugs as well.

Remember that the single most important factor in VD cure is *prompt treatment.* If you have noticed any symptoms or have any suspicions whatsoever, don't guess and don't wait around. Go directly to a VD clinic or private physician. Anyone who suspects that he or she has been exposed to VD will be examined and treated promptly.

And: return to your doctor or clinic for a follow-up test after your initial treatment. You have not been totally "cured" until your second test shows up negative.

Q. If you are cured of VD once, does this mean that it's harder to cure if you get it again?

A. Not necessarily. If you happen to come up with a second case of syphilis or gonorrhea, which is diagnosed and treated early, the cure should be no more complicated than it was the first time.

But if you contract repeated cases of VD, the chances for complications do increase (since you could become sensitized to drugs used in treatment, or develop an allergic reaction).

Anybody who gets repeated cases of VD should really ask *Why?* Repeated cases evidently mean you're not treating yourself, your partner(s) and sex with the respect they deserve.

Q. I know that women can get gonorrhea without showing any symptoms. Can the same thing happen to men?

A. Yes. Asymptomatic gonorrhea (that is, gonorrhea with masked symptoms, or with no symptoms at all) in men was not identified until the early 1960's, but it has been appearing with increasing frequency in the last few years.

Thus, women are not the only "silent carriers" of gonorrhea. Men who have been exposed to the disease but show no symptoms should not rule out the possibility that they may have a quiet case of VD. Again, a visit to a clinic or private physician is called for.

Q. So if you get VD, the word has to be passed on to any and all you have had sex with . . . but how do you tell a friend something like that? Is it best to do it in person or by telephone? (How about a letter?)

A. No matter what method of communication you choose, it's difficult. But let us emphasize how very important it is to tell. The damage resulting from a case of untreated syphilis or gonorrhea can last a lifetime—or even end a life. And often the *only* way a person can find out about a possible infection is from his or her partner.

How do you tell? First, do a bit of psychological preparation. Remind yourself that you're doing something which is honest, considerate, and absolutely necessary. Also be aware that while VD is a serious problem, it is not the end of the world. It is curable and, if treated early, will not leave behind any lasting physical damage. With these thoughts in mind, consider what makes you most comfortable and what will make it easiest for your partner to deal with the news. It may seem easier to you to pick up the phone rather than face someone in person; but if she (or he) takes your call when others are at home, a difficult situation may be created.

And please—no messages left with roommates or other third parties. That's not only cowardly; it's just plain cruel. Even if you are angry at the other person because you're sure that's where *you* got infected, remember, it takes two to spread those germs—you didn't *have to* get into that relationship.

Q. Is it true that washing the genitals before and after sex and urinating afterward can reduce the spread of VD?

A. The syphilis germ can be present on the skin, and it may enter a tiny scratch in someone else's skin, so washing may help. The germ of gonorrhea is always inside—urethra, vagina, uterus, etc.—and it is thought that urinating after exposure might carry some germs out of the urethra that have just entered. Such attempts to prevent infection, however, don't amount to much compared to using condoms properly and—best of all—not being exposed to the risk. Condoms do *not* protect against the herpes virus, which is much smaller than bacteria. And herpes in a way is the worst of these ailments because it is generally regarded as "incurable" despite many research efforts: certainly it is by far the most resistant to treatment—and the most worrisome to those who contract it!

Q. How many different sexually transmissible diseases (STD's) are there?

A. In its excellent pamphlet, "Conquering the Silent Epidemic: The Challenge of the 80's," the American Social Health Association (260 Sheridan Ave., Palo Alto, California 94306) lists twenty. If you can pronounce them all you are sober and swift-tongued: Syphilis, gonorrhea, herpes simplex, nongonococcal urethritis and cervicitis, trichomoniasis, group B streptococcal disease, cytomegalovirus, condyloma acuminata, candidiasis, pediculosis pubis (crab lice), scabies, molluscum contagiosum, lymphogranuloma venereum, chancroid, granuloma inguinale, hepatitis B, shigellosis, giardiasis, amebiasis, and hemophilus vaginalis.

However, as we've tried to stress throughout this chapter (which one of our young friends has labeled the *"scary but necessary"* chapter), the best advice for avoiding all twenty of these sexually transmissible diseases can be given in just one single word: CAUTION.

14
Minoring in Sex

Sex is not something that just comes naturally. It improves with learning.

Michael Schofield

Reporting to the Family Planning Association conference in London in 1971, British psychologist Michael Schofield said that nine out of ten boys and girls in their teens would fail exams in birth control methods, venereal diseases, or basic sexual physiology.

These are subjects in which the failures become marks on people's lives, not just on report cards.

In his recent research on the sex lives of 600 young adults, aged twenty-five, Schofield found that the most common problems were worry about sexual performance and anxiety growing out of their loss of interest in sex. "Thousands of young people have a vague sort of dissatisfaction," he said, contrary to the impression given in the media that everyone is having a "sexual ball most of the time . . . going from one sexual triumph to another" except possibly those who don't have the right car, or the right bath oil—which is what the advertisers would have you believe. Most of all, Schofield concludes, the young people want sex education, and regret they weren't given it sooner.

The following column by Art Buchwald is an amusing but sharp assessment of the state of traditional sex education in the U.S.A.

Soda Fountain School *

There is a big flap going on in the United States right now over the question of teaching sex education in our schools. The educators are mostly for it and the ultraconservatives, including the John Birchers and the DAR, are mostly against it. I usually like to stay out of controversial matters as I hate to answer my mail, but in this case I have to come out for teaching sex education in the schools.

This is a very personal matter with me. I had no formal sex education when I was a student, and everyone knows the mess I'm in. If there had been a Head Start program in sex education when I was going to public school, I might have been a different man today.

When I was going to Public School 35 in Hollis, N.Y., we got all our sex education at the local candy store after three o'clock. The information was dispensed by thirteen-year-olds who seemed to know everything there was to know on the subject, and we eleven- and twelve-year-olds believed every word they told us.

Some of it, I discovered later on, did not necessarily happen to be true. For example, I was told as an absolute fact that if a girl necked with you in the rumble seat of a car, she would automatically have a baby.

This kept me out of the rumble seat of an automobile until I was twenty-three years old.

There were some other canards of the day, including one that the method of kissing a girl on the mouth decided whether she would become pregnant or not. Every time I kissed a girl after that, I sweated for the next nine months.

The sex experts at Sam's Candy Store had an answer for every problem that was raised at the soda fountain. These included warnings that if you did certain things you would go insane. Most of us were prepared to be taken off to the booby hatch at any moment.

There was obviously no talk about birds, bees, flowers or animals. We couldn't care less what happened when they were doing it. Our only concern was what happened to human beings, and from what our thirteen-year-old instructors could tell us, it was all bad.

Those of us who escaped insanity and shotgun weddings were told we would probably wind up with a horrendous disease that would be passed on to our children and their children for generations to come. There were twenty-five ways of catching this disease, including shaking hands with someone who knew someone who had it.

You can imagine the nightmares these tales produced. There seemed to be no escape. You were doomed if you did and you were doomed if you didn't. After one of these sessions at the candy store, I seriously contemplated suicide. There didn't seem to be any other way out.

Now the worst part of my sex indoctrination was that when I turned thirteen I became an instructor myself and passed on my knowledge to eleven- and twelve-year-olds at the same candy store. They listened in awe as I repeated word for word what I had been told by my "teachers," and I was amazed with how much authority I was able to pass on the "facts" of sex education as I knew them.

Upon becoming thirteen, they in turn taught the younger students. Heaven knows how many generations of Public School 35 alumni went through life believing everything they had learned about sex at Sam's Candy Store.

The fact is that, while the sex education at Sam's served a purpose, we were all emotional wrecks before we got to high school.

So, on the basis of my own experience, I don't think we have much choice in this country when it comes to sex education. In order to avoid the agony and pain my fellow classmates and I went through, we either have to teach sex in the schools, or close down every soda fountain in the United States.

Sex education is highly controversial, but not with young people. It has always been something of a problem for parents, educators, clergymen, and even doctors, all of whom are concerned with the mental, physical, and moral development of the upcoming generation.

Teen-agers are vitally concerned with sex information. Whatever their major interests may be in school, most students are also minoring in sex. The educator's response to this yearning for learning has not been particularly helpful until now, which in part explains the need for a book like this in the 1980's.

For various reasons parents do not usually teach many of the facts of sexual life, and outside sources of information are needed. Nevertheless, the greatest blessing a young person can have in learning about sex (or any other subject of emotional and moral consequence) is parents who are sensitive, open-minded, and honest. Sensitivity means that parents will not overburden their youngsters with either

personal detail or excessive moralizing, and will know what is best left
to more neutral or more expert sources. The best moral lessons are
taught by example, which is the important factor in home sex education. Of course, young people are not and should not be privy to the
details of their parents' sex life. By setting an "example" we mean
giving leadership in such broad aspects of sex education as: equal
regard for and treatment of the sexes, truthfulness combined with tact
in personal relations, taking responsibility for the consequences of
one's actions, and a healthy attitude toward the body and its pleasures
within limits of good taste and discretion.

Some teen-agers say they can talk about any subject with their
parents, including sex, and are pleased and grateful that this is so.
Many find sex a difficult subject to discuss with parents, and still
others find their parents unavailable for discussion. A few teen-agers
say that they are embarrassed by their parents' efforts to communicate
about sensitive topics such as sex, and are glad when the awkward
discussion is over. Teen-agers normally go through a phase in which
personal communication with parents about sex is very difficult.
Many parents report trying to bring up the subject, only to be turned
off by a shrug, embarrassed look, or "Oh, I already know all that."
Neither you nor your parents should be upset by apparent blocks to
communication. It is a mistake to force sensitive discussions. Parents
can simply leave the door open for conversation (but closed on their
personal sex life and sex history), making sure that there is at least
one good book on sex available in the home. Youngsters who would
like to talk to their parents about sex but find that the effort always
fails usually have to accept this as a different kind of fact of life. Many
young people, realizing that they are going to have to take the initiative in their own sex education have become active in asking for sex
education programs, helping to publish sex education booklets, and
so forth.

Schoolteachers have a special kind of problem in being effective in
sex education. They may be quite expert on the factual side, and they
may have sound attitudes and a willingness to hear the feelings and
concerns of different students. But, teachers are often afraid to communicate honestly in open discussion for fear of antagonizing school

authorities or parents or other members of the community who may
be opposed to sex education or certain aspects of it. In a few instances
where 90 percent of the parents have shown support for sex education,
a vocal, aggressive minority of 10 percent has made the teaching of the
subject all but impossible. Meanwhile, teen-agers go on picking up
information from their friends and others slightly older, from the
newsstand, and from movies. The majority of students lose their
chance to discuss sexual matters with a respected adult because of
censorship by a minority of parents.

Even when sex education is available, certain topics are likely to be
missed. Dr. Sadja Goldsmith and her colleagues found in a sample of
sexually active girls under eighteen that one-third had taken a course
in sex education at school, and another third had discussed sexual
topics in other classes. But no relationship was found between the
girls' knowledge and the extent of school or home sex education they
reported! One factor did relate to a girl's knowledge: her age. Evidently, sources outside home and school are very important.

The topics most often discussed by the girls at home or in school
were menstruation, pregnancy, and childbirth. Intercourse, birth control, and venereal disease were discussed by little more than 50 percent of the girls, but abortion, orgasm, and masturbation by only
about 25 percent of them. Over 95 percent of the girls approved of
birth control being taught in the schools. Their knowledge of contraception was poor, and their practice irregular, as in the surveys we
reported earlier. This particular study, reported in *Family Planning
Perspectives* (January 1972), also explored beliefs of girls about masturbation, the topic least discussed. Less than half knew that masturbation is normal and nothing to worry about. The rest thought it
might be harmful to your body or mind, or even prevent a normal sex
life later on. Note: These are girls having sex with boys. It could be
that ignorance and fear about masturbation contributes to earlier
experience with intercourse, experience which is lacking in adequate
preparation as evidenced by poor contraceptive practice and high
rates of pregnancy.

A third group of likely sex educators are the clergy, who are expected to supply guidelines for moral development, including sex

education. Many clergymen have been willing and eager to speak out on the subject, but often their guidelines are rigidly based in traditional doctrine rather than in the reality of the adolescent in the modern world. This is not to say that tradition is irrelevant, but that it is the sensible mixture of tradition with new ideas that makes a subject lively and meaningful for the student.

Doctors might be expected to exercise leadership in the area of sex education, but only recently, thanks to pioneers like Mary Calderone and Harold Lief, have medical students had courses specifically on sex and sexual problems during their training for the M.D. degree. Doctor William Masters and Mrs. Virginia Johnson provided much of the impetus for this development with their unprecedented research on sexual problems. It is clear that the medical profession has neglected normal sexual function and has not met its responsibilities for protecting and promoting sexual health. Nevertheless, many doctors, nurses, and health educators have helped young people, individually and in classroom or community group settings. It is to be hoped that physicians and other health workers will increasingly participate in this important aspect of health promotion and mental health.

As teen-agers you are consumers of education services. You should be aware that health education is the best pathway to good health. A system that allows people to become ill or unbalanced before they can get help is not a sound system either from the standpoint of economy or human decency.

This is a time of transition for all of the professions that do or could play a role in sex education. There is reason to hope that in the future students will receive sound sex information. But in the meantime we have a long way to go.

The Report of the Commission on Population Growth and the American Future (1972) concludes: "Recognizing the importance of human sexuality, the Commission recommends that sex education be available to all, and that it be presented in a responsible manner through community organizations, the media, and especially the schools." The Commission recognizes that parents are the preferred source of sex information and cites a study in which the overwhelming majority of those interviewed confirmed that they would like to have learned about sex at home. However, parents actually served as a source of sex information for only twenty-five percent of the men interviewed, and for forty-six percent of the women.

Teens Speak Out

Harriet Surovell, a high school student, had this to say at a public hearing of the Commission on Population Growth and the American Future: ". . . the refusal to provide education will not prevent sex, but it certainly will prevent responsible sex."

At the first government-sponsored family planning conference to include teen-agers as a majority group (New York, 1972) Michelle Dotts of Evander Childs High School in the Bronx said:

Pregnancy is harder physically, emotionally, financially, and mentally on teen-agers than it is on adults. It is the duty of the schools to educate us on sex. The whole system of sex education has to be revised. Teachers should not be so condescending, so mechanical . . . the rights of teen-agers are being infringed upon . . . the right to life, liberty and the pursuit of happiness, and it's up to you to see that we get these services if we are to live in peace, love, and brotherhood.

Dr. Frank Beckles, then director of the National Center for Family Planning Services, replied to the young people:

Let us make it legal for young people to make those decisions that affect their very lives. They go to war, they can now vote. Let us now make it possible for young people to have access to advice and services in drug programs, reproductive control programs, sex education programs, and VD programs.

Leslie Dixon, who graduated from San Francisco's Lowell High School in 1972, wrote an article for the school paper which was reprinted in the San Francisco *Chronicle* on April 17 of that year. She said, "Straight sex education is really worthwhile because there are always kids who don't know the facts." But she criticized the available textbooks. For example, on dating, which the textbooks dwell on: "The kind of dating where the boy calls up, comes to the door for you, pays your way somewhere, just isn't my thing and it's not a lot of kids' thing." She deplored the scare tactics the books used to deal with drugs, venereal disease, and pregnancy. "If kids are given misleading information like that, they won't believe what they are told about really bad drugs." She polled 100 Lowell students, all of whom had taken family-life courses. Of those, 93 thought sex education should be taught in the high school; the same number said they did *not* feel that the family-life texts and films they had seen in the courses constituted an impartial presentation of facts. Finally, she found that 90 percent of the 100 believed in sex before marriage, as against 10 percent who did not.

Let us turn for a moment to a much earlier source of statements about sexual learning. One girl who had had three affairs by the age of twenty said, "I think the time is long past for discussion, but why don't parents see that their young children need instruction or see that they get accurate information before they reach the terrible adolescent self-conscious stage?" Another girl said, "My parents insist that they did not mean to teach me that sex is shameful, but that was the impression they gave me." An Eastern college boy said, "I feel that there is a definite lack in sex education, especially by the parents. If the parents do not care to inform their children, they ought to have a competent authority do so."

These statements, typical of those heard today, came from a survey of 1,300 American college students published a generation ago: *Youth and Sex* by Dorothy D. Bromley and Florence H. Britten (1938). Some things haven't changed much. In that sample, half the men and one-quarter of the women (college juniors and seniors) had had premarital intercourse. Two-thirds of those students while still in high school knew something about birth control methods, and in addition had heard about or knew girls who had abortions. More than half the students reported that they had received no sex education from their parents, and only a small number felt that they could discuss sexual problems with their parents. Of this group, 64 percent of the women approved of sexual relations before marriage. Three-quarters of the men were willing to marry non-virgins.

Some Problems in Sex Education

The need for sex education is not new, but it is more explicit now among young people, more outspoken, and probably more universal. Even youngsters who have considerable sexual experience may still need sex education in a discussion format. A ghetto youth of nineteen, the father of a two-year-old boy, asked, "What do I tell my son about sex, when he gets to be eight or nine years old, without saying anything—you know—nasty?" One aspect of traditional sex education that you ought not to be subjected to in the future is the scare technique. For years we have had evidence that it doesn't work, and yet people still try it. In fact, very often the scare technique backfires. Students either turn off the message altogether or conclude that the teacher is misinformed. Special presentations meant to scare students away from drugs have been followed by a rise in drug use. Students today are rightly demanding truthful discussion of serious problems, and an end to the withholding of relevant information.

In sex education there are some key areas where young people are too often not given the whole story. 1. It is certainly true that sex can lead to a tragic unwanted pregnancy, *but* this can be avoided by the effective use of contraceptives, which, after all, are widely and successfully used by adults. 2. It is true that if you have sex you may be exposing yourself to venereal disease, *but* with complete information about prevention, symptoms, and treatment, the risks are greatly reduced and the incidence of the disease can be lowered. 3. It is true that premature or foolish sexual involvements can cause emotional unhappiness, *but* there is no evidence that premarital sex *per se* is harmful, and responsible premarital sex may be socially helpful because it makes it easier for young people to complete their education and begin their careers before embarking on marriage or parenthood. 4. It is *not* true that masturbation is abnormal or harmful; it is a healthy form of sexual release. It is not just for "kids." Adults masturbate for the same reasons young people do: because it's often preferable to no sex, to sex with whoever's available, or to sex with someone you care for when the time or situation isn't right.

In addition to the basic physical facts about the body and reproduction, the above are some of the subjects you also have a right to hear discussed helpfully and honestly.

Another change young people look for in sex education is less censorship of sexual issues in all aspects of the curriculum. Traditionally, sex education courses have been lodged in departments of physical education, or home economics, or biology, or sometimes in social studies. Every subject has its sexual aspects, and sexual themes can be important in literature, the arts, politics, languages—you name it. Instead of taking advantage of the interrelatedness of sex with these many topics, teachers often miss or even avoid the sexual aspects. You hear a great deal about history being made on the battlefields and very little about history being made in the bedrooms. This can lead to comical situations. One student in a parochial school told us that his history teacher had mentioned in passing that Madame de Maintenon had a great influence on the king of France. The teacher was stumped, though, when one of the students asked, "Why?"

Most students are kept strictly away from the great erotic and ribald writers like Boccaccio, Rabelais, Casanova, and Henry Miller. And they are even frequently kept unaware that most great writers have something to say about sex. William Blake, Shakespeare, John Donne, Goethe, Walt Whitman, Simone de Beauvoir—to name a few —have written things of lasting value about human sexuality, works which would not only be helpful in a discussion of sex, but also would bring a greater appreciation of these writers as sensitive human beings and powerful artists. See, for example, *Erotic Poetry,* edited by William Cole (1963); and *The Universal Experience of Adolescence* by Norman Kiell (1964).

You may be told that people don't want to talk about sexual subjects in public, but assuming that the discussion is neither prying nor vulgar, this doesn't seem to be true in most cases. For example, to take quite a controversial subject, a study of "self-prescribed contraceptive education by the unwillingly pregnant" was published in the *American Journal of Public Health* (May 1972) by Dr. Jean Thiebaux. Eighty single women who had applied for abortion were interviewed.

They were mostly middle-income girls, but more than half of them, although pregnant, had never discussed birth control with their physician. Most of the respondents indicated that a comprehensive health course with frank presentation of sexuality, including birth control, was the preferred source of this type of information. The peer-group school setting was the most widely preferred, and age thirteen or fourteen was generally chosen as the time that contraceptive education should begin.

In a recent national opinion poll covering 1,708 respondents, men and women seventeen and older, nearly 90 percent believe that birth control should be made available to all who want it, and about 60 percent approve of contraceptive education in public schools; however, about 80 percent favor population courses in schools, a matter which we will discuss later. It is ironic that more are willing to have courses about population problems in general than about the individual's prevention of pregnancy!

Population is easier to teach than sex, since it is less personal. But if the point of teaching about population is to influence behavior, then sex must have its share of time, too.

It is a great joy to have important questions answered, and to be able to answer them well. Karl de Schweinitz, author of the sex education classic *Growing Up,* wrote in the journal *Mental Hygiene* (1931):

The desire to know is its own justification. The systematization of knowledge is one of the bases of civilization. Sex education is inevitable. Children are born without either facts or point of view. They reach adult years with both. To bring this process of acquisition within the bounds of method, even though the secret of that method be its informality, is to place it in the way along which all scientific progress has been achieved. This, together with the clearing of the mysteries and the ignorances that puzzle and give anxiety to the child, is sufficient reason for sex instruction.

In the appendix we include a listing of resources in sex education including family planning and population education. Sound sex education may be as close as your telephone. In many communities hospitals or health departments have installed health education tape

recordings on many subjects, including sex. These are accessible by
telephone. Many localities have crisis hotlines which are staffed by
trained volunteers who can either answer your questions or refer you
to someone who can. The VD National Hotline also can help you with
questions relating to sex and birth control. See the appendix (pages
259–267) for a list of helpful organizations. The leader in sex education has recently affiliated with the Department of Health Education,
New York University: Founded and led by Dr. Mary Calderone, it
is the Sex Information and Education Council of the U.S. (SIECUS),
at 84 Fifth Avenue, New York, N.Y. 10011. SIECUS regularly reviews
books, films, and tapes so that parents, educators, clergy, health
professionals, and anyone else can find the best available materials.

15
What's Normal? What's Moral?

> Just a little while ago I saw two people kissing. I am almost fourteen, these people were my age. . . . Other than this I haven't really seen any other people having sex relations besides kissing. I have seen frogs, bees, and dogs having intercourse, but that really doesn't have any effect on me because it seems that with animals it's not really a personal experience.
>
> Jane L.

Only human beings can think about sex, make and break laws about it, love with it and hate with it. Only human beings worry about whether sex is right or wrong.

On the subject of sex, there's never been agreement about what's normal and what's moral. This is hardly surprising, since there's never been agreement about the meaning of the terms "normal" (or "sane") and "moral" (or "right"). What is accepted as true for one period of history or place may be rejected in another. But even though no one can give absolute answers to questions about morality and normality, one can at least avoid some approaches that seem to be destructive or contradictory.

Human sexuality can be viewed at three levels. The first has to do with being a person: personhood, personality, humanity. You are a person, a human being, first, and a sexual being second; it is not really possible to separate the two, any more than it is possible to separate wind and air—but we do it for purposes of discussion. The well-balanced person is a sexual being whose humanity guides his/her sex life and whose sex life enriches his/her humanity.

Unfortunately, in some places, sex still is a factor in discrimination

for and against *persons,* just as color or religion or language sometimes is. And a person may be treated by another not as a human being
but as a sexual thing, or sex object. Discrimination against a person
because of femaleness or maleness is sometimes called "sexism" (like
"racism"). The recognition of male sexism, or chauvinism against
woman, is an important issue today, but not as new as you might
think, nor has it been protested by female voices only. For example,
in the early twentieth century George Bernard Shaw wrote:

It is not surprising that our society, being directly dominated by men, comes
to regard Woman, not as an end in herself like Man, but solely as a means
of ministering to his appetite. The ideal wife is one who does everything that
the ideal husband likes, and nothing else. Now to treat a person as a means
instead of an end is to deny that person's right to live.*

At the second level, after being human, you are masculine or feminine. "Masculine" and "feminine" include all the sex-related aspects
of personal life; i.e., the roles which cultures assign to male and female
for work, family, and social life (and which might be quite arbitrary
from the standpoint of biology). Males drive trucks, females teach
nursery school . . . but not always. Women cook most meals, but many
cooks are men. Actually, you grow up taking from and imitating both
parents, both sexes; if fortunate, you will have strengths from both
parents and important aspects of personality from both sexes—you
will be, in a sense, bisexual. (Better education, changing technology,
and men's and women's liberation are opening a much wider range
of choices to both sexes. That means more freedom, and that's good.
Why shouldn't women be able to say, "Childbearing is not for me. I
can't do that and go to sea, or become Chief Justice!" And why
shouldn't a man be a kindergarten teacher or nurse, and be able to
weep when saddened?)

At the third level, you are male or female biologically, although
your anatomy—so important from the moment of birth in the way
you are brought up and the way you think of yourself—is not as
different from that of the "opposite sex" as most people believe. The

*G. B. Shaw, "The Womanly Woman," in *The Quintessence of Ibsenism.*

similarities between the two sexes are greater than the differences.

But there are biological differences which are constant and socially significant: Women carry and deliver babies; men, if sexually aroused, can impregnate women. Male arousal (erection and orgasm) is necessary for intercourse and reproduction. Female sexual response, desirable as it is, is hardly related to fertility at all, and intercourse can even be forced on a woman against her will (rape).

Anatomy and Sexual Function

Sex determination can be thought of as a hairsbreadth difference. The same tissue that becomes scrotum in the male becomes the genital labia in the female. The tissue which becomes the penis in the male becomes the clitoris in the female: Both penis and clitoris have erectile tissue and are the focus of sexual excitation; in the male, the organ also contains the urethra, while in the female it does not.

The clitoris and penis are both crucial in sexual response. The clitoris is much smaller than the penis but has a comparable number of nerve endings, so it is even more sensitive than the penis. Therefore, women often prefer indirect rather than direct stimulation of the clitoris during sex. Only the lower one-third of the vagina has nerve endings for sensation, so the length of the penis has no bearing on female sensation, contrary to popular myth. Not the length of the penis, but the quality of pressure and movement around the clitoris, labia, and pubic area is important for female arousal and orgasm (sexual climax, or "coming").

Until recently many "experts" believed that the woman's enjoyment of sensation in and around the clitoris was not normal, which led many women to feel guilty and many lovers to have unhappy times in bed. Important research by Masters and Johnson, among others, showed that the old-fashioned experts who approached sex with preconceived ideas about what it *ought* to be were wrong. This not only points up the need for an accurate understanding of human sexuality, but also shows how necessary it is for lovers to communicate with each other about what gives them pleasure.

But does knowledge and discussion take the mystery out of sex?

Hardly! If so, you would expect doctors and nurses to be pretty jaded and tired of the whole thing—they not only study the reproductive system inside out, they see a great deal of sexual anatomy in the examining room and on the operating table. And they hear a good deal about sex if they take an interest in that aspect of their patients' lives. Are they bored with sex? Not unless they have some problem with sex. There is no more reason to expect boredom by exploring the mystery of sex than there is to expect a musician to become bored with Beethoven or a naturalist to become bored with birds and trees. Of course it *is* possible to run anything into the ground—Beethoven, nature, or sex—but not *because* one learns about it. The approach may be too narrow. Or you may have been hoping that learning about sex is the key to friendship or love—and it isn't. Being "good at" anything—music, sports, sex—is an asset to friendship but not a substitute for love and friendship. On the other hand, love and friendship don't exist, at least for very long, without interests that can be shared. The mystery of sex is like the mystery of many other natural marvels. Understanding such marvels gives us greater appreciation, not less. The secret of a good sex life is not ignorance or innocence of the facts, but the unfolding of loving intimacy between two people who continue to care about each other and to cherish their relationship. That will provide all the life, spontaneity, and passion that sex expresses best.

Sexual learning begins at birth. The touching, cuddling, and loving —physical and emotional—that we receive as infants are basic to our normal development as well-functioning sexual adults.

Animals raised from birth without the kind of closeness and skin stimulation provided by the normal mother will, as adults, fail to function sexually. Their sex instinct, in other words, is blocked by lack of normal experiences *during infancy.* The same is true for human beings: Without sufficient cuddling, touching, and closeness in infancy, the trust and enjoyment of closeness later on can be upset. There is, then, an essential input for normal sexual development that comes in earliest infancy.

Attractiveness and Responsible Seduction

It's normal to want to be attractive. But that simple truism hides a
multitude of not-so-simple problems which rarely are talked about in
our society. Until the 1960's brought the Beatles, unisex, and the
natural look, American teen-agers—and adults—lived with very narrow ideas of good looks and sex appeal. In reality, ideas of attractiveness vary in different societies: A woman in certain African societies
does not cover her breasts but would be considered indecent if she
showed her thigh in public; here we have the reverse. Furthermore,
sex appeal, TV-style, and being sexy, or sensual, in bed are two
different things.

Advertisers have always used our wish for attractiveness to sell
their products. Increased openness about sex means that today toothpaste can be promoted on the basis of *sex appeal* along with soaps,
cigarettes, cosmetics—you name it. But the sales efforts not only cater
to concerns about looking, smelling, and feeling sexy; they create or
strengthen attitudes. Advertising has convinced millions of women to
douche or use genital sprays in spite of sound medical advice against
these practices. Apart from selling people on things they don't really
need, advertising maintains an obsession, public and private, with
physical attractiveness that is dangerous because it leaves out so
much: the psychological, or *personality,* factors in being attractive,
and the consequences—not always happy—of trading on sex appeal.
True sex appeal, like beauty in art, is a blend of the "materials" you
have and what you do with them. It lasts beyond newness and youth.

The overemphasis on physical attractiveness fostered by advertising
can be harmful to those who have it as well as to those who don't.
A good-looking, well-endowed girl may find herself viewed more as
a sex object than she likes; it may be hard for boys to see through to
the person inside because of their fixation on the outside packaging.
A beautiful girl may sometimes be treated like an untouchable prin-
cess, at other times like an object for hot sexual pursuit—depending
on the male, the circumstances, and her own dress and manner. The

situation is comparable for good-looking men: They may have an easy time being "popular" but not necessarily an easy time forming good, solid relationships. As for the plainer folk, those poorly endowed, or those with obvious handicaps, they have to "make it" socially on their personality qualities rather than looks—not always a disadvantage, though it may sometimes feel like one. People who *feel* very insecure about their attractiveness—whether they are good-looking or not—may be prone to try sexual adventures as an ego boost. The unattractive (or insecure) girl may take a lot of boys to bed; the fellow driven by insecurity "scores" with girls no matter how he feels about them. These people may have a lot of sex, but also a lot of shabby or sordid sex which can't help anybody's ego, or sex attitudes, very much.

A word about responsible seduction—leading another person toward a sexual relationship. Sexual love depends on trust and honesty between partners. Yet the pressures of sex, coupled with inexperience and insecurity, sometimes cause people to engage in deceptions, even with the "loved" one. It may not be deliberate or conscious: A girl may, to compete for a particular boy, take him to bed although she doesn't like sex, in order to hold him, or because she loves him and is willing to suffer! A fellow may pressure his reluctant girl by asking her to *prove* her love, or saying she may be frigid if she doesn't go all the way. This is not responsible seduction. Nor is it responsible when a girl wears a low-cut dress with a high-cut hem and wonders why the guys get hopped up or nasty; she may not consciously want to arouse them, but she *does* control what she wears, and has to take responsibility for what, by usual standards, would be called "suggestive." Responsible seduction means letting a person know that he or she is attractive to you and making yourself attractive to that person, with a view toward sex. And if it is really responsible, then before you have gone all the way, you will have decided how not to have an unwanted pregnancy.

In a continuing relationship many people, young and old, are concerned with how to remain seductive, how to be both good friends and good lovers. Today naturalness and openness are frequently stressed, and this is a fine approach as long as it isn't confused with doing away with privacy and modesty. If you're completely "natural" you may, for example, be leaving bathroom doors open. It's a better idea to keep associations with the genital region special and erotic rather than commonplace.

Masturbation

Sexual self-stimulation might better be called "solitary sex." Recent writing on the subject has become quite tolerant, and masturbation is now recommended by some authorities as an important step in normal sexual development, and in sex therapy. Most young children explore their bodies and discover some especially pleasing sensations from the genitals, although probably nothing approaching adult orgasm. Parents sometimes overreact to this and instill shame and guilt at an early age. It would be enough to tell children that this is something they ought not to do in public, just as we teach them to undress in private. Modesty, or a sense of privacy, can be taught without teaching shame or guilt.

If solitary sex can be helpful, how did masturbation get such a bad name? In *The Psychology of Adolescence* (1962), Dr. John E. Horrocks writes: "Among the ills attributed to masturbation have been overfatigue, loss of weight, loss of potency, cancer, ulcers, loss of athletic ability, loss of social competence, insomnia, death, insanity, feeblemindedness, pimples, bad breath, weak eyes or loss of sight, paleness, stooped shoulders, neurasthenia, dizziness, and susceptibility to disease."

A few centuries ago "experts" argued as to whether a man's blood or his seminal fluid was the more essential to long and vigorous life! People thought each ejaculation spent some of the essential life substance, so masturbation would be "losing it" wastefully. (Women weren't even supposed to have sexual feelings, so there wasn't much said about their masturbating. And women didn't write books—nor did they study medicine or argue theology until quite recent times. Teen-agers weren't heard from either, on important questions.)

The Old Testament story of Onan (*Genesis* 38:7–10) was for a long time interpreted to mean that masturbation is a sin—spilling or wasting the seed. But new biblical studies indicate that Onan's sin was not solitary sex but deceiving his brother's widow and refusing to impregnate her (he probably used withdrawal).

Medical books, not so long ago, taught that masturbation caused insanity. This conclusion was reached because disturbed mental patients could be seen openly masturbating in the wards of insane asylums. Doctors jumped to the conclusion that masturbation *caused* them to lose their minds. Today we know better: Some people who have lost their mental faculties masturbate publicly, but that act is merely a *symptom* of disturbance, not a cause. Other people, quite normal, may be doing it more often but in private, with no ill effects.

If you look up masturbation in a dictionary just a few decades old, you'll find definitions like "self-pollution" or "self-abuse." Those are terrifying words! It follows, if solitary sex is self-pollution, that regular sex must be polluting the other person! Pretty grim, but that's what many people felt, even—or especially—the authorities, until very recently. You may wonder why more people didn't crack up, not from masturbation, but from the frightful pressures against normal sexual expression, of which, for many people, solitary sex is a part.

Masturbation is normal in that most people do it or have done it. Is it *moral?* Increasingly, the answer is Yes, even from church leaders. It certainly is moral according to the criterion of not harming anyone. But the individual who thinks it is morally wrong cannot feel normal and "right" about solitary sex. He or she may choose abstinence from sex—all sex—and this is quite compatible with good health and good morals. It's unusual as a total commitment, but that doesn't make it wrong or abnormal in the psychiatric sense.

Most young people, however, do not make this choice. They masturbate as a release from sexual tension, and to learn about sexual feelings without making the more serious commitment of entering a sexual relationship.

For those who accept solitary sex as morally acceptable, there is still the question, "Can it be overdone?" Or, "Can't it be detrimental to sex relations later?" Like many other activities, it can be overdone, but who's to say what the limit is? If masturbation is compulsive, i.e., if you can't get through a day without it, then there may be something psychological that needs looking into—not so much being oversexed as being afraid of sexual tension or needing to prove one's potency all the time. If you're doing it more and enjoying it less, that suggests a problem. Also, if you're very guilty or ashamed, and can't stop feeling that way *or* cutting down on the masturbation, then it's an obsession rather than a release.

Masturbation in groups is different from solitary sex. Most of you have probably heard of the "circle jerk," a contest to see who can reach a climax first. This reduces sex to a crude game and may interfere with lovemaking. Practice for loving requires the opposite of speed—rather, enjoying sex leisurely, having the time and control to be considerate of your partner. A masturbating contest is an exercise in voyeurism and exhibitionism in a homosexual context.

Another kind of problem that turns up is in the fantasy life, the mental activity, that goes with masturbation. Is it pleasant? (It should be.) A person should be able to enjoy a fantasy—daydream—of sex with an appropriate partner. Some people are very restricted in their fantasies, and cannot allow themselves a really desirable partner. They have to use pornography, or imagine a whorehouse, or get it over with as rapidly as possible. For such individuals, solitary sex is a release of tension physically, but doesn't help in enabling one to make love with a cherished partner. If you are "locked" into disturbing fantasies, discussion with a trusted counselor would be advisable.

Some people find themselves aroused by thinking of a partner of the same sex. This *may* be a sign of homosexual tendency, but the question then is, Do enjoyable fantasies occur with the opposite sex, also? And what else is going on in the person's life at the time? (Homosexual dreams sometimes alarm people more than they should. An occasional one is perfectly normal.) If fantasies are primarily homosexual, and there is no apparent reason (or even if there is—such as a good friend moving away), some counseling help is in order. See the Appendix for counseling resources.

Does a fantasy of someone other than your girl or boyfriend mean you are unfaithful? No: The difference between thought and act is fundamental. If you can't even think about other people once you are in a particular relationship, then your relationship becomes a mental prison. There is a great difference between thinking about sex with someone else and having it. Solitary sex, with thoughts and fantasies freely allowed, is not an act of infidelity. But if you engage in fantasies of someone else while in bed with your partner, that indicates a problem—a need to be less than fully intimate. Also masturbation can be used in a hateful way, to withdraw from a person spitefully or with hostile fantasies, and that is another sign that something is wrong with the relationship.

There remains a common-sense caution on the physical side. Sometimes masturbation does become "self-abuse" because people put foreign objects in the urethra or vagina, or rub the penis with something rough or unclean. Physicians can list a large variety of objects people use in or around their genitals, only to end up in their offices because something is stuck inside, or caused an infection or injury. The hands or any object that touches the genitals should be clean in order to prevent infection. In general, one's hands should be kept clean, and especially should be washed after going to the bathroom. And the genitals and anal area should be washed every day.

Thomas Edwards Brown, writing in *Pastoral Psychology* (May, 1968), quotes a ghetto youth: "A guy who's not interested in making women, he's got something wrong with him. He must still be playing with himself like a little kid, or else maybe he's queer." As Brown points out, young people who share that belief are under a lot of pressure to have intercourse, and they frown on masturbation. But the costs of intercourse are high when people are immature, and the advantages are with those who can postpone it when the time is not right. Substituting masturbation does not mean you're queer or just a kid.

Petting

In between solitary sex and intercourse is petting. We have presented some statistics on it; it is a time-honored practice which can lead to sexual release for one or both partners in what is called "petting to climax." Theologian Richard Hettlinger, in his book *Growing Up With Sex* (1972), views it as an important compromise given the choices of premarital intercourse, abstinence, masturbation, or petting without release. Some teen-agers worry that problems can result from petting to climax, but, as with masturbation, such problems are more the result of worry than cause for worry. Of course, if it's the "wrong" partner, if petting dominates the relationship, if guilt is strong, then you may need to cut back on petting or make some other changes—possibly with help of a counselor.

Sexual Problems

Many young people have sexual problems that worry them a great deal—lack of interest, impotence, frigidity, and premature ejaculation. A few words about each of these will at least clarify the terms. For more information you may consult a fuller work such as J. L. McCary's *Human Sexuality.*

Lack of sexual interest may or may not be a problem. Insecure people are the most vocal about their sexual exploits, some of which may be embellished in the telling, so you should not be too hasty to compare yourself with others in these matters; if you insist on worrying that you are below par in experience or desire, it would help to talk with a counselor experienced in work with young people and in talking about sex. Meanwhile, you should be aware that sexual feelings in everyday life are a good barometer of general feelings; if you are depressed, angry at your partner, grieving for a lost love, sick, or thoroughly engrossed in something else, don't expect to be sexually eager. If you are afraid of letting someone else be close to you, guilty about sexual feelings, or attracted only to inappropriate or unattainable people, then your sexual lassitude may be a sign of a deeper problem which may require counseling help.

Impotence refers to the male's inability to achieve an erection and consummate intercourse. Sometimes he will have an erection but promptly lose it, or it will be a partial (not firm) erection. Probably every male experiences impotence at some time in his life; it can be very upsetting but can be a helpful clue to important feelings. If a male can achieve erection and orgasm in masturbation, with a pleasant fantasy of intercourse with an appropriate partner, he can be reasonably confident that he will not have a problem. Petting with arousal is another sign of potency. If a male is anxious about impotence and sets out to prove himself, anxiety itself may cause him to fail, or a bad choice of partner may, so that a casual pickup may not be a fair test.

Frigidity, or lack of orgasm in the female, is somewhat comparable to the above: Can the girl become aroused under suitable circumstances? Does she have an appropriate partner? Can she reach orgasm by herself with appropriate stimulation and fantasy? If not, is she emotionally ready for intercourse? Female orgasm seems to be more responsive to delicate shades of emotion than male orgasm, and it can be interrupted at any point (unlike the male orgasm, which reaches a point of no-return). Some girls have pleasure but no peak, and they are not sure whether it is orgasm or not; and the intensity of feeling varies from one time to the next. Multiple or prolonged orgasm is possible for some women, while almost all men have a period of twenty to thirty minutes of non-arousal after a climax.

If a woman is having intercourse without orgasm, is her lover in tune with her, sexually—in addition to being someone she cares for and trusts? Is he a good lover, able to wait for her to be aroused before entering, and then taking enough time for her to reach a peak before his climax?

Unless the woman feels no arousal under any circumstances, worry about frigidity is probably premature. Women, even though they have greater sexual capacity than men, often take longer than men to discover and develop their sexuality. Relaxation, patience, experience are needed. These are very difficult to achieve if you panic, start changing partners compulsively, or approach each sexual encounter with anxiety and tension over the issue of an orgasm. For this reason many sex counselors advise couples *not* to have intercourse for a while: to start sex play by concentrating on what gives pleasure, and to proceed slowly from pleasure to pleasure.

Premature ejaculation is the term used for the problem in which the male reaches his climax very quickly—sometimes even before entering the vagina, usually a matter of seconds or a minute or two afterward. It is frustrating to his partner, who is left unsatisfied, and to him, since the mutuality of the act is lost and he feels helpless to control it. This happens to most men at one time or another, and especially to the young, inexperienced, or abstinent male. It may also be a sign of insecurity or hostility.

Treatment of premature ejaculation has been very successful using a conditioning technique carefully studied by Masters and Johnson. Their treatments have also been very helpful in many cases of impotence and frigidity. In all cases they treat a couple, not an individual, since they find the relationship to be of the essence: People must be motivated to cooperate with treatment and able to trust each other and the therapists.

One other condition infrequently encountered is the opposite of premature ejaculation. It is called ejaculatory incompetence, and refers to a condition in which the male cannot reach a climax during intercourse, although he may be able to by other stimulation. He can maintain intercourse for a long time, but it is not particularly pleasurable for him. Treatment is indicated and is usually successful.

A few words about drugs and sex. Shakespeare wrote that alcohol increases the desire but decreases the performance. So do a number of other compounds. Sex is a natural high, and there are no true aphrodisiacs. Yet some people either want or need the aid of a chemical to enhance sex or, in some cases, to make it possible. Obviously, if you need to be drugged to enjoy sex, something is wrong.

Is there a connection between the rise in drug use and changing sexual attitudes and behavior? Possibly so, but not necessarily the way people usually think. Since sex is a marvelous high but not a guaranteed one, it can be elusive and frustrating, even disappointing and painful. People who are not sexually fulfilled may turn to drugs either to ease the pain of disappointment or to escape into other kinds of bodily pleasures as a substitute. Most drugs, like alcohol, probably have a depressant effect on sexual function, although, like alcohol, they may be accompanied by a euphoria that hides the pain, despair, or anger. Some young people, wary of commitment or involvement, or incapable of emotional intimacy, look for easy-come, easy-go relationships but remain dissatisfied because they are emotionally barren. Sex with strangers, or instant intimacy, has something in common with the drug scene, in which people feel they can become intimate through "vibes" with the help of chemicals or altered states of mind. We're skeptical.

Homosexuality

Homosexuality is the preference for a lover of the same sex. In our culture homosexuals have always been considered evil, sick, or inferior, and only recently have Gay Liberation movements begun to appear. Homosexuals are up against considerable discrimination—inability to find good jobs or housing, if their sexual preferences are known. Progress is being made toward understanding without prejudice. In 1973 the American Psychiatric Association officially removed homosexuality from the disease category. "Homosexuality per se is one form of sexual behavior and, with other forms of sexual behavior which are not by themselves psychiatric disorders, is not listed in this nomenclature." The San Francisco Association for Mental Health had this to say about prejudice:

> The Association views social intolerance, discrimination, and ostracism directed against any minority as inimical to the mental health not only of the affected minority but of the community as a whole. In this context, the Association deplores the archaic laws, discriminatory employment practices, and other forms of oppression and repression which serve to impose upon the homosexual members of the human family—both women and men—something less than equal status.

In a free country there should be no laws restricting private acts of consenting adults just because they deviate from the norm, when no harm can be shown to result from those practices.

In every group there are people who deviate from the norm. Deviation can be up or down, left or right, better or worse; it means *different,* and why not have variety? *Some* deviations are destructive of life, limb, human rights, or property and cannot be tolerated by society: Murder, for example. Drunk driving. Rape. Child molestation. But homosexuality? It cannot be said to be destructive. Arguments are raised that it is unnatural, or sacrilegious. Well, playing the piano is "unnatural," and so is driving a car. But playing the piano, which is also done by a "deviant" minority, is praiseworthy, and driving a car, which is a rather dangerous habit, is regarded as absolutely necessary.

There are always to be found in society some people, and sometimes many people, who strongly, irrationally fear deviations of a particular kind, or even of *any* kind. Differences in religion, language, political beliefs, and many other types of behavior may upset many people to the point that they try to convert the minorities or suppress them. Extreme fear of deviance usually reflects insecurity. Most of you have probably met people who are obsessed with a hatred of homosexuals; they can't keep off the subject. Most of you are probably aware that such people are not very secure in their own heterosexuality. The laws against homosexuality reflect this kind of fear. But there is no rational reason for them in a pluralistic society. You may personally find the idea of sexual contact between males (or females) quite distasteful. If so, that's understandable. Most people in our society are taught to feel that way. Even most homosexuals don't expect you to celebrate their life style—just to live and let live.

Homosexual feelings and the reaction to them cause quite a few difficulties in our society, especially for men, who are supposed to be friends in a "buddy" sense but tough rather than tender with each other, and not too close or expressive in an emotional or physical sense. The "taboo" against male tenderness can interfere with father-son relationships, male friendships, and even heterosexual relations.

Homosexual panic means an extreme, almost paralyzing anxiety or fear resulting, usually, from intense conflicts over attraction to a member of the same sex. As feelings of closeness, even love, build up between friends, there may be a longing, or unconscious wish, for physical contact, accompanied by an opposite emotion of dread, or disgust. Instead of canceling each other out, the two feelings stretch the emotions to the breaking point—although the individual may not be aware of what is happening. An experienced counselor, usually a psychiatrist, is needed in such crises, although milder conflicts may be resolved without help. Nevertheless, such feelings, as you can see, may cause damage by wrecking a friendship as it becomes close.

Mixed feelings, or conflict, or "ambivalence," is a universal human condition. For an illustration, see John Knowles' novel, *A Separate Peace*.

What causes homosexuality? This is a favorite question from young people; there is no simple answer. To give an idea of what's involved, you might ask what causes *heterosexuality!* Not simply one's genes, not simply one's mother, not simply any of the factors that are sometimes called "the cause" of homosexuality. Homosexuality may be the result of some inborn difference causing, for example, a shift of hormone balance; it may be the result of upbringing, in which preference for the same sex, or distaste for the opposite sex, was built into the developing child's personality; it may be a combination of inborn factors and experience. Probably there are several kinds of homosexuality, and each of the conditions mentioned can sometimes be a cause. The same principle—several different causes and combinations of causes—probably accounts for many of the major deviations in human behavior, including, on the negative side, schizophrenia and, on the positive side, genius in music, mathematics, or some other field.

You may wonder whether homosexuals can or should be treated medically or psychologically. That depends on whether they wish to be treated, and if so, for what. If a person is miserable about his sexual adjustment, and the misery is not simply due to social prejudice, then he is a candidate for therapy to explore the roots of his sexual identity, feelings, and relationships with a view toward change.

"Unusual Sex Acts"

Are there *any* deviations of which we disapprove? Yes: anything which involves force or violence, cruelty, coercion, invasion of privacy, or exploitation as part of sex. Rape, molesting children, exhibiting oneself, peeping on others (voyeurism) are all unacceptable. No one can claim the freedom to do those things, because they violate the rights of others. This also applies to obscene phone calls and any kind of sexual harassment.

What about "unusual" sex acts—oral-genital contact, for example? Or suppose people enjoy slapping or spanking each other? The mar-

riage guidebooks nowadays say that anything two consenting adults
enjoy is all right. We agree, with one warning: Sometimes one partner
will tell the other, "Look, it says here that anything we want to do
is all right. So what is the matter with *you?* Why don't you want to
do it?" That's *not* what the books mean. That's arm-twisting, or
browbeating, and not part of a loving approach. There are a lot of
things that people don't enjoy, or not yet anyway, because they are
not ready. People's reservations should be respected; if you rush
people into sex or into particular kinds of sex, you'll probably only
convince them that you are selfish and that the act is "abnormal" or
"wrong." Worse, you may cause a serious psychological reaction. For
those of you who are reluctant to have sex at all, or to try any
particular thing: If in doubt, leave it out. If you go along with something against your better judgment and you don't like it, then you are
at least 50 percent responsible, right? If that happens, chalk it up to
experience, but say "no" or "not yet" the next time.

Chastity, Fidelity, Jealousy

For real chastity is a state of mind, a way, not of foregoing love, but of
evaluating it. Such chastity is not easily had. It is a product of culture and
freedom; and it is not necessarily in agreement with our prevailing sex traditions. As judged by those traditions it may even appear unchaste. For mere
conformity to a prescribed code, a real chastity substitutes moral responsibility, common sense, good judgment, and a sincere desire to respect other
people's rights. It would base sex conduct on ethics, not on a compulsory
morality which has never heard of ethics and which cares nothing for what
is genuine in conduct.*

Our traditional religions and many state laws demand premarital
chastity and postmarital fidelity. No sex before marriage; after marriage, no sex with anyone but your spouse. These rules have been
spoken and broken for a long time. For some of those who broke the
rules, the major consequences were unwanted pregnancy, a ruined

---

*Judge Ben Lindsey and Wainwright Evans, *The Companionate Marriage* (New
York: Boni & Liveright, 1927).

reputation, and sometimes a ruined life. (Women suffered far more than men.) For others there were apparently no negative consequences.

Suppose there is no danger of pregnancy, or VD, or being found out. Is there still good reason to observe these rules? There simply is no way to predict the consequences of rule breaking in an area that is so private and so complex psychologically, at a time when attitudes toward sex in society are changing so rapidly.

We cannot point to evidence showing that harmful results or good results come from breaking or keeping the rules. In the chapter on abstinence we gave some guidelines that might be used in individual cases. The most important is to not deceive or hurt yourself or others.

However, you should *respect* the rules held dear by others even if you don't observe them in your private life. This means respecting the opinions and beliefs of others who hold to the rules, just as they must respect your decisions about your private life.

One can argue for sexual restraint without being anti-pleasure or pro-puritan. It is never wrong to say No to sex if you have doubts; indeed, if you go ahead in the face of strong doubts, conscious or unconscious, your body may refuse, resulting in impotence or frigidity. Conversely, it is wrong to bulldoze or browbeat someone into having sex. Sometimes honest doubt or restraint, instead of being respected, is ridiculed. There's nothing loving about that, and the person who gives in to sex despite strong doubts is bound for disappointment.

Other people may argue that tolerance for premarital sex may lead young people to throw away restraint. This isn't very likely. Young people have been told No officially for a long time. It hasn't worked very well as a deterrent, and the consequences for individuals and society have been terrible. On the other hand, many young people have much more freedom today and still choose to put off sex until they're married or at least more mature and independent.

Jealousy may or may not be a bad state of mind. A certain amount of jealousy and possessiveness is a sign of emotional investment, caring. If you are so casual about "love" that you can leave it at the drop of a hat without feeling loss, anger, or jealousy, then the "love" is counterfeit. The capacity for joy and intimacy entails the risk of separation and sorrow. People who can't risk such loss can't risk the investment of love, and may justify their "cool" with attacks on fidelity and jealousy. Of course, jealousy can go too far: Anyone who converts marriage or any relationship to a prison because of extreme jealousy reduces the rights of the partner, who becomes an appendage, a nonperson. People should be able to make choices; they often, though not always, choose to be faithful.

This is true even of sexual "rebels." We again quote D. H. Lawrence, a trailblazer in the sexual revolution, to show that enthusiasm for sex does not rule out sexual fidelity. He's on doubtful ground in calling fidelity an "instinct," but what he has to say is what many people feel:

. . . All the literature of the world shows how profound is the instinct of fidelity in both man and woman, how men and women both hanker restlessly after the satisfaction of this instinct, and fret at their own inability to find the real mode of fidelity. The instinct of fidelity is perhaps the deepest instinct in the great complex we call sex. Where there is real sex there is the underlying passion for fidelity. And the prostitute knows this, because she is up against it. She can only keep men who have no real sex, the counterfeits: and these she despises. The men with real sex leave her inevitably, as unable to satisfy their real desire.*

Moral Development

For many people, being "good" is merely a matter of "doing as you are told." Little children, of course, have no other standard for right and wrong than what they are told; for the two-year-old, the word "no" is the first mini-lecture on morality—and an important one.

Moral judgment develops with age, just as do other faculties of the mind. Most of the great psychologists have been concerned with the nature of moral choices and behavior—William James, Sigmund Freud, Erik Erikson, Jean Piaget, and B. F. Skinner are prominent

*"Apropos Lady Chatterley's Lover," *op. cit.*

examples. Recently Professor Lawrence Kohlberg of Harvard University has studied the progression of moral thinking in young people and adults. The most elementary moral state of mind is doing what an authority says because he says it. Later on comes the sense of doing something because it is good or right, basing the rightness on certain beliefs: who the authority is, or what the outcome of an action will be, or whether a decision is in harmony with certain principles. At more advanced levels of moral judgment reached by adolescents and adults (but not even all adults), thinking about what is right will sometimes lead to conflict with authority. An example is the case of a person who is told to carry out a mission which he believes is unethical. But his job depends on it. Does obedience or conscience—internal moral judgment—come first?

A society cannot function without laws and authority (anarchists might take exception to this statement). People must be protected against violence, exploitation, invasion of privacy, etc. But, most important, they must develop responsibility for their own actions in relation to each other and the wider world. It is not enough for adults to do as they are told. They must have their own standards, which they believe in and are willing to stand by.

Responsibility in sex—or anything else—requires knowledge and self-control. Self-control means the ability to decide and do something even when no one's going to punish you for not doing it. Knowledge includes understanding yourself and the other person, and anticipating the consequences of your behavior. Some guiding moral principles that are common to many different points of view include: Forced choices are not as good as free choices; knowledge is better than ignorance; each individual is morally responsible for his own life—to the extent that he or she has the knowledge and the power to make choices; do no harm and tell no lies (to oneself as well as others). There is nothing original about these principles, but they are a lifetime challenge to observe. The power to harm with sex is considerable, just as the power to love is great. The temptation to alter the truth is great in matters of strong emotion such as sex. But without truth there is, in the long run, no trust; and without trust, no love.

Until you have developed your own principles to guide you, you will lean on others, or be uncomfortable. Don't worry, and don't hurry. There is plenty of time for sex. Against the danger of "missing out" is the danger of spoiling something beautiful.

Psychological health and moral responsibility go together. Sanity is not mere adjustment to the world, to what authorities tell you. There are enough things out of adjustment in the world to make *changing* those things morally right and very sane.

In his preface to the book *Emotional Problems of the Student,* Erik Erikson, one of this century's leading psychologists and moral thinkers, offers a description of true sanity and individuality. He quotes these words from one of his famous predecessors in psychology, Professor William James:

. . . I have often thought that the best way to define a man's character would be to seek out the particular mental or moral attitude in which, when it came upon him, he felt himself most deeply and intensely active and alive. At such moments there is a voice inside which speaks and says: This is the real me!

This is a state of self-confidence that does not depend upon guarantees, a way of being certain enough even in the face of uncertainties. Given the changes of today and tomorrow, this kind of mental health is what the world needs more of. Elsewhere Erikson says, "young people, if they know where they are going, can take sexuality, also, in their stride."

16
The Future of Marriage and Parenthood

I feel that the task of transforming a house into a home is one that should be shared fifty-fifty between husband and wife.

My mother knew nothing about birth control or the importance of spacing children, health-wise or population-wise. To me this is very important because I feel very strongly that the husband-and-wife relationship should come before that of the children.

How will I react to some of the strange things my children might want to do? What will attitudes about sex, marriage, drugs, race relations, etc., be twenty years from now and will I tackle problems sensibly? . . . Being a parent isn't easy now, and in the future, I don't think it will get any easier.

The three teen-agers quoted above were responding to a questionnaire sent to leaders of the Future Homemakers of America. Their views were among those appearing in "How Does Youth Envision the 1984 Family?" by Jacque Boyd (*Journal of Home Economics,* November 1972). The sense of change and uncertainty is there, but so is a feeling of confidence that young people can tackle sensibly the problems that face them.

The oldest institution in society is the family and it is also the newest, because it is being started all over again by new individuals as the generations move on. The functions of the family, its strengths and weaknesses, change with the new stresses and stimuli of changing times.

Families used to be larger. A woman would have more children—starting at about age seventeen, a new baby every year or two. The average early American couple had seven or eight children, but many died young. Grandparents, aunts, uncles, and cousins were usually nearby, even in the same house or on the same farm. This bunch of relatives is called the extended family. In the twentieth century the predominant family style has changed, and the grouping is mother, father, and their children—called the nuclear family, not because we are in the nuclear age but because this is the kernel, core, or nucleus of the family. Families aren't so large anymore, but there are more and more of them. Children are healthier, and almost every child grows up to start another family.

In the days gone by of life on the farm or in the village, growing up was not easy, but in some ways it was more predictable. It was possible to predict that farms and villages would still be the basic communities, and that raising children would go on pretty much as when the parents were being raised. The parents and grandparents and extended family and village leaders could teach children what they needed to know—at least to get by. Successful, respected adults could show the way for the next generation to be successful.

The nuclear family, especially in the city, is separated not only from many relatives but from family tradition, "tried and true" ways of doing things. With modern industry, communications, transportation, health, and education, family life is changing. Many traditions are broken or changed so that people can earn a better living, whatever that may be. Boys and girls can get the education they will need to make *their* living when they grow up; even if they are rich they will need an education to get along in the world, to understand what is happening, to be able to plan for the future.

Today even educated parents are not sure how to teach their children what they will need to know. Traditions are shaken; science and technology are changing so many things in life. Schools, television, books, newspapers, and magazines are doing more and more of the teaching. But families are still important: They are responsible for developing the personalities and values of the next generation.

We do not predict the disappearance of the family as a primary institution of society. We do predict that some changes will be seen. In the past few decades the word "family" has been rigidly defined: a legally married man and woman and their own biological child or children. The framework of the family has been so rigid, in fact, that not all individuals could fit within it. Rising divorce rates indicate the failure of many marriages and the breakup of many families. But new family forms are emerging. Consider the couple with adopted rather than biological children, the child-free couple, the group of single and married people who live (and sometimes work) communally, the man and woman who live together in a stable unmarried relationship. These are "families" too. And if society can begin to accept and define "family" in a more flexible way—to account for a variety of life-styles —the family as a social unit will actually be strengthened.

Before You Wed, Use Your Head

Marrying during the teen-age years means assuming more of a burden than most young people are really ready to do. It's unrealistic for someone to try to make a sound lifetime contract (that's fifty years if you live to the expected age of seventy!) after only a few years— maybe three or four—of close contact with the opposite sex. Most marriages in the United States have been contracted by people under twenty-two. By the age of twenty-one, half the women who will ever marry have already done so—at least this was true in the recent past. But twenty-five or older would be a better time to form a marriage (this is the average age in a number of industrialized Western countries).

It is a good sign that age at marriage is now rising in the United States, and as a result the divorce rate should go down. This optimistic prediction is based on the well-known fact that teen-age marriages have the highest divorce rate, about one of every two breaking up, compared with one in four marriages contracted *after* twenty-one.

There is simultaneously a large increase in the number of young adults who want and expect to have fewer children. These trends suggest a more sound and stable basis for family life, a more careful entry into marriage and parenthood by more mature people.

Americans are among the "marryingest" people on earth. Until recently more than 95 percent of all Americans went down the bridal path at least once. Why such a high percentage? Can it be that the marriage relationship is appropriate for practically everyone, that practically everyone is suited to be a spouse? No—yet many people unsuited for marriage, or at least not ready for it, get married anyway. In the past people often married because of social pressures, or impulsiveness. For that reason alone, we would expect a rather high divorce rate now, and, indeed, the United States leads the world both in its teen-age marriages and in its divorce rate. If, instead of a 95 percent marriage rate, we had a rate of 80 or 85 percent, probably everyone would be better off. Many marriages do not survive even five or ten years, and many of these, particularly among young people, should never have occurred at all. With better birth control available to young people, these impulsive and coerced marriages should (and do) decrease in number with an increase in general welfare, including the welfare of the institution of marriage.

George Bernard Shaw, in the Preface to *Getting Married*, wrote: "When two people are under the influence of the most violent, most insane, most delusive, and most transient of passions, they are required to swear that they will remain in that excited, abnormal, and exhausting condition continuously until death do them part."

Young people today are moving away from the romantic extreme in this parody. More of them are living together and postponing marriage. Some of your elders are worried about this, and even alarmed, because they fear that you may not marry at all. It's true that in the past decade there has been a large increase—more than one-third—in the number of women remaining single into their mid-twenties. There is also an increase of young couples who marry but postpone childbearing for several years.

This is not really so radical, nor is it a bad sign for the future of marriage and the family. In fact, the idea has been seriously considered for many years. Judge Ben Lindsey of Denver proposed it in 1927 in his book *The Companionate Marriage*. He pleaded for the right of everyone to do as the privileged were doing: have "legal marriage, with legalized Birth Control, and with the right to divorce by mutual consent for childless couples, usually without payment of alimony." The idea won the praise of Bertrand Russell in his very relevant book *Marriage and Morals* (1929), but it raised havoc in many quarters. The idea of using birth control prior to the first pregnancy is just now taking hold—but fast! As recently as 1960 most couples did not do so. By 1970 perhaps the majority did. Your generation almost certainly will.

Lawmakers are reluctant to establish new barriers to the marriage of young people, although in California recently an effort was made to require premarital counseling for couples under a certain age. Even then, and even in states where there are higher age limits for marriage, the minimum-age limits are commonly breached when, for example, the girl is pregnant. Pregnancy may be a common reason to get married, but it is an unfortunate reason and is correlated with later marital unhappiness and failure, as you would expect.

You have heard often enough that the divorce rate is high, and going up. Later marriage and parenthood should help reduce that rate, although the effects may not be evident statistically for some years (about half of all divorces take place after seven years of marriage). The divorce rate must also be viewed in the light of several other factors, including the improved social, educational, and economic status of women; the easing of outmoded and cruel divorce laws; higher expectations of men and women for happiness in marriage. The divorce rate is an indicator of unhappiness but represents an action taken to reduce unhappiness—often by people who are much more mature than when they married.

Unhappy couples should make a serious effort to resolve their problems, with professional help if necessary—especially if they have children. Children do suffer to some extent when their parents separate or divorce. Nevertheless, some children who would otherwise have to grow up in the shadow of severe marital conflict would be harmed less if the parents dissolved their bad marriage and moved on to a more peaceful life, either alone or in a more successful remarriage.

One million children have been affected annually in the past several years by divorce—too many children and parents to be counseled even if they wished to be; there aren't enough professional counselors to go around. Prevention is the only answer. Meanwhile, if you are struggling with the breakup of your parents' marriage (or if a young person you know is having this problem), see *The Boys and Girls Book About Divorce* (1970) by Dr. Richard Gardner, a leading child psychiatrist.

Most divorced people remarry—so marriage as an institution seems to be alive and well. Indeed, more people have been getting married, and staying married longer, than in past generations. People live longer; there are far more thirty-year, forty-year, and fifty-year wedding anniversaries. In this connection, an important long-range consideration is the age difference between husband and wife. Traditionally the male is a few years older than the female spouse. Since men on the average die sooner than women, the result is a substantial period of widowhood in store for most wives. What does this have to do with young people? A great deal, if you look forward to a long and happy life.

Why should he be older than she? If both are mature enough to get married, then the age difference ought to be a matter of independent judgment, not habit or tradition. And if more wives were as old as, or older than, their husbands, we would not have the sad situation of 9 million widows compared to 2 million widowers which currently exists in the United States.

Parenthood and Child Rearing

In 1972 a sensible new law went into effect in Virginia providing that all persons who apply for marriage licenses in the state be given a health department pamphlet on birth control, "The Right Way to Plan Your Family." At least one state senator was not happy about the new program. He said:

The day you go to get your marriage license is a singularly inappropriate time to be handed a pile of stuff telling you how not to have babies. Here's a guy and a gal getting ready to go on their honeymoon; you know what they're thinking about, and the clerk starts laying pamphlets on 'em. That just isn't the right time. Why can't they send it along in the mail later? Everybody ought to be entitled to one unplanned baby anyway. And what about the people who are going down there to get the license because they didn't know about birth control? How do you think they're gonna feel?

We appreciate the dilemmas the senator is raising. But young people, although "entitled" to an unplanned baby, should not have to have one as often as they did in past generations. The Virginia law is good, but still too little and too late for many young people.

With the exception of couples of child-bearing age during the Depression years of the 1930's, all but 5 to 10 percent of the married couples in the United States have had children. This pattern, too, shows some recent change. A few years ago only one percent of married couples in this country said that they wanted no children. Now on college campuses as many as 10 to 15 percent of the students are saying that they do not wish to bear children, according to Dr. Marjorie Lozoff of the Wright Institute in Berkeley. Parenthood and child rearing are vocations of major importance which also represent lifetime commitments. Some of you will wonder why people marry if they don't want children.

The value of companionship in marriage is highly regarded by many people; after all, a couple in love are in love with each other, not their potential children. In a good marriage as much (or more) time is spent in adult relationships as in parent-child interaction; this is more the case as family size becomes smaller, people live longer, and children become independent (in some ways) sooner than they used to, with many opportunities to take part in activities outside the home.

It is a good thing for marriage, the family, and society that more people will have fewer children or no children. There are still more children in our society and in the world than are well cared for. You have all heard grim statistics on child neglect, child abuse, and children in institutions. There is no real women's liberation, either, as long as women are tied mainly to childbearing and child rearing. If instead of 85 to 95 percent of couples having children, the figure dropped to 70 or 75 percent, then the quality of parenthood could decidedly improve, and more women could take an important part in other areas of life.

There are decided advantages to delaying parenthood, spacing births about three years apart, and having small families. Although there is a good deal of prejudice against the only child, there is no evidence to support the commonly held opinion that only children are always spoiled. On the contrary, the only child outranks all others in achievement, and probably in adjustment. Of course, only children need outside social experiences (all children do), but their parents are in a good position to enter the child in play groups and nursery schools of the best quality. Only children have a greater likelihood of getting into college and the professions, and of being listed in *Who's Who;* also, they are less likely to become psychiatric patients. A strikingly high proportion of astronauts are only children. There is no reason for anyone to think it "wrong" to have one child only—but it will take a while for the old ideas to disappear.

Research studies exist showing the relative advantages of being born and raised in a small or a large family. The small family, with long intervals—three or more years—between births, seems most desirable. Both health and mental health are better in children whose parents have more time, energy, and money to spend on them. (For a review of research studies see the *American Journal of Public Health,* January 1970, or *The New York Times Magazine,* March 8, 1970.) An important British study of thousands of children—*Home and School* by J. W. B. Douglas (1964)—shows that intelligence, school achievement, physical growth, and health are all favored by smaller family size.

The spacing and number of children affects parents, too. Sociologist Harold T. Christensen of Purdue University finds a strong correlation between happiness in marriage and family planning. When children are born during the first year of marriage, the divorce rate is higher than when childbirth is postponed until later (*Journal of Marriage and The Family,* May 1968). Professor Lee Rainwater of Harvard, in *Family Design* (1970), reports that marital adjustment itself has a lot to do with the success of birth control. It all adds up to the conclusion that better marriage means better family planning, and better family planning means better marriage. Getting off to a good start is very important.

Being a good parent is much more than a matter of maternal or paternal instinct. *Parenthood is a difficult task as well as an exciting one, and those who undertake it should do so thoughtfully, with more caution and deliberation than in any other decision they ever make.* No one we know would argue otherwise. Yet only now are the majority of young couples able to make this principle a reality in practice!

Financial columnist Sylvia Porter, whose *Money Book* is a valuable guide to almost everything including family planning, states that the annual cost of rearing a child is 15 to 17 percent of a family's income. Considering the loss of income by the mother who gives up a job (or pursuit of a career) to care for her child, the investment required by parenthood is enormous, financially as well as emotionally.

Professor Ronald Freedman of the University of Michigan has shown statistically that young couples whose pregnancies occurred before marriage never caught up financially with similar couples who waited for children until after marriage, particularly those who waited for two years after marriage. Premarital pregnancy is a serious barrier to dollars-and-cents security. Early pregnancy represents, in a sense, a denial of equal opportunity. Well-to-do couples have always been able to arrange for abortions, but other people saw their ambitions and dreams wiped out by premature parenthood. When forced marriage and unwilling parenthood occur family life starts off on the wrong foot.

Parenthood is one of many creative life careers; it is not the right choice for everyone. Many people worry that it is the responsible young people who really ought to be parents who are deciding not to be parents. The fear is that everything they could teach a new generation will be lost. But in our experience many people who choose not to be parents are very active and effective in helping children: They may act as parents for children who need them; they support efforts to help poor and handicapped children; they teach; they fight for greater justice for young people under the law. There are many ways in which a young adult can serve as a guide for the children of the next generation. There are many ways to be a "parent"—not all of them involve a pregnancy.

Adoption is an approach to parenthood that is receiving considerable attention today. The adoptive parent who wants a newborn, white infant will find that there are fewer available now than in the past. But there are older children, children in foster care, handicapped children, and some from racial minorities and other countries who need parental care.

For a long time adoptive parents have been made to feel like second-class parents, although that's quite irrational. It reflects an overemphasis on biological reproduction, which is really the animal part of child rearing. The more important part is raising a child—the psychological, uniquely human part. As child psychiatrist Lili Peller put it: We should no longer talk about "real parents" and "adoptive parents"; instead, we should talk about *birth* parents and *real* parents. To the child the real parents are the ones who raise him, not the ones who gave him his genes. If you cannot consider adoption, you may not be ready for parenthood. *In other words, if you can't be a real parent, you shouldn't be a birth parent.*

Foster care is another way to engage in parenthood, but on a temporary basis. There are perhaps 300,000 children in foster homes or institutions at any one time in this country, and many children suffer from being transplanted periodically from one home to another. Arrangements for a more permanent family life for these children would help, and more people should be available for foster care in cases where sudden illness, accident, death, or other emergencies devastate a family. With the extended family scattered all over the country, there is great need for better organized, quickly available foster care. Good foster parents could, as their experience grows, be in a position to take care of children with more serious problems, including predelinquent children, children with mild to moderate emotional problems, unwed pregnant girls, and children with other special needs, including the handicapped.

Young people could serve apprenticeships with foster parents to learn about child care before starting a family. Indeed, every high school should have a child care center for preschoolers, so that all teen-agers, male and female, could have an intensive experience learning about child development. Ideally they would not only work with children in the nursery school setting, but would also visit their homes and help their parents at mealtimes, in the evenings, and on weekends, so that they could learn the skills and responsibilities of child care. Babysitting is not really a sufficient preparation for parenthood, and many youngsters—especially boys—miss even that.

For those of you who want to be parents, an intensive work-study program of child care would teach much-needed skills. Remember, raising children has never been easy. Why is Dr. Spock's *Baby and Child Care* a continual best seller? "It is easy to become a parent, but hard to be one" (Wilhelm Busch, a nineteenth-century German poet and illustrator).

Single Parenthood

In very recent years there has been a trend toward being more open about unmarried pregnancy and parenthood. Should young single parents keep their children rather than place them for adoption? While we favor the right of teen-agers to make important decisions and assume responsibility, we question the wisdom of parenthood during the teen-age years or even before age twenty-two. It is difficult to make a decision with such long-range consequences when you have so little life experience. Some eighteen-year-olds are more mature than some twenty-five-year-olds, and there is no hard-and-fast test of personal maturity and readiness for parenthood. But as a guideline, age is much better than nothing. In a period of history when small families are both popular and necessary, *there is no rush to become a parent at such an early age, and there are many good reasons why parenthood should be postponed.* If some people are "mature enough" at eighteen, they'll be better still at twenty-five. Why commit those precious years to parenthood, when there are so many other things to do first that can't be done later?

Nevertheless, many young people, married and unmarried, are becoming parents. And young parents—single or married—face a serious challenge which the community should help them meet.

In general, it is best if a child has two mature parents. But this does not mean that all single people who keep their children have made poor decisions. It is probably less important whether a parent is married than whether that person can meet the challenge of parent-hood with competence and love. Mature single people can be good parents, and many want to have or adopt children. There is no reason they should not if they can support, care for, and love the child. For most teenagers, though, there is no practical way to both make a secure living and take good care of a child.

Sex Choice and Genetic Technology

Science and technology makes it possible for couples to influence, if not absolutely determine, whether they have a boy or girl child. The hazards of this possibility are obvious. There tends to be a preference for boys, at least for the firstborn, and it could result in an imbalance between the sexes which might have serious social consequences later on, e.g., when it's time for the girls and boys of the new generation to marry. But there is value in the ability to choose the sex of offspring, because there are many cases in which parents continue to have children in the hope of getting one of a particular sex. It would be an advantage all around if couples who already have one child and wish to have one of the opposite sex would avail themselves of a technique that could increase their chances. Such a technique has been described in the chapter on rhythm. Parents who are attempting to balance the present sex composition of their family, however, should remember that each child is a unique person, and his or her sex is only a secondary matter.

There is also a new technique called amniocentesis which is being used to reduce the number of seriously defective children who are born. A doctor inserts a needle into the womb of a pregnant mother to withdraw some amniotic fluid with cells that can be examined to locate a genetic defect. In case such a defect is found, the parents *may* decide to abort that pregnancy. Some couples will take their chances, asserting that abortion is wrong and that they value the opportunity to care for a handicapped child. But for most people the burden is too great, and society has many handicapped children who need—and are not getting—special attention right now.

Although developments such as amniocentesis are interesting and important, the greatest improvement in parenthood, physical and mental, will occur when everybody who has children does so only as the result of informed and responsible choices. New technology will not make up for the principle of *informed consent for parenthood*. When everyone has the information and means to effectively plan pregnancies and provide realistically for family needs, there will be much improvement in the experience of parenthood and childhood. This is a happy outcome to anticipate for everyone—individuals, their families, and the larger society.

Alternative Life-Styles

Women—and men—have recently begun to question the traditional roles assigned to the sexes in our society, and most of us will never be quite the same again. Even men who still look forward to their "masculine" role of breadwinner, and women who cling to the usual "feminine" role of homemaker, will be affected by the fact that others are beginning to see things differently.

The changes in traditional sex roles are already reflected in matters of boy-girl etiquette. In the first six months of 1972, Ellen received more than fifty letters from boys and girls who explained how they divided dating expenses. (The year before there was not one such letter.) There are also quite a few letters from girls who, as a matter of course, ask boys for dates. "I no longer just 'indicate an interest,' " one girl wrote; "if I like a boy, I ask him out."

The following advice on "Manners for Humans" was given in *Ms.* magazine (July 1972):

A woman does not wait to be asked out by a man. She feels free to make the first move.

Whether he asks her or she asks him, she should feel free to pick up the whole tab, half of it, or whatever her pocketbook will allow. If a man can't accept this, he's not in tune with today.

A woman should feel free to ask a man to dance. Some women feel they should be able to dance with other women. Some feel they should lead when they know they dance better than the man. Some think the leader role should be exchanged. Do what comes naturally.

Men do not rise at the table and help women sit down. This is a dreary custom.

Men do not open car doors, help women in and/or out, and then close the door.

Anyone can hold doors open for anyone else.

While ten years ago a campus funnyline was "He wants to graduate with a Ph.D., she wants to graduate with an MRS" (implying that the ultimate achievement for an educated woman was a prefix indicating that she was married), many women today are choosing the new symbol "Ms.," which, like "Mr.," does not indicate whether or not they are married. Leading young career women are keeping their maiden names along with their husband's name (Brenda *Feigen* Fasteau, Carol *Eisen* Rinzler) or not changing their names at all when they marry: Midge Decter, Margaret Mead, Elizabeth Herzog.

Regarding terms referring to women, one feminist has said, "There is one word for an adolescent or adult female, and it is not girl, chick, dame, broad, or lady. It is *woman.* Any other term is condescending and disrespectful."

These surface symbols carry meaning. Traditional "etiquette" is viewed as a program for treating women as childlike, dependent creatures who cannot put on their own coats; changing a woman's name when she marries symbolically removes her identity and independence.

The changing traditions of etiquette and names also signal that some deeper changes are occurring in male-female relationships. No longer is *she* the only one to lift a kitchen sponge or *he* the only one to bring home a paycheck. Couples are sharing household duties and financial responsibilities—and these couples are not always married.

Here's what three high school Merit Scholars think about changing roles:

The man will remain the provider, the woman the mother and caretaker, but the bounds to these roles won't be so great. As far as changing my own life-style, I'll probably be meeting fewer damsels in distress but more women who have definite ideas and plans for their future. They will not be husband-hunting in college—but planning a career.

Chester P., New Orleans

I really don't think that sex roles will be affected to any great extent. Regardless of what one does, the female will still carry the child. Hopefully, what will be affected will be the traditional occupational roles. I support the movement, though it will not have any large effect on my life since I never discriminate because of sex (except in dating).

Jerry S., Overland, Missouri

Women's Lib has already succeeded in altering my group to form a close family. Boys and girls are able to relate to one another as friends, not girls fearing other girls as competition and always having a love relationship. Recently we girls had a cottage which the boys naturally frequented. The boys did the cooking and cleaning readily and pretty evenly with the girls. In my relationship with my boyfriend, we are much more open and honest. I can call him and invite him out on an outing as well as his inviting me.

Very often we go dutch. By both sharing costs and ideas we are able to do a greater variety of things. I am also spared of feeling I owe him anything. I don't find that we play games with each other, as a typical male-female role. I also hope the Lib movement will help me get professional respect, equal payment and equal competition for a job.

I am not certain of my future at the present time, because I am changing my mind so rapidly. Marriage is very far off. I would consider taking up housekeeping with a man sooner than marriage—along the lines of a trial marriage. I will limit my childbearing to two, but if I can afford it, I will adopt as many as I can provide for. I will adopt any nationality or race. I also will continue my career. My husband and I will split household duties according to understandings before the marriage. I hope the marriage will be very liberal and flexible. I also would like a sort of communal living. Not a farm where we are self-sufficient, but just a larger family unit. A house of friends so that the children would be able to love and relate to several adults, while still knowing who their parents are.

Judith B., Albion, N.Y.

And Birgitta Linner, Swedish marriage counselor and author, told the 1972 American Orthopsychiatric Association meeting: "We have to remember that as women have been deprived of the responsibility in the society—men have been underprivileged emotionally, not having had the possibilities to be close to children and therefore prone to stagnate as emotional persons."

Not everybody has or wants the usual family. For example, we know of:

Four married couples who share a large house and who, among them, have two children.

Two couples (not married) who share a California apartment and have no children.

A divorced mother of three who lives communally with other women in Seattle.

A forty-year-old woman in Chicago who has lived (unmarried) with the same man for fifteen years and who has one child.

We're not about to judge which life-style is "best." On any happiness-and-fulfillment scorecard we could draw up, all would be winners if their way of life was chosen freely and maintained willingly.

Should society attempt to encourage and maintain an "ideal" or preferred life-style (marriage plus children) when countless thousands do not find it satisfying? Just because the nuclear family works well for *some* is not a reason to force everyone into it.

America's schools, and its social and economic systems, are organized as if to support the nuclear family unit. Often the support is more apparent than real: The expectations "When you get married . . ." or "After you have children . . ." do not make sense unless people have real understanding of and preparation for these commitments. Young people are waking up to this faster than some of their elders.

Fidelity or Freedom: The Loving Compromise

Most people continue to marry for life, because in their lasting commitment they have something which they treasure very much and would not trade, even for "lost" bachelor freedom or a new start with somebody else. There are values in lifelong marriage which for many, if not most, people surpass other possibilities. On the other hand, people who find themselves in an unwise or ill-conceived marriage suffer something akin to hell on earth. There is no need to praise or blame marriage itself. Real partners, married or not, do not take each other for granted, and must recognize the possibility of the marriage failing or two people growing apart as they mature. They do not, however, treat this possibility as a probability, and they are committed enough to work on problems, and to be supportive of and interesting to each other, as the years go on. This very attitude of *not taking a partner for granted* is perhaps the best stimulus to good marriage that exists. For this reason, women's liberation and men's liberation will do much to improve the quality of American marriage and family life.

A tolerant view of sexual relations outside of marriage is that of Alex Comfort, British physician, novelist, and social critic (author of *Sex in Society,* 1963, and *The Anxiety Makers,* 1967, and editor of *The Joy of Sex,* 1972). Writing in *Center Report* (December 1972), he said:

All that can be certainly predicted for the future is that the variety of patterns will increase as individuals find the norm that suits them. For some, parenthood will still be the central satisfaction, carrying with it the obligation of giving the children the stability they require. For others, sexuality will express total involvement with one person. For others, one or more primary relationships will be central, but will not exclude others, in which the recreational role of sex acts as a source of bonding to supply the range of relationships formerly met by kin—an old human pattern in which sexual contacts were permitted between a woman and all her husband's clan brothers, or a man and all his wife's titular sisters.

In *The New York Times Magazine* (August 13, 1972), two leading experts on marriage and divorce had this to say:

I think if I came back in a hundred years I'd find marriage here in some form or other, whatever they may be calling it. The one-to-one commitment is hard as hell, but no viable alternative presents itself that is as rewarding, as intimate and as significant.

Dr. Laura Singer

The young people . . . feel so alone, they want to merge quickly, and when it's a drag they split. It's obsolescence applied to human relationships: Use it, throw it away. What's sad is that they never learn. They repeat the pattern again and again, and never find what they're looking for.

Dr. Paul Vahanian

Dr. Jessie Bernard, a renowned sociologist, writing in *The Future of Marriage* (1972), said:

Marriage is the best of human statuses and the worst, and it will continue to be. And that is why, though its future in some form or other is as assured as anything can be, this future is as equivocal as its past. The demands that men and women make on marriage will never be fully met; they cannot be. And these demands will rise rather than decline as our standards—rightfully —go up. Men and women will continue to disappoint as well as to delight one another, regardless of the form of their commitments to one another, or the living style they adopt, or even of the nature of the relationship between them. And we will have to continue to make provision for all the inevitable —but, hopefully, decreasing—failures of these marriages to meet the rising demands made on them which we can unequivocally expect.

According to Dr. Bernard, people want "excitement, freedom, new experiences on the one hand, along with security and stability on the other. But they cannot have it both ways." Commitments mean compromises, and she sees "people shaking their fists at the restraints they need and know they must have."

In days past, there was little need to defend fidelity because it was not under open attack. Nowadays you hear critics of marriage, of romantic love, of jealousy as an emotion, and even of commitment in relationships. We can't go into all the arguments here, but no one should be railroaded away from his sense of what is right. Listen to the arguments, but if you still feel that you want your partner to be faithful and you want to be faithful, then don't settle for less. Most people seem to value fidelity, although they may have a hard time saying why, or convincing a skeptic—it's such a personal matter.

For further discussion and argument on the theme, see *Sexual Latitude: For and Against* (1971), a collection of essays edited by Harold H. Hart. In the same series is *Marriage: For and Against* (1971), also edited by Mr. Hart.

Because it's a shame when people *compromise* their ideals or principles in life, the word has become a bit tainted. You'll need it in marriage and family life—in love, friendship, and everyday human relations—but you don't have to sell your soul. The word originally means "promise together" and refers to a mutual commitment made before a third party, as in arbitration. Rabbi Gustav Buchdahl of Baltimore teaches that the family is the place where you learn *the art of legitimate compromise.* The word *legitimate* tells you that no sacrifice of integrity is required; on the contrary, the ability to make legitimate compromises is of the essence in maintaining your basic rights and respecting others' at the same time.

17
Sex, Population, and Planet Earth

We have forgotten how to be good guests, how to walk lightly on
the earth as its other creatures do.
                    The Stockholm Conference, *Only One Earth,* 1972

Long ago, our planet got started racing around space tied by gravity
to the sun. Things took shape as we know them now after millions of
years of volcanic heat and glacial cold. Some molecules came to life:
Atoms of carbon, hydrogen, oxygen, and nitrogen joined in such a
way that they could transform energy to matter—sunlight to plant
fiber. The molecules formed cells that moved, ate, rested, reproduced,
and died. Such is life.

One-cell plants and animals inherited the earth from steam, lava,
ice, and stone. And after generation—and generations of generation
—complex and specialized forms of life appeared, and inherited the
earth. Then man appeared, and thought himself landlord of the
planet.

But man, the only thoughtful living thing, now knows that he is just
a tenant here on earth; the lease is held by silent forms of life which
got the whole thing started and keep it going without thinking. These
mindless creatures demand respect—Albert Schweitzer called it Reverence for Life. Like grains of sand or flakes of snow, simple forms
of life are small—but taken together, formidable. They are not mean,
but there are terrible risks in violating their laws, nature's laws.

Man-made laws must be in harmony with nature's law and order.
Over the ages our ancestors learned to obey some of nature's laws, and
made nature bow to some of their inventions. Early on, people

thought little about the balances in nature. They simply found that some places made better homes than others. A few hardy souls live on high mountains where the air is thin, or on hot, dry desert, or in the Arctic, where ice never melts. But people usually gathered near good sources of food and water. Later they developed the transportation to obtain necessities from a distance and elaborate trade systems to pay for them. Power sources like dammed rivers helped to raise the standard of living, giving electricity for light at home, and for running factories and offices, trains and movies, radio and newspapers and television; but such production uses up resources and dumps waste products on or over the earth.

The ability to concentrate and harness nature's energy led to the growth of industries and the replacement of human labor by machine labor. When industry grows, people tend to move to the industrial and commercial centers—cities. Because of industry, farms can produce more with less human toil, using tractors, harvesters, and other machines. Farm workers have to look for new jobs—in factories, in trades (as plumbers, electricians, barbers), or in human services (nursing, teaching, sales, taxi driving). Most opportunities are in or near cities, so the world is fast becoming urbanized.

Cities can be beautiful or ugly, or a mixture of both. They can make people happy or miserable. When thousands of people live close together, they can enjoy benefits that small villages of a few hundred cannot provide: good schools and libraries, hospitals and clinics, sports stadiums and professional teams, concert halls, museums, and theaters, art and entertainment from everywhere.

But when thousands live close together, they also have problems: how to get enough clean air and water, space for children to play, and peace and quiet; how to get across town or away from the city; how to get rid of garbage and trash.

We have come a long way from the time when the earth was a globe of green forests and fresh oceans. Partially as a result of our "high" standard of living, we have become familiar with such phrases as "human survival" . . . "crisis in human ecology."

Ecology refers to the natural housekeeping of living things on the planet—the balance of nature. It comes from the Greek word *oikos,* meaning "house." To our generation and yours falls the task of putting our house in order.

Green forests, fresh oceans? Some can still be found. But, increasingly, the garden spot that was the earth, and the myriad forms of life which live on it, fall victim to that big-brained but thoughtless tenant. We are cutting down enough trees each year to lay a ten-foot-wide boardwalk thirty times around the earth. A road is chopped through the lush Amazon forests, a huge pipeline now crosses Alaska. DDT sprayed over the eastern United States falls in England's rain. Particles of soot and sulfur thinly blanket even the icecaps of the North and South poles. Sewage is dumped into rivers, pesticides damage the land—and all wastes eventually reach the oceans. We face, tomorrow, a world without wolves, a world without whales. We are destroying our household.

In nonindustrialized countries today, life is still relatively simple. The peasant who lives in China or India does not disturb the land very much. The Asian peasant woman does not throw away bread wrappers and orange-juice cans; her child does not cast away broken plastic toys, junior furniture, and disposable diapers. The average citizen of China does not drive a car.

Demographers use the term "Indian equivalents" to explain that the birth of *one* American child is more destructive to the planet than the birth of *fifty* Indian children. So, it's nice to be concerned about birth control in India, but for planet earth and the U.S.A. we have a mission to accomplish here at home.

During his lifetime, each American child will consume:

9,000 pounds of wheat

10,150 pounds of meat

56 million gallons of water

28,000 pounds of milk and its by-products

100,000 pounds of steel

1,000 trees . . .

And each will produce 150,000 pounds of garbage. (Who's going to dig the hole to put it in?)

It's the luxury-class passengers on "spaceship Earth," not the plain folk, who use up the most goods and discharge the most waste products per capita.

The sea has always seemed limitless, and immune to man's destruction. As late as 1818 the British poet Byron wrote:

> Roll on, thou deep and dark blue ocean—roll!
> Ten thousand fleets sweep over thee in vain.
> Man marks the earth with ruin—
> His control stops with the shore.

That, too, has changed. Some 3,000 chemical compounds have been added to earth's atmosphere by man—but we are dumping as many as *half a million* polluting substances into the oceans. (These include 200,000 tons of lead, 5,000 tons of mercury, and one million tons of oil *each year,* plus large amounts of sewage, detergents, pesticides, and industrial chemical wastes.) Swiss oceanographer Jacques Piccard estimates that, in the last twenty years, we have destroyed 30 to 50 percent of all life in the oceans, including the ocean plants which produce most of our planet's oxygen. And the rate of destruction is increasing.

The Population Explosion

Surely the earth, that's very wise, being very old, needs not our help.
                              Dante Gabriel Rossetti, 1870

The earth is dying. We must all direct our attention toward limiting its population, ending its exploitation, and making it a fit place to live.
                              Tony Wagner, senior,
                              Friends World College, 1970

A lot has changed in 100 years. In 1870 the population explosion was beginning—but practically nobody realized it. Now, in the 1980's, everybody knows there is a population explosion—but nobody's quite sure how to stop it.

An explosion may begin with a fuse that burns very slowly. During the early millennia of life on earth, forests grew and oceans teeming

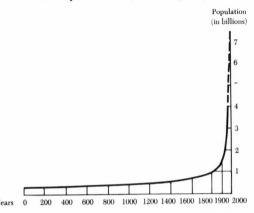

World Population Growth, from the Beginning

with life washed over the globe untroubled by the presence of men. If early communities of men despoiled one area (filling a river with too much sewage, over-hunting one forest area), they could always move on, for the earth seemed boundless. For hundreds of thousands of years the population of the earth grew slowly. There were many births, but disease, famine, and other natural disasters, as well as wars, served to keep numbers in check.

The population "fuse" reached the "bomb" in the 1800's, when modern medicine began to prevent deaths in infancy and childhood. More children survived at least to the age of reproduction, and had their own children. More of these children were also kept alive through further medical discoveries, to produce yet more children—and so on through the generations.

The population "explosion" occurred because man discovered effective means of *death prevention* but did not simultaneously discover and use effective means of *birth prevention:* Louis Pasteur preceded Margaret Sanger; penicillin came before the pill. Survival rates soared as death rates plunged, and the relationship between man and his planet was altered for all time. Man, among all earth's creatures, said to Nature, "I will not necessarily die when you decree it," and, saying this, man ceased to be a child of Nature—and has become, in fact, her adversary.

Suddenly the "boundless" earth became small indeed.

Perhaps you know the figures; perhaps you've seen the charts.

It took from the beginning of time until A.D. 1830 for the earth to acquire its first billion human inhabitants. But it took only one hundred years (from 1830 to 1930) to add the second billion, and only thirty years (1930 to 1960) to add the third billion.

By 1980—another twenty years—we passed the 4 billion mark!

The preceding chart shows us that if these population growth rates continue, earth could be carrying more than 7.5 billion passengers during your adulthood—by the year 2000. (By that time, given the huge numbers of human beings who would be at reproductive age, a *ninth billion* of people could be added in just five years!)

Notice how the time it takes to double the population has shortened. Even so, the danger is not obvious to many people. Think of a pond being overgrown with algae; suppose the algae double their number each day, and the pond will be covered in thirty days. On day twenty-nine, the pond will be only half covered!

It is hardly likely that we can reach a population of 9 billion, for even now the planet is showing clear signs that it is over burdened. Polluted air and water, extinct species of animals, depleted and poisoned oceans—all are now facts of life (and factors in a sophisticated scientific guessing game as to whether, and for how long, life can continue).

Even if you do not live near a factory or a freeway, you breathe polluted air. True, air pollution is more intense near industrial centers, but pollutants disperse: They do not stop at city limits or national boundaries, and they never leave the atmosphere! All air pollutants produced by man remain "trapped" in the thin lower layer of atmosphere which also contains our breatheable air. These pollutants have already decreased the amount of sunlight that our earth receives, and are causing changes of climate which we do not fully understand. A 1968 UNESCO conference concluded that man had only about twenty more years before the planet would begin to become uninhabitable due to air pollution alone.

Pollution is worldwide.

The Lake of Zurich is dying like Lake Erie; the Rhine is as polluted as the Hudson. Forests deep in Sweden are withering under acid rains bearing sulfur from the Ruhr, while all of California's ponderosa pines may die from sulfur dioxide and other components of automobile exhaust. Raw sewage greets surfers at Waikiki Beach. Sturgeon and caviar are disappearing from the Caspian Sea; the Baltic Sea's vital oxygen content is dropping at an alarming rate. In Milan ordinary workers have to wear gas masks. In some parts of Rome's Tiber River a fish will die in fifteen minutes. The grizzly bear, the whooping crane, and the Atlantic salmon have joined the list of endangered species on the route to extinction—along with the national symbol of America, the bald eagle.

A food crisis faces many countries.

In an effort to expand world food production, scientists presented us with DDT, and people began to use it widely in the 1940's. Later we began to notice that where crops were sprayed, songbirds died; where residues washed into rivers, fish disappeared. In the spring of 1971 sixty sea lions washed up dead onto the coast of California north of San Francisco—3,900 parts per million DDT in their tissues. (There is DDT in your body tissues, too.) We must face the unpleasant fact that, even if all nations ban DDT and other persistent pesticides *now,* residues will continue to run off into streams and oceans for many years.

Underlying all these planetary problems is overpopulation. Various science-fiction writers have described a future of "standing room only," but overpopulation is not a question of density per square mile. (All 4.2 billion people in the world today could fit into North America.) The overpopulation problem is one of *resources,* and one of *technology.*

For example, if present trends continue, world reserves of oil may be exhausted in thirty years; natural gas may be exhausted in twenty years; iron, in eighty years; lead, in fifteen years; gold, in fifteen years; and copper, in twenty-five years.

And what of air and water? They are resources, too. The Royal Bank of Canada, foreseeing water shortages, has called water "the central material problem of mankind." Earth's rather small supply of fresh water is being rapidly reduced, as man removes fresh water from the continents faster than the hydrologic cycle replaces it. We reduce the oxygen content of our atmosphere every time we cut down a forest —and, as population grows, we cut down more forests: to provide housing, school buildings, hospitals, furniture, and highways.

Technology intensifies the impact of human beings on the planet's resources and life-support systems. (One paper mill, for example, uses as much water as a city of 50,000 people.)

Primitive man had a minimal impact on the earth: with his simple fires and food, he required only about 5,000 calories of energy a day. Modern "civilized" man, with his vast array of appliances and manufactured goods, requires about 200,000 calories of energy a day! (Think of the factories that are necessary to provide you with clothing, cars, radios, records, hair dryers, electric lights, and processed food.)

In terms of our impact on the planet, the United States is the most overpopulated country on earth! With about 5 percent of the world's population, we use about 40 percent of the world's resources consumed each year.

The United States, of course, is not the only nation doing more than its share of consumption and pollution. Britain, for example, also has a high rate of resource consumption. Anyone who doubted the seriousness of the population problem was startled to read headlines in January 1972, when thirty-three leading British scientists warned that a world environmental catastrophe was near. *All* of these scientists signed a statement saying that "the breakdown of society and the irreversible disruption of the life-support systems of this planet— possibly by the end of the century, certainly within the lifetime of our children—are inevitable." *All* urged Britain to stop building roads, to tax the use of power, and to *cut her population in half.*

Meanwhile, the U.S. Commission on Population Growth and the American Future concluded that there were *no* identifiable benefits to be derived from further population growth in this country; and the most massive study of world systems ever undertaken was completed at the Massachusetts Institute of Technology. Echoing the conclusions of his British counterparts, MIT scientist Dennis Meadows declared simply: "All growth projections end in collapse." (See *The Limits to Growth,* 1972).

Some took comfort from the fact that shortly after the MIT study was released, a national survey of fertility in this country indicated that our birth rate was down. However, the birth rate is calculated on a larger-than-ever base population! In the United States our *rate* of growth is slowing, but our *real numbers* continue to rise.

In 1972 United States birth rates and the birth expectations of young couples were at a new low, consistent with eventual zero population growth (ZPG), that is, the point at which population is stabilized at a certain level. ZPG will not come for seventy more years, however, even if every couple from now on only replaces itself with an average of two children. Meanwhile, we continue to add to the population, because the number of couples is so large. We could reach ZPG sooner only if couples averaged less than two children—a possibility, since non-parenthood, adoption, and the one-child family are gaining acceptance.

Social problems, as well as environmental problems, are caused or aggravated by overpopulation. Many see overpopulation as a threat to world peace. Stanford psychologist P. G. Zimbardo sees a connection between anonymity and aggression in the pressures of urban crowding.

Some say, "Reduce urban congestion by redistributing the population. Move city dwellers to the countryside." However, if city dwellers move *en masse* to rural areas, they will simply transform these rural areas into other cities and take with them their urban problems, even if on a smaller scale. "Spreading out" the population is going to mean that more forests will fall to the bulldozers. And, while trees produce oxygen, houses and roads do not.

Cities *are* spreading out, in any case. The eastern and western seaboards are close to being completely urbanized. Chains of cities extend for thousands of miles to form what social scientists call a "megalopolis."

Some who have tried to escape urban pressures by finding a pastoral setting have been disappointed. One of these, a young writer, said:

"South of us, Interstate 91 is being blasted through the hills. At night, part of the sky glows an eerie green from the towers of light over a supermarket parking lot. A few years ago, we were safe in Vermont from the urban monster. Now, we're not so sure. . . ." (*Time,* August 15, 1971)

Overpopulation seems certain to further a variety of social and environmental ills and inconveniences, from crime, congestion, and higher taxes to community breakdown and poisoned air.

Intelligent criticism of these points is hard to find. Ben Wattenberg, writing in *World* magazine (July 1972), argues that there is no real crisis, and that there is danger in blaming social problems on population. Biologist Barry Commoner believes that misuse of resources is more important than population growth. Of course there are many problems which must be solved independently of the population problem—no one really disputes that! But overpopulation is one of the biggest threats, and aggravates most other problems.

The situation seemed so grave to college graduate Stephanie Mills that, surveying the world from her standpoint in the middle of the twentieth century, she said, "The best thing I can do for mankind is never to have children."

"As an ex-potential parent," Stephanie continued, "I asked myself, 'What kind of a world would my children have? Not very clean, not very pretty. Sad, in fact.' "

Well, then, the question—can the world be saved?

For many years a stock cartoon character was a robed figure carrying a sign "The World Is Coming To An End." The phrase is not so funny anymore. Perhaps the person carrying the sign was right.

Whether or not the world can survive depends on you. The situation is quite unfair. Generations which preceded you wrote a lot of big checks on the future; you are being handed the bills. We taught you to like toasters and hair dryers; we didn't tell you what they cost. (They have a price beyond the dollars you pay for them—their cost in resources, their cost in pollution.) We made you accustomed to gasoline-powered transportation, and we didn't tell you the price of that, either. (Part of that price is the destruction of the Alaskan wilderness.) We taught you, in sixth-grade history books, that nothing

could ever go really wrong in America, because we were so clever;
now things are going wrong. There's something else we didn't tell you,
because we're just realizing it ourselves, and some of us don't realize
it yet: Because we overindulged in parenthood, many of you or your
children may be deprived of it.

Having a child used to be an automatic adult activity. Now it's a
moral dilemma.

Some letters we have received, and some comments we have heard,
may show how some of those of your generation are facing this
dilemma:

I've just started to understand the population problem, and I think it represents a kind of ultimatum: *don't* (reproduce) or die. . . . How can we organize
enough to do it? Even if we get our heads together here, what about kids our
age in other countries? These are things I'm going to have to talk about with
all my friends. I'm not sure just what I think about it yet.

Marie K., age eighteen

I used to think I wanted to have three children—three. You can't have dreams
like that anymore.

Joyce M., age eighteen

I told my dad I'm never going to have kids. I told him there's no way the
world is going to be fit, in my lifetime, to bring kids into. He said I'd change
my mind when I was twenty-one or so. I have news for him—I don't think
so.

Kenneth A., age seventeen

Children? We're not sure. We're going to wait five years and then decide.
We want to see what happens in five years. If *everybody everywhere* starts to
take the population crisis seriously, and population stops growing—well,
then it might be safe for us to have a child someday, and know that he'll
survive.

Roland and Helena J.,
just married, both age twenty-one

My mother had four children (I'm the last), then ended up joining Zero
Population Growth. She suggested to my sisters and me that we should only

have one child. I don't think I'm going to have even one, though. That way maybe my sister can have two—she really wants kids.

Linda S., age fourteen

Kent has applied for a vasectomy and can get it, since age of majority in California is age eighteen. We're going to adopt American Indian children. Why have your own children when you can give homes to children who are already here—who might not have homes otherwise?

Kent and Michelle B., ages nineteen and twenty

What worries me is that some of my classmates think there's going to be a magical scientific solution. We've been taught to believe that American ingenuity and inventions can solve anything. But sometimes these brilliant scientists only mess things up more. Look at DDT, and the Aswan Dam. People call me a pessimist. I don't think you can just dismiss uncomfortable facts as pessimism.

Donna Mc.C., age seventeen

I hereby serve notice to whom it may concern—particularly my parents—that they will not get many grandchildren from me. I hereby resolve to have a very small family—two children at most! I intend to let everyone my age know of my decision, so that maybe others will start to feel the same way. We *can* stop the population crisis!

Sandra D., age fifteen

It would be personally repugnant to me to nurse my *own* child at my breast and watch hundreds of starving children in other countries on TV. . . . I could not do it.

Dominique F., age eighteen

Finally, here is a letter we received from Paula R., age seventeen:

I have read the MIT computer study *The Limits to Growth.* Can I tell you something? I was not surprised. Oh, I didn't know all the facts and statistics —but I did know that things are dying. Every year there are fewer birds at my bird feeder. Man may die too. Gertrude Stein called your generation "the lost generation." Is my generation "the *last* generation"?

We hope not. It seems to us that there is some basis for thinking we can survive—simply because most of you who have written to us seem keenly aware of the problem. We think you can be counted on to act differently, and more responsibly, about reproduction than past generations have.

There are several indications that your generation will use birth control methods, and ideas for new life-styles, to bring about a better, less populated world.

A number of recent surveys have shown that more men and women of college age than ever before intend to have no children, or only one or two. Another hopeful sign is that many young couples who *do* plan to have children intend to *wait* for a number of years after marriage. This, in itself, would help to slow the rate of population growth.

Zero population growth is a popular goal among those concerned about our population crisis. We suspect it will not be for long. It is becoming increasingly apparent that *zero population growth is not enough!* It would have been a fine goal for our nation in 1850 or in 1900. Now, it may be too little, and too late.

"Negative population growth," or a reduction in *our real numbers,* seems a more desirable eventual goal. Many writers in the field say that our population *now* exceeds desirable limits.

Our population now, in this country, is about 212 million. Demographer Lincoln Day, for example, holds that it would have been "better" if the American population had stopped growing at 150 million, and that such an "optimum" population would afford the individual "serenity, dignity, order, leisure, peace, beauty, elbow room . . . necessary to the cultivation of the whole person."

Stewart Udall, former Secretary of the Interior, agrees.

Wayne Davis, of the University of Kentucky, believes that "we have far more people now than we can continue to support at anything near today's level of affluence."

Referring to world population in 1969, the Committee on Resources and Man (of the National Academy of Sciences) suggests, "A human population less than the present one would offer the best hope for comfortable living for our descendants."

The problem of "too much, too many" becomes clearer day by day. In fairness to the future, there should be banner headlines in the newspapers of all world capitals which proclaim, "WORLD OVER-

POPULATED!" There are not, but the news in the headlines carries the same message.

For example, here are two headlines for wire-service stories dated September 18, 1972:

ECONOMIC GROWTH HAS NOT EASED POVERTY'S GRIP, WORLD BANK SAYS

OVER 300 MILLION SUFFER FROM MALNUTRITION, U.N. NOTES

Reading closely, you find the relationship between overpopulation, poverty, and malnutrition. Here, for example, is the first story:

ECONOMIC GROWTH HAS NOT EASED POVERTY'S GRIP, WORLD BANK SAYS

Washington (Reuter's): The earth's burden of poverty is probably increasing despite impressive growth in production and income in the developing nations, the World Bank said yesterday.

It warned, in its annual report, of underlying social and economic problems, such as rapid population increase, high unemployment. . . .

And the second:

OVER 300 MILLION SUFFER FROM MALNUTRITION, U.N. NOTES

Rome (Reuter's): Between 300 million and 500 million people in the world are suffering from malnutrition—the same number as fifteen years ago, the United Nations Food and Agricultural Organization said yesterday.

The organization said there had been a small percentage decrease in the world's undernourished, but the number had remained the same because of an increase in population. . . .

Think of other headlines you have seen: "Pollution Still a Threat" . . . "Power Shortages and Brownouts Likely This Summer" . . . "Urban Crime at Record High" . . . "Unemployment, Inflation

Plague Job Force" . . . "Zoning Change Disputed by County Residents" . . . "Commuters Face More Freeway Traffic" . . .

Don't these problems all relate to overpopulation?

If county residents resist a zoning change that would change a green park to an industrial park, is the real issue zoning—or overpopulation?

Inevitably, we must ask the question, What is to be done about the population problem? Can the problem be solved in time by *individuals freely choosing* to limit or postpone their families, by *individuals freely choosing* adopted children or child-free life-styles?

In our opinion: Yes.

It's true that some experts have suggested that voluntary policies may not work. (Biologist Garrett Hardin puts it tersely: "Given policies of voluntarism, non-cooperators will outbreed cooperators.")

Certainly, with regard to birth control, there are many options our society might choose. We favor some or all of the policies within each of the following categories except the last; if the policies in the first four categories are adopted, those last, final measures should not be necessary.

I. *Make voluntary birth control fully available, to all who need and want it.*
Attach birth control clinics to all hospitals.

Provide birth control services as part of student health services at all high schools and colleges.

Make more funds available for family planning among the poor; provide services at no cost.

Make voluntary sterilization readily available to those who desire it.

II. *Modernize social policies regarding population and reproduction.*
Intensify educational campaigns regarding overpopulation: in schools, and on national and worldwide television. In schools, relate overpopulation to other courses of study (economics, psychology, family life).

Encourage child-free life-styles, delayed parenthood, and small families.

Remove pro-natalist bias (attitudes favoring parenthood) from textbooks and the popular media.

Improve career opportunities for women, so that more women *could* choose a role other than the maternal one.

III. *Provide incentives to encourage fewer births.*

Change tax laws by removing deductions for biological children. (Presently, our tax laws provide *incentives for parenthood;* these tax laws, created in another era, no longer serve a useful purpose.)

Reward child-free couples with cash payments. (Suzanne Keller of Princeton, among others, has suggested this.)

Reward men who decide to have a vasectomy. (One advocate of this policy, sportscaster Jim Bouton, suggests $1,000 as an amount.)

Lessen tax burdens on the unmarried.

Place an escalating tax on children—adding, perhaps, $600 to taxable income for the first child, $1,200 for the second child, $1,800 for the third or later children.

IV. *Provide international incentives.*

Limit immigration, encourage emigration, in order to emphasize the seriousness of the population crisis to all countries.

Increase foreign aid in the areas of health and education, family planning information and services. Increase training programs in population and family planning for students and health workers. Support research and development programs abroad, consistent with the needs of various cultures and political systems.

V. *Enact legislation to control parenthood or make birth control compulsory (not recommended, but discussable).*

Issue child licenses—similar to marriage licenses, but provided less casually.

Pass other legislation regulating family size and fertility.

Put an anti-fertility chemical in drinking water which requires an antidote if conception is to take place.

You should ask yourself which policies *you* favor; your generation will have to make important decisions regarding population control. Will population control be voluntary—or a matter of law? If voluntary: Which voluntary individual choices should be encouraged, what incentives offered? How, and *how soon?*

We have not attempted here to give you all the information for reaching a decision. We hope you will examine the references suggested at the end of the book and include the facts about the population crisis in your frame of reference for discussions and personal decisions in the coming years.

We hope that you will *act*. Tony Wagner, one of the young men quoted in this chapter, began to be concerned about the ecology of revolution in the midst of the many reform movements of the 60's. He wrote:

... we can argue the merits of third-party politics, coalition movements, and student-worker alliances until doomsday, but in the coming years, there is only going to be *one meaningful* alliance—the grouping together of people who are totally committed to the affirmation of all life on this planet; not only human life, but plant and animal life as well.

We hope that you will help to forge that alliance, for yourself and those who will follow.

Most people will have sex relations thousands of times during their lives. If the human race is to survive, childbirth will follow sexual intercourse very rarely—on the average about twice during a couple's sex life of forty years or more. The small family, with births well spaced and not too soon, thrives in health and happiness. Too many bright futures have been dimmed in adolescence by accidental pregnancy. The babies haven't turned out as well as they might, either.

Contraceptives, including the pill, the condom, the IUD, and the diaphragm, are modern tools which separate the mechanics of biological reproduction from the human aspects of love and sexual intimacy. We know that man will wear out his welcome on earth if he fails to use these tools. If we have reverence for life, we will make fewer babies and cherish them more. And we will be free to discover the countless miracles of harmony in sexual love, without disturbing the miraculous harmony of nature's household, Planet Earth.

Appendix
Where To Turn for Help
and Information

Birth Control Services

Planned Parenthood Federation of America, Inc. is a nonprofit, voluntary agency with local and regional offices nationwide. Laws vary from place to place, but if teen-agers are served anywhere in your locality, Planned Parenthood will know about it, if it does not operate a program for teens themselves. PPFA specializes in contraception, and operates a reputable and nonprofit abortion service in New York City; it provides abortion counseling in many other localities. It also provides information about sterilization. In addition, it will be helpful to you about education programs on family planning and population. We list the regional offices, lacking space to include all the local affiliates. Try the phone book or call Information for your city or town; if you don't succeed, call the nearest regional office. All Planned Parenthood clinics serve teen-agers, and many have developed special educational or service programs for teens. We list a few of these in each region just to indicate how widely available these programs are across the country.

Planned Parenthood Regional Offices

Great Lakes Detroit: 313-962-4390
Illinois, Indiana, Michigan, Minnesota, Ohio, West Virginia, Wisconsin.

Check these teen programs: Columbus, Grand Rapids, Milwaukee, Minneapolis.

Central Dallas: 214-350-8663
Arkansas, Iowa, Kansas, Louisiana, Missouri, Nebraska, New Mexico, Oklahoma, Texas.
Check these teen programs: Austin, Des Moines, Columbia, Fort Worth, Tulsa.

Southeast Atlanta: 404-262-1128
Alabama, Florida, Georgia, Kentucky, Mississippi, North Carolina, South Carolina, Tennessee, Virginia.
Check these teen programs: Atlanta, Augusta, Charlotte, Memphis, Nashville, Sarasota.

Western San Francisco: 415-777-1217
Alaska, Arizona, California, Colorado, Hawaii, Idaho, Montana, Nevada, North Dakota, Oregon, South Dakota, Utah, Washington, Wyoming.
Check these teen programs: Eugene, Phoenix, San Francisco, Santa Cruz, Seattle, Tucson.

North Atlantic New York City: 212-541-7800
Connecticut, Delaware, District of Columbia, Maine, Maryland, Massachusetts, New Hampshire, New Jersey, New York, Pennsylvania, Rhode Island, Vermont.
Check these teen programs: Baltimore, Cambridge, Morristown, New York City, Rochester, Trenton, Washington, D.C.

For addresses and telephone numbers of other helpful organizations, see the pertinent chapter or the list which follows in this appendix. One model program deserves special mention here—it combines comprehensive health and counseling services for teens under one roof: The Door, 618 Avenue of the Americas, New York City. 212-691-6161. Open 2–10 P.M. weekdays.

Other Personal Problems

In time of personal crisis—health, pregnancy, emotional, or family problems—think first of resources at hand, starting with your parents. Many young people find more support at home than they anticipated in their panic. Help with health problems can be found through your doctor or local health department; your school or college (which usually has both health and counseling offices); a reputable social agency such as Family and Child Services (accredited social workers have A.C.S.W. after their names, and at least some in a good agency will be so accredited); a church (many have helpful programs of service and counseling); or a Florence Crittendon home (in the case of a pregnancy for which abortion is not desired or not possible).

Most state and local health departments have active venereal disease programs. You can call first for information if you are hesitant to simply go there. Private physicians are becoming more aware of VD and its treatment; the specialist in VD treatment, especially syphilis, is the dermatologist; urologists are more likely to be expert in the treatment of gonorrhea; but a good general or family practitioner will be able to handle the vast majority of cases.

For emotional problems, think again of home, school, doctor, church or synagogue, social agency. A trusted adult counselor may be found there. For more specific help—e.g., with symptoms of severe depression (including suicidal thoughts), extreme anxiety, sleeplessness, drug problems, or a major disturbing change in personality or behavior—psychiatric or professional psychological help is indicated. You can obtain information through your local or state medical society or health department. If there is a medical school near you, the department of psychiatry is usually an excellent and inexpensive resource. If there is a university nearby, it may have a clinical psychology program with therapy or counseling available to people in the community. You may also have a community mental health center near you, or a child-guidance clinic (don't be put off—such clinics handle problems of people up to eighteen, and many are changing their names to reflect that fact).

It is sometimes too difficult to telephone or go for help when you want it. Remember, you do not have to give your name until you're sure the person or agency will give you the information or aid you need. You can ask ahead of time what the policy is regarding keeping your name private, and in particular not telling your parents or school. If you are too embarrassed, you can have a friend call for you. Unfortunately we cannot guarantee that every agency, health department, doctor, and so on will always be cooperative. But more and more are trying to be helpful and to respect the rights of teen-agers.

If you don't know what to say, you might use the following straightforward approach: "Hello, my name is Bill (Jane). And I have a question (or problem) about ——. Is there someone there who can help me with this? Can you refer me to someone who can help?"

Hotlines are available now in many localities, and also nationally, on toll-free lines. We have listed two dealing with abortion and VD; another is the National Runaway Switchboard: 800-621-4000 (Illinois: 800-972-6004).

If there is no great urgency, you may write for information on sexual and emotional questions to The National Institute of Mental Health, 5600 Fishers Lane, Rockville, Md. 20852. It can also supply you with information on various problems relating to mental health and illness, and also on the training required to enter one of the mental health professions. One further hint: If your problem involves you and your parents—if you are living at home, it usually does in some way —try to locate a family therapist, or someone who will spend some time with you and your parents. You may wish to have counseling for yourself, privately, and this is fine; a good family therapist will keep the individual sessions completely separate from those with the family, keeping strict confidences while helping you and your parents— and possibly brothers and sisters—negotiate some new ways of solving problems.

Another important resource is the National Mental Health Association, which has 850 affiliates across the country. Look up National Mental Health Association in your local phone book or write to

NMHA, 1800 N. Kent St., Arlington, Va. 22209. This organization does not provide services but will help you find what you need.

Literature, Films, Speakers, and Other Information

Planned Parenthood is the best single source of information on birth control, as SIECUS is for sex education. The most useful reference on birth control is *Contraceptive Technology* by Robert A. Hatcher, M.D., et al., which is updated every two years. A number of colleges have published handbooks, and especially notable for teens are the pamphlets and books produced under the direction of Dr. Sol Gordon; these are available from Ed-U Press, P.O. Box 583, Fayetteville, N.Y. 13066. "The Optional Parenthood Questionnaire" is a self-help device to guide the thoughtful person in making one of life's most important decisions: whether or not to have a child. It, and other relevant material, can be obtained from the National Alliance for Optional Parenthood, 2010 Massachusetts Avenue, N.W., Washington, D.C. 20036. Consumers Union, which publishes the excellent monthly *Consumer Reports* also has just updated its book *The Medicine Show* (5th ed., 1980), in which you can find what you need to know about everyday health problems and products.

Many good films are now being produced, although it is still easier to learn about space technology than sex! Schools may not be able to show some of the best films because approval is required at so many levels by so many people. Other places to see them include your church or synagogue, YMCA and YWCA, library, community center, health department, mental health center, or Planned Parenthood —which may be the place to borrow the film also. Some excellent films are: "Linda's Film" (about menstruation); "Am I Normal?" (about male puberty); "Love Carefully" (about all forms of birth control); "VD: Old Bugs, New Problems", and an Academy Award winner (best short film), "Teenage Father." SIECUS, the National Council on Family Relations (in *Family Relations* quarterly each January), and *Science Books and Films* will keep you up to date with reviews of new films.

Most teen publications have some intelligent articles on sex and population issues nowadays. Many newsstand magazines have reliable information. *Family Planning Perspectives* is an excellent magazine put out by Planned Parenthood—of interest to the serious student.

The health and advice columns of newspapers can be useful. *Today's Health* is put out for the general public by the American Medical Association. A number of excellent easy-to-read booklets on health, mental health, and family planning (list available) can be obtained from the Channing L. Bete Company, Greenfield, Mass. 01301. Public Affairs Pamphlets, 381 Park Avenue South, New York 10016, is another good source (e.g., see "The Rights of Teen-agers as Patients").

General books on adolescence abound, but there are a few gold mines which yield a treasure of psychology, history, and literature. Two are by Norman Kiell: an anthology, *The Universal Experience of Adolescence* (New York: International Universities Press, 1964; also a Beacon press paperback) and *The Adolescent Through Fiction* (International Universities Press, 1965). The first is crammed with fascinating fiction and biography. The second, a smaller book, is mostly commentary but has a bibliography of hundreds of titles of novels about teenagers. Robert Bremner's three-volume *Children and Youth in America* (Cambridge: Harvard University Press, 1970–71) is the definitive documentary history of young people in the United States.

Probably all good books on sex should be considered good books on mental health. The reader seeking a general introduction to psychology and psychiatry might start with books by such well-known writers as Karl Menninger, Erich Fromm, and Virginia Satir. Some of the references that follow will be of greater interest to professionals and teachers than teens themselves; we include such titles because teens will benefit indirectly.

Books on sex for young people range from quite conservative—those of Evelyn Millis Duvall—to the very liberal, such as those of Eleanor Hamilton and Wardell Pomeroy. In between are those of Eric Johnson, Richard Hettlinger, Helen Southard, and Ann Landers. Newly on the scene are Alex and Jane Comfort's *The Facts of Love* (he wrote *The Joy of Sex*) and Helen Singer Kaplan's *Making Sense of Sex* (she is a leading sex therapist). Our book does not deal with the biology, anatomy, and physiology of sex and reproduction, but many books and films do that very well. Professor Warren R. Johnson's *Sex Education and Counseling of Special Groups* (1975) deals with problems of the mentally and physically handicapped. Lorna and Philip Sarrel have written on sexual development and sex therapy in the college population in *Sexual Unfolding* (1979). Advanced sex education for men and women, respectively, comes in Bernie Zilbergeld's *Male Sexuality* and Lonnie Barbach's *For Yourself.* Couple relationships are addressed in *The Pleasure Bond* by Masters and Johnson and *A Couple's Guide to Communication* by John Gottman et al. (Research Press, Champaign, Illinois 61820). *Our Bodies, Ourselves* is a modern classic on health and self-help.

In the population and ecology area there are *The Report of the Commission on Population Growth and the American Future* (Washington, D.C.: U.S. Government Printing Office, 1972; also a New American Library paperback) and *Population, Resources, Environment* by Paul and Ann Ehrlich (San Francisco: Freeman, 2nd. ed., 1972). *The Population Activists's Handbook* (Collier/Macmillan, 1974) and *How To Influence Your Congressman* by George Alderson and Everett Sentman (Dutton, 1979) are important guides to action in an area which you know by now is controversial and rapidly changing. Without intelligent activism the world will decline rapidly; would you help prevent a sad ending, please?

The following list is not complete by any means, but indicates the range of sources for information—books and booklets, magazines, standard-setting, position-stating, annual meetings or conventions, audio-visual materials, professional training and career advice, etc. When writing for information, always send a long, stamped, self-addressed envelope.

American Home Economics Association
2010 Massachusetts Ave., N.W.
Washington, D.C. 20036

American Medical Association
535 North Dearborn St.
Chicago, Illinois 60610

American Public Health Association
1015 15th St., N.W.
Washington, D.C. 20005

American Social Health Association
260 Sheridan Ave.
Palo Alto, California 94306
VD Hotline: **800-227-8922**

American Association for Marriage
and Family Therapy
924 West 9th St.
Upland, California 91786

Catholic Alternatives
45 West 45th St.
New York, N.Y. 10036
Teen Hotline: **212-921-9111**

Center for Population Options
2031 Florida Ave., N.W.
Wahington, D.C. 20009

Consumers Union
Orangeburg, N.Y. 10962

Metro-Help, Inc.
2210 North Halsted St.
Chicago, Illinois 60614
National Runaway Switchboard: **800-621-4000**

National Abortion Federation
110 East 59th St.
New York, N.Y. 10022
Consumer Hotline: **800-223-0618**

National Council on Family Relations
1219 University Ave., S.E.
Minneapolis, Minnesota 55414

National Education Association
1201 16th St., N.W.
Washington, D.C. 20036

Population Reference Bureau
1337 Connecticut Ave., N.W.
Washington, D.C. 20036

Sex Information and Education Council of the U.S. (SIECUS)
84 Fifth Ave.
New York, N.Y. 10011

Zero Population Growth
1346 Connecticut Ave., N.W.
Washington, D.C. 20036

Index